OXFORD

THÉR

MW00653174

ÉMILE ZOLA was born in Paris in 1840, the son of a Venetian engineer and his French wife. He grew up in Aix-en-Provence, where he made friends with Paul Cézanne. After an undistinguished school career and a brief period of dire poverty in Paris, Zola joined the newly founded publishing firm of Hachette, which he left in 1866 to live by his pen. He had already published a novel and his first collection of short stories. *Thérèse Raquin*, the work in which Zola's mature style becomes recognizable for the first time, appeared in 1867. In 1871 he published the first volume of his Rougon-Macquart series with the sub-title *Histoire naturelle et sociale d'une famille sous le Second Empire*, in which he sets out to illustrate the influence of heredity and environment on a wide range of characters and milieux. It was, however, not until 1877 that his novel *L'Assommoir*, a study of alcoholism in the working classes, brought him wealth and fame. The last of the Rougon-Macquart series appeared in 1893 and his subsequent writing was far less successful, although he achieved fame of a different sort in his vigorous and influential intervention in the Dreyfus case. His marriage in 1870 had remained childless but his extremely happy liaison with a young laundress in later life gave him a son and a daughter. He died in 1902.

ANDREW ROTHWELL was educated at Oxford and in Paris. He has published widely on nineteenth- and twentieth-century French literature, including a book on the modern poet Pierre Reverdy. His translations from the French include works by contemporary poets Jacques Dupin and Bernard Noël, and the philosopher Francis Jacques. He is now Professor of French at Swansea University.

OXFORD WORLD'S CLASSICS

*For over 100 years Oxford World's Classics have brought
readers closer to the world's great literature. Now with over 700
titles—from the 4,000-year-old myths of Mesopotamia to the
twentieth century's greatest novels—the series makes available
lesser-known as well as celebrated writing.*

*The pocket-sized hardbacks of the early years contained
introductions by Virginia Woolf, T. S. Eliot, Graham Greene,
and other literary figures which enriched the experience of reading.
Today the series is recognized for its fine scholarship and
reliability in texts that span world literature, drama and poetry,
religion, philosophy and politics. Each edition includes perceptive
commentary and essential background information to meet the
changing needs of readers.*

OXFORD WORLD'S CLASSICS

ÉMILE ZOLA

Thérèse Raquin

Translated with an Introduction and Notes by
ANDREW ROTHWELL

OXFORD
UNIVERSITY PRESS

OXFORD
UNIVERSITY PRESS

Great Clarendon Street, Oxford OX2 6DP

Oxford University Press is a department of the University of Oxford.
It furthers the University's objective of excellence in research, scholarship,
and education by publishing worldwide in

Oxford New York

Auckland Bangkok Buenos Aires Cape Town Chennai
Dar es Salaam Delhi Hong Kong Istanbul Karachi Kolkata
Kuala Lumpur Madrid Melbourne Mexico City Mumbai Nairobi
São Paulo Shanghai Taipei Tokyo Toronto

Oxford is a registered trade mark of Oxford University Press
in the UK and in certain other countries

Published in the United States
by Oxford University Press Inc., New York

© Andrew Rothwell 1992

The moral rights of the author have been asserted

Database right Oxford University Press (maker)

First published as a World's Classics paperback 1992
Reissued as an Oxford World's Classics paperback 1998
Reissued 2008

British Library Cataloguing in Publication Data

Data available

Library of Congress Cataloging in Publication Data
Zola, Émile, 1840–1902.
[Thérèse Raquin. English]
Thérèse Raquin/Émile Zola; translated with an introduction and
notes by Andrew Rothwell.
p. cm.—(Oxford world's classics)
Translation of: Thérèse Raquin.
Includes bibliographical references.
1. Rothwell, Andrew. II. Title. III. Series.
PQ2521.T3E5 1992 843'.8—dc20 91–25532

ISBN 978-0-19-953685-6

7

Printed in Great Britain by
Clays Ltd, St Ives plc

CONTENTS

For Siân

INTRODUCTION

WHEN *Thérèse Raquin* was published in 1867, it caused rather a scandal. This violent, red-blooded story of adultery and murder among the lower orders shocked a middle-class readership accustomed to delicate psychological intrigue and veiled titillation, and conferred upon Zola a quite undeserved reputation as a pornographer. But for the young man of twenty-seven vying to make a name for himself in the Parisian literary world, publicity of any kind was not to be spurned; indeed, it seems that he actually orchestrated the press campaign against *Thérèse Raquin* himself. A number of years as a freelance literary and art critic for regional newspapers had given him a keen sense of polemical cut and thrust, as well as nourishing his pronounced talent for self-publicity, while a period of dire poverty in the early 1860s had left him with a burning determination not to fail in his chosen profession. He had already written two novels and a volume of short stories in his spare time, while working in the advertising department of Hachette, the bookseller and publisher, before giving up this lifeline in 1866 in order to earn a living solely by his pen. Throughout 1867 he worked slowly on *Thérèse Raquin*, conscious that it was to be 'the masterpiece of [his] early years' (as he wrote prophetically to a friend), while at the same time dashing off a pot-boiler serial novel, *Les Mystères de Marseille*, designed simply to keep him alive. When it eventually came out in volume form, amid the stultifying social conformity and hypocrisy of the Second Empire, and with the threat of prosecution for indecency hanging over its author (Zola's reference in the preface to 'these times of freedom in the arts' (p. 5) is clearly ironic), *Thérèse Raquin* was a runaway success: the first edition sold out in under four months. A year later, after one more 'experimental' novel (*Madeleine Férat*), Zola was already working on the monumental twenty-volume cycle Les Rougon-Macquart which was to dominate his life for the next fifteen years and for which he is now so justly celebrated.

While it may have enjoyed a *succès de scandale* at the time, *Thérèse Raquin* has endured with subsequent generations for different reasons. A work of intense atmosphere and unremitting tension, it builds a compelling drama out of a minimal plot, few characters, and the most basic of human motivations, the sex drive, in its crudest form. For all its strong story-line and direct presentation, however, the book remains highly ambiguous and unsettling. Zola's allusive, often euphemistic portrayal of sex and violence may have lost much of its power to shock today, but there is still something distinctly disturbing about the way he draws his characters, and the attitude he invites his readers to adopt towards them. Thérèse and her lover, Laurent, murder her ineffectual husband Camille in pursuit of their lust and self-gratification, only to find their relationship degenerating into horror and mutually inflicted torture. Yet we find ourselves largely unable either to sympathize or to condemn, for throughout this tense and lurid drama Zola works hard to deny the reader two key privileges which centuries of increasingly refined psychological literature had accustomed him or her to enjoying as of right: those of identifying with the characters' motives and feelings, and of judging their actions. This deliberate frustration of the 'legitimate' expectations with which any reader approaches realist literature has led as great a critic as F. W. J. Hemmings to dismiss *Thérèse Raquin* as an immature work; while recognizing its 'dark poetry', he writes in his pioneering book *Émile Zola* that the novel lacks 'the kind of human appeal which is normally a necessity if the novelist is to compel the interest of his readers'.[1] Yet Zola's aim was precisely to make a radical break with the prevailing literary norms of human interest and moral judgement, and to write an experimental work which would utterly undermine the novel's dependence on conventional psychology. The extent to which he succeeds in making us accept the would-be scientific basis of his alternative system of character portrayal is a matter of debate; what is beyond question, however, is the disturbing power of the novel which it allowed him to write.

[1] F. W. J. Hemmings, *Émile Zola* (2nd edn., Oxford, 1966), 38.

Zola explained some of the principles of his new approach in April 1868, in a preface to the second edition of *Thérèse Raquin* which was to become a landmark manifesto for Naturalism, the literary movement which he was working busily to establish and which has since become synonymous with his name. The importance of this preface, which purports to be simply a defence against charges of immorality, is considerable, for it condenses many of Zola's theoretical concerns and demonstrates, however self-assertively, the powerfully determining effect that they had on the composition of the novel. As I hope to show, *Thérèse Raquin* is in fact saturated on every level—plot, setting, descriptive technique, causality, characterization—with the techniques and metaphors advocated and exploited in this and Zola's other writings on Naturalism. Therefore, while it would be quite wrong to look to this preface for a complete account of his intentions and methods, it would be equally wrong to reject it out of hand as irrelevant, as critics hostile to any notion that an author might legitimately have a theory of his or her own production have tended to do. It is easy to dismiss Zola's at times irritating insistence on 'scientific' doctrine, but that would be to miss the possibility of a more fruitful interplay, essentially metaphorical rather than literal, between his theory and his practice.

In January 1868 *Thérèse Raquin* had been severely criticized in *Le Figaro* by a friend of Zola's, Louis Ulbach (writing under the pseudonym 'Ferragus'), as 'putrid literature';[2] the author's unhealthy preoccupation with lust, corpses, and decay was not only disgusting and immoral, wrote the columnist; it was an outrage against good taste. In fact, Zola may well have put him up to this attack himself in order to engineer an opportunity of publicizing his own views in a refutation. In any case, he riposted with an assertion of the principles of 'scientific analysis' and 'objective truth' upon which the book was based. It was, he claimed, simply 'a study in physiology', 'an example of the modern method' (p. 5), and the novelist had proceeded in the manner of a medical lecturer performing a public dissection; there was no question of gratuitous sex and violence, for he had merely opened up the living

[2] 'La Littérature putride', *Le Figaro*, 23 Jan. 1868; repr. in Zola, *Thérèse Raquin*, ed. Henri Mitterrand (Paris, Garnier-Flammarion, 1970), 39–44.

bodies of his characters as surgeons open up corpses, to find
out what was going on inside. This appeal to scientific rationalism and apparently perverse use of dissection metaphors in
defence of a work of literature has consistently irritated those
critics who retain an essentially Romantic notion of the artist
as an inspired and intuitive genius; indeed, this is by and large
the view on which we still fall back today, although it is historically conditioned and Zola was already reacting against it explicitly. Many have therefore tried to set up a dichotomy in Zola's
work (and above all in *Thérèse Raquin*) between 'reason' and
'imagination', always to the detriment of the former. They
usually argue that, if Zola was a great imaginative artist, it
is because he could not help overflowing the constraints of
theory and writing whatever seemed intuitively necessary, even
where it contradicted his scientific principles. He has even been
accused of opportunism, bad faith, and deliberate mystifi-
cation. Yet in his case the opposition between science and
art is a false one, for not only did he believe that his ideas
were in the mainstream of progress in his day; he also made
them the foundation of his Naturalist aesthetic, of which the
manifesto and first major showcase was to be *Thérèse Raquin*.

The term Naturalism has generated more literary debate
in the century or so since it was coined than almost any other.
Originally a naturalist was—and still is—a person who studies
nature, whether as a scientist or, more commonly in Zola's
day, a wealthy amateur enthusiast. But the word Naturalism
also had a long-established meaning in philosophy, applying
to any school of thought which took 'natural', material reality
as its first principle (philosophical Naturalism is therefore the
opposite of Idealism). By the mid-nineteenth century the word
already had a limited aesthetic sense as well: Baudelaire had
applied it somewhat disparagingly to painting which sought
merely to copy nature, as opposed to the more colourful,
Romantic, and imaginative approach of artists whom he cham-
pioned such as Delacroix (a generation later, Zola took the
opposite view, defending the 'crude' realism of Manet and
other modern painters). Zola took these three sets of related
ideas and connotations (scientific enquiry, materialism, pictorial realism) and brought them together to form the relatively
precise literary 'doctrine' which is now so closely linked to

his name. He first used the word Naturalism in print in a
eulogistic article about the great literary critic, philosopher,
and historian, Hippolyte Taine, which appeared in *L'Événement* in July 1866. In calling Taine the 'naturalist of the moral
world',[3] he was projecting on to the critic the image of scientific enquiry into the human mind which he himself was soon
to adopt explicitly as a novelist when he pledged allegiance,
in the preface to *Thérèse Raquin*, to 'the methodical, Naturalist
school' (p. 5) of writing. It was also Taine whom he had in
mind when anticipating what the 'great critics' (ibid.) would
say about his novel; in fact, he had already received from the
great man a letter broadly praising *Thérèse Raquin*, but also
containing some general criticisms which Zola virtually quotes,
without acknowledging their source, in his preface.

This was the great age of Positivism, the philosophical movement founded by Auguste Comte (1798–1857). Positivism
held that everything in the universe would one day (and sooner
rather than later, for such was the optimism of the times) suc-
cumb to scientific explanation, on the basis of observation and
reasoning. Great strides had been made in discovering the
underlying principles of the physical and earth sciences; Cuvier
had succeeded in imposing a workable system of classification
on the overwhelming variety of animal types, and Darwin's
Origin of Species (1859) had proposed for the first time a coher-
ent theory of their evolution. Zola saw that the 'general progress
of the century' lay squarely in scientific enquiry, and that the
race was on to apply comparable methods to the vastly more
complex fields of human behaviour, psychology, and society.
In this enterprise, in which he saw himself participating as
a novelist, his great model was medicine. Having been until
the mid-nineteenth century very much an art, based on trial
and error, medicine was now being established on an empirical
scientific footing by the doctor and eminent philosopher of
science, Claude Bernard, and his work was clearly a direct
inspiration to Zola in the composition of *Thérèse Raquin*.

[3] 'Livres d'aujourd'hui et de demain', *L'Événement*, 25 July 1866; repr.
in Zola, *Œuvres complètes*, ed. Henri Mitterrand (15 vols.; Paris, Cerce
du Livre précieux, 1966–70), x.563–5 (p.564).

Zola was not the first exponent of what became known as the 'medical novel', only the most purposeful and radical. Two years before the publication of *Thérèse Raquin*, the brothers Goncourt had published *Germinie Lacerteux*, an 'objective' study of the breakdown through neurosis of a real person, their elderly maid; 'Ferragus' was to attack this book as a precursor of Zola's own 'putrid literature', but Zola himself had reviewed it with warm approval. Less than a decade earlier Zola's most admired role-model, Flaubert, had brought out *Madame Bovary*, which had shocked by its detatched analysis of the heroine's states of mind, and the gruesome and dispassionate detail in which her death from poisoning is described. In a contemporary review of the book, the influential critic Sainte-Beuve (who himself had studied medicine) had made the oft-quoted remark: 'anatomists and physiologists, I find you wherever I look',[4] which suggests that this was already felt to be a distinct, if controversial, class of novel at the time. However, it was perhaps Balzac (d. 1850), author of the monumental *Comédie humaine*, who provided Zola with the most potent model of the 'scientific' objectives and methods of the modern novelist. While Balzac's theoretical metaphors were drawn from the field of zoological classification, the achievement of an earlier generation, rather than from medicine, Zola read his intentions in a way which brought him into line with his own 'physiological' preoccupations of 1865–7, the seminal years for Naturalism. In a paper delivered in 1866 to the Congrès Scientifique de France at Aix, he presented Balzac enthusiastically as

the anatomist of the soul and of the flesh. He dissects man, studies the play of his passions, interrogates every fibre, analyses the whole organism. Like a surgeon, he feels neither shame nor repugnance when exploring our human sores. His only concern is for the truth, and he lays out before us the corpse of our hearts. Modern science has provided him with the tools of analysis and the scientific method. He proceeds like our chemists and mathematicians, breaking down actions, determining their cause, and explaining their effects; he operates according to fixed equations, accounting for his observations by

---

[4] Closing remark from his 1857 review of *Madame Bovary* in C.-A. Sainte-Beuve, *Causeries du lundi* (Paris, Garnier, n.d.), xiii. 346–63 (p.363).

studying the influence of different environments on individuals. The
title most appropriate to him is that of Doctor of Moral Science.[5]

In this extremely partial, not to say distorted, evocation of
Balzac, we observe a powerful strategic displacement and
reduction of the mental ('soul', 'passions', 'moral') to the
physical ('flesh', 'fibre', 'organism', 'corpse'), performed via
the mediating metaphorical term 'heart' (which, as the conventional seat of the emotions, has, so to speak, a foot in both
camps). This manipulative procedure of displacement,
together with the obsessively reiterated vocabulary of dissection
and the (physical and metaphorical) 'profundity' of scientific
analysis which it purports to make available, strongly prefigure
both Zola's critical discourse about *Thérèse Raquin*, and some
of the specific ways in which he went about composing the
novel.

Apart from the fact that physiology was 'in the air' at this
period, Zola was influenced more directly by his reading of
Claude Bernard's *Introduction à l'étude de la médecine expérimen-
tale*, published in 1865, which eventually led him to write the
essay *Le Roman expérimental* of 1879. In this manifesto from
his second and greatest campaign in support of Naturalism,
which follows on directly from the concerns of his 1868 preface
to *Thérèse Raquin*, Zola took over everything Bernard had said
in justification of his medical philosophy and applied it to the
novel, simply substituting the word 'novelist' for 'physiologist'.
He presented the novelist as an 'experimental moralist' whose
field of investigation was 'the human body in its cerebral and
sensual functions, both healthy and morbid';[6] like the physiologist in his domain, he wrote, the novelist should seek the
simple rules of cause and effect governing our most complex
behaviour, setting up hypotheses and then testing their accuracy as his story unfolds. The higher mental and moral functions
were assimilated and reduced to manifestations of the body,
to be explained rationally as symptoms of our healthy or
morbid physical states, thus reversing the accustomed value
hierarchy. Like the physiologist also, the novelist would find
that the rules governing behaviour emerged more clearly if

[5] See Guy Robert, '3 textes inédits d'Émile Zola', *Revue des Sciences
Humaines*, 51 (1948), 181–207 (p.204); my translation.
[6] *Le Roman expérimental*, in *Œuvres complètes*, x.1175–1204 (p.1191).

he investigated exceptional, pathological subjects such as those
suffering from neuroses (the term was in widespread popular
use by this time) rather than healthy people, for such deviations
from the norm revealed the norm itself all the more directly.
This largely explains the frequently-observed 'exaggeration'
in the character-drawing of Zola and his fellow Naturalists.

Two related points in this retrospective account of Zola's
theory and practice are of particular interest for *Thérèse Raquin*.
In the first place, the novelist is not concerned with questions
of taste, nor is it his role to make moral judgements; he simply
pursues what the preface calls his 'quest for truth' (p. 2)
(although literature does retain a didactic and moral function
at one remove, for, in exposing the causes of neurosis and
the antisocial behaviour associated with it, the novelist is performing a service to society). Secondly, the view of human
reality as a scientific object which Zola presents in *Le Roman
expérimental* is a mechanistic and deterministic one. His
'experimental psychology', or 'interior physiology', which aims
to lay bare the laws by which the 'intellectual and sensual
cogs'[7] of man's brain are made to turn, takes Claude Bernard's definitions of physiology as literally applicable, directly
transferable, to the domain of the human mind. In this controversial perspective, mental phenomena were no longer myster-
ious, metaphysical processes different in kind from physical
ones and so inaccessible to scientific enquiry; they became
in theory as predictable and testable (in the framework of a
novel) as any other observation about the physical world. The
notion of the mind as a mechanism governed by cause and
effect as a machine is by gears (a caricatural illustration of
which is provided by the 'mechanical corpses' (p. 24) of Mme
Raquin's Thursday receptions) shows how extreme was the
materialism to which Zola subscribed at this stage in his career
(partly, no doubt, because taking such a radical, to many people outrageous, point of view was a good way of attracting
public attention). Of course, his apparent attempt to solve
at a stroke what philosophers have always called the 'mind–
body problem' was on the face of it hopelessly naïve, although
it anticipated in an interesting way both the early

[7] Ibid. 1185.

twentieth century's success in setting the study of psychology on a quasi-scientific footing, and the distant dream of modern neurology that we might one day understand the 'wiring' of the brain well enough to give a physical account of phenomena such as memory. But the real importance of Zola's materialist stance for his Naturalist aesthetic was strategic, in that physiology and its underlying ideology of scientific rationalism provided him both with arguments with which to attack conventional psychology (and the normative moral values which it concealed/imposed), and with the legitimizing metaphors on which to base a replacement for it. Of all his novels, it is in *Thérèse Raquin* that this radical materialism is most consistently and uncompromisingly applied.

The comfortably stable psychological categories and models which prevailed in the literature of Zola's day (and in many ways still do) went back to the prestigious work of seventeenth-century moralists such as Pascal, La Rochefoucauld, and La Bruyère. Theirs was a highly abstract view of man, based on introspection and privileging the mind over the body; they sought to bring out what was universal in human behaviour and codify it in terms of an interlocking network of vices and virtues, passions and duties, which were in theory entirely independent of individuals and circumstances (though in practice they presupposed an educated, aristocratic, male subject with no material constraints on his existence). Although the advent of Realism in the thirty years or so before Zola began writing had brought a marked departure from the generalizing abstraction of the classical thinkers, and a new interest in individuals and their predicaments, the categories of behaviour and motivation employed by Balzac, Stendhal, and Flaubert, not to mention a host of lesser novelists, were still substantially the same. Zola, and the philosophers of his time, rejected such pre-established explanations and the moral values underlying them as inappropriate to a modern society, unrealistic and essentially metaphysical. Later, in *Le Roman expérimental*, he was to proclaim: 'metaphysical man is dead, our whole field of enquiry is transformed by physiological man',[8] and from *Thérèse Raquin* onwards he resolved to make physiology

[8] Ibid. 1203.

the instrument of the novel's liberation from 'metaphysical' psychology. But, in the state of scientific knowledge at that time, his project to identify the physiological 'cogs' of the mind could never be more than conjectural. The challenge, and the originality (for this is where the Romantic notion of artistic inspiration comes back in), were therefore to imagine a hypothesis plausible and powerful enough to 'deconstruct' human motivation in a convincingly physiological way. In this enterprise, *Thérèse Raquin* was to be his laboratory.

How, then, could mental phenomena be derived directly from physiology? Zola's answer was an extremely bold one. Following on from the theories of Taine, he decided that there were two crucial facts about individuals which the novelist could profitably explore: their inbuilt disposition or temperament, and the effect on that temperament of the particular surroundings, or environment, in which they lived. The importance of this latter aspect for the way *Thérèse Raquin* is organized will be examined below. Zola's hypothesis to account for the former, the notion of an inherited or acquired disposition (the distinction is not clearly drawn), looked back to the ancient theory of temperaments which had been used in the medieval period to explain different people's tendency to behave in different ways. 'In *Thérèse Raquin* I set out to study, not characters, but temperaments' (p. 1), he announces near the start of the preface, thereby clearly marking his distance from the psychological assumptions and methods of character-drawing used by other novelists of his day. In medieval theory, each of the four temperaments (sanguine, melancholic, lymphatic, bilious—though the names vary) was traditionally thought to be characterized by the predominance of a particular body fluid or 'humour' (blood, and different types of bile) which determined such things as one's physical appearance and overall mental disposition, or temperament. Of course, the theory of temperaments had long since been overtaken and discredited by more sophisticated psychological models, so it might at first sight seem astonishing that Zola the 'scientist' should have taken this step backwards into pre-scientific history. His detractors certainly regarded the whole business as no more than a manœuvre by an immoral writer, a spurious and subversive attempt to dissociate psychology from morality and thereby justify his circumvention of the 'natural' canons of taste and decency as enshrined in traditional psychological description. Although this was undoubtedly part of his purpose, however, the theory in fact had a number of other advantages which were much more crucial.

The first of these was that, as the modern French sense of 'mood' (*humeur*) might suggest, the mythical 'humours' of medieval psychology and medicine seemed to bridge the terminological gap between mental and physical realities, in much the same way as the word 'heart' in Zola's homage to Balzac (quoted above). Temperaments therefore seemed to promise a concrete model, and a vocabulary, by means of which the novelist might explore the 'interior physiology' of his characters; they would allow certain quasi-medical 'laws' to be internalized and the inner workings of the mind to be explained in apparently scientific terms, with no need to appeal to ordinary psychology. In reality, of course, Zola's 'interior physiology' was to be a literary rather than a scientific construct, dependent on a limited range of physiological terms which carried a highly conventional psychological charge in addition to their literal (physical) meaning. By systematically using such terms in their literal sense to account for characters' temperaments and motives, he would manage both to displace psychology into the physical domain and to create an impression of novelty and disorientation in readers accustomed to 'mentalistic' psychology. So the overall technique, however audacious it may appear, remained a simple one based on some very ancient metaphors. Zola's original achievement in *Thérèse Raquin* is that he applied these metaphors single-mindedly and forcefully enough to create the appearance of a complex quasi-scientific 'system' out of what is, in reality, merely a verbal artefact, at the same time challenging accepted notions of the nature of the novelist's craft and his moral responsibility to uphold social norms.

The other key advantage of the temperaments theory, the final piece of the jigsaw which allowed materialism, physiology, and scientific cause and effect to be brought into play together in the creation of a new type of novel, was its powerful inbuilt determinism. In *Thérèse Raquin* all the characters' feelings and reactions are so directly dictated by their initial temperament, seen in purely physical terms, that they have almost no freedom either to choose how they act, or to develop as people; from start to finish they are what they are, and their actions unfold, in Zola's eyes, with absolute inevitability. This too brought him much hostile criticism, for it seemed to many as if he were deliberately and subversively absolving his characters of any moral responsibility for their actions. However, his justification for this was again that, since he was setting out to explore the 'deep', physiological roots of mind, rather than the civilizing metaphysical constructs of ordinary psychology, he was naturally interested only in those hidden, powerful impulses dictated by temperament of which the individual was largely unaware, and which were therefore by definition beyond the control of his or her moral sense. Although the much more satisfactory theories developed by Freud and others half a century later now make Zola's temperament-based view of such unconscious impulses seem rather weak to us, it should be remembered that in his day this was a very radical and innovative approach for a novelist to take, with no guarantee at all that it would work. Nor is it surprising that so many of his contemporaries, accustomed to more conventional novels, should have failed (whether deliberately or not) to understand his intentions, although it must at the same time be admitted that Zola doubtless foresaw the outrage he would provoke, and did nothing to lessen it. Conventional psychological novels had always made much play with their characters' dilemmas and choices, and the often unexpected ways in which their experiences led them to grow and mature (though in reality they are subject to an equally strong but concealed determinism, the pre-existing teleology or 'sense of an ending' which the novelist imposes on his plot). In *Thérèse Raquin* Zola deliberately rejected the wealth of resources available within this tradition, insisting instead that the way his protagonists behaved under the pressure of surroundings and circumstances (the other key element in his theory) was totally predetermined by their physiological make-up. In so doing, as his critics were quick to point out, he seemed to be setting out thoroughly to dehumanize them.

In the preface to the second edition Zola makes absolutely no attempt to defend himself against this charge; on the contrary, he goes out of his way to stress that Thérèse and Laurent were in fact hardly people at all, defining them as individuals utterly dominated by 'their nerves and their blood' (see below), 'devoid of free will and drawn into every act of their lives by the inescapable promptings of their flesh'. They are, he says, 'human animals, nothing more' (pp. 1–2), governed solely by an instinctive and selfish urge towards physical satisfaction. In this too he was echoing Claude Bernard's *Introduction*, which had defined man as 'an animal machine acting under the influence of heredity and environment' (Zola's paraphrase of 1879),[9] and in fact *Thérèse Raquin* can be read as a direct experiment in giving literary expression to Bernard's anti-humanistic theories. Throughout the book the narrator is at pains to tell us that the murderers do not think, they merely act in instinctive accordance with their own drives and impulses (though this does not exclude a certain animal cunning which allows them, in their own interests, to act out a part), and this profound lack of self-awareness clearly precludes any possibility of their experiencing guilt for their actions. They certainly realize that they have infringed the rules of society and will be severely punished if found out, but Zola presents this as simply a reaction of self-preservation; what eventually leads to their downfall is not guilt, but a (by modern standards somewhat vague and improbable) 'nervous disorder' caused by the shock of murdering Camille.

However, the line between physical sickness and moral self-torture is a fine one for the novelist to maintain, as Zola seems to recognize when in the preface he refers to 'what I have been obliged to call [the characters'] remorse' (p. 2). This is not just a problem of vocabulary, for it again raises the question of how the obsessional relationship between the central characters in the last third of the book is to be motivated in other than psychological terms. In fact, though, Zola's resolute insistence that Laurent's remorse 'was purely physical' (p. 130) is less unconvincing to the reader than it might sound, for he develops in the course of the novel a physiological system of character-drawing complex enough to carry considerable conviction. His intention was certainly that *Thérèse Raquin*

[9] Ibid. 1190.

should not have any obvious moral message, and the fact that
he forces us to suspend judgement on the guilt or otherwise
of the protagonists makes it to a large extent an amoral book.
This is spelled out clearly in Chapter XXVIII, when Thérèse
and Laurent go back in harrowing fashion over the murder
itself, trying to force each other to admit responsibility. Their
acrimonious debate is referred to explicitly as an 'imaginary
court case' which 'never came to a verdict' (p. 175), Zola
anticipating the reader's desire to put the characters on trial
and guiding him or her to the conclusion that a combination
of temperaments in particular circumstances is the real culprit.
Yet, although Zola is at pains to avoid explicit condemnation,
the book's general drift does contain an implicit message (animal lust leads inevitably to hatred and death) which in turn
reveals the conventional nature of his own underlying moral
assumptions. Moreover, as recent feminist criticism has
pointed out, the author's moral 'impartiality' itself is actually
more apparent than real, for he seems unable to avoid presenting Thérèse, against the book's ideology of moral neutrality,
as the pernicious female who, unlike Laurent, 'knew what harm
she was doing' (p. 44). In fact, Zola's work generally shows
him to have been unable to escape from the restrictive 'angel'/
'mother'/'devil' female stereotypes which pervaded the literature and the moral value-system of his day.

   Having examined the origins, intentions, and implications
of Zola's theory of temperaments, let us now turn to its practi-
cal implementation in *Thérèse Raquin*. As we are progressively
informed by various narratorial interventions throughout the
book, the three characters in the triangular relationship which
forms the novel's centre each represent a different temperament. Thérèse herself, strong, alert, and full of smouldering
passion, is of a 'nervous' disposition; Laurent, robust, imper-
turbable and sensual, is 'sanguine'; while Camille, feeble,
sickly, and thoroughly inadequate, is 'lymphatic'. The whole
drama arises from an incompatibility between Thérèse and
her husband which, in her restricted and unnatural circumstances and environment, throws her temperament off balance.
Having been destabilized in this way, she instinctively seeks
a new equilibrium in a relationship with the entirely compatible
Laurent, whom she in turn provides with the sexual satisfaction

that his passionate nature craves. But, following the murder of Camille, which is necessary for this beneficial situation to be perpetuated, both she and Laurent are again thrown off balance by their terror of discovery, and in this situation of stress they begin to acquire aspects of each other's temperaments in the unsuccessful search for a new equilibrium. This interplay of complementary and conflicting temperaments, which Zola insists rather heavy-handedly in Chapter XVIII is 'a psychological and physiological fact' (p. 99), acts as the well-spring and mechanism of the whole plot, which thus unfolds with a kind of inevitability that Zola doubtless intended to be seen as genuinely tragic. It is as if the external forces of fate (the vengeful gods) in Greek tragedy, or the inner, self-destructive 'fate' of irresistible psychological yearnings in the seventeenth-century theatre of Racine, had been literally incarnated, in *Thérèse Raquin*, in the bodily cravings of the characters, or what Zola terms 'the fatalities of their flesh'.[10]

The inevitable working-out of these conflicts is heroically sustained throughout in purely physical terms, though on occasion with less than plausible results. (When, for instance, Laurent has a nervous breakdown under the influence of Thérèse's temperament, a side-effect of which is that he finally becomes a real artist, we are told that his formerly fleshy body grew thinner and his brain became enlarged!) But we should remember that this occasionally naïve-sounding writing, like all Zola's 'physiological' explanations in *Thérèse Raquin*, needs to be read on a literal and a metaphorical level simultaneously. This is particularly true of the key terms 'blood' and 'nerves', which define the temperaments of Laurent and Thérèse. Like the word 'heart' in Zola's Balzac lecture, both stand half-way between the physiological and mental domains, as physical terms historically loaded with conventional behavioural and emotional connotations. The blood, pumped round by the heart, seat of the passions, becomes literally a vehicle and indicator of sexual excitement, as well as characterizing individuals as more or less passionate by nature (thus Camille's sickly, pallid complexion also betrays an absence of ardour); while the nerves are at once a physiological system for the

[10] As Zola puts it in his next novel, *Madeleine Férat* (1868); see *Œuvres complètes*, i. 689–896 (p.812).

transmission of sensory data to the brain and, in reverse as it were, a physical reflection of heightened emotional states of the mind such as excitement or stress. In this context it is worth pointing out that the French word *nerfs* also means 'sinews', so that a person who is 'nervous' is probably, like Thérèse, excitable but also tough and resilient, rather than fragile, as English usage would lead us to expect. We are told that Thérèse has 'hot' African blood in her, Laurent's neck pulses redly when he is aroused, their nerves are 'stretched to breaking-point' by the tension they are going through, and so on; in each case, an apparently commonplace piece of symbolism is used as part of a consistent system which allows the author to account for inner states in a purely physical manner. In general, we are rarely told what the characters think or feel in an emotional sense, only what they feel physically, what their sensations are (the distinction is clearer in French, which has different words for the two types of feeling). Thérèse's anxiety in the shop, for instance, is not stated as such but evoked by the 'feverish pricking sensation' in her hands (p. 24), while after the murder, beads of sweat form in her hair at the memory of it; on the journey back from Saint-Ouen the terrible 'bond of blood and fear' (p. 90) which will unite the murderers is symbolized by a hand-clasp through which blood seems to circulate between their bodies, and both later find their heads filled, not with guilt and confusion, but with 'clouds of acrid vapour' (p. 54).

A further physical–symbolic resource of this kind, and one which adds greatly to the flexibility of the 'temperamental' novelist's options, is the description of facial features. Balzac had been the first to make systematic use of physical portraits in his novels, on the fictional justification that he was describing real people from observation (whereas he was actually creating 'types' whose characters could be 'deduced' from their appearance). In the same way, Zola's 'portraits' are done not from life, as we might expect from a novelist with such a reputation as an arch-realist, but, as Henri Mitterrand has shown, in accordance with a pre-existing grid of contrasting values which symbolically reinforce the system of temperaments.[11] The

[11] Henri Mitterrand, introduction to the Garnier-Flammarion edition of *Thérèse Raquin*, 30–2.

various aspects of each physical portrait are made into a system of differential signs which combine to point to the individual's temperament. Thus, for instance, Camille's mouth gapes open idiotically, in life as in death, while Thérèse and Laurent have firm, expressive lips; their eyes are black and fiery, while his are round, blue, and vacant; their hair is dark and vigorous, his lank and colourless; their complexion is healthy and full of vitality, his sallow and lifeless, and so on. This system of descriptive signs, of which many other examples could be found, extends to such aspects as the characteristic postures in which the characters sit (Thérèse crouches down, as if ready to pounce, while Camille usually lounges), and above all the way they look at each other. Because of their 'expressiveness', we tend to regard the eyes (in life as well as, for instance, in portrait-painting) as a kind of 'mirror of the mind', the point of intersection between a person's external appearance and their inner emotions and thoughts, and this makes them ideally suited to Zola's physiological system. When one character stares at another in a particular situation, as they do with increasing frequency as the book progresses, we are able to read into that simple action a corresponding accusation, or motives of complicity, fear, or hatred, without the need for any intervention by the narrator. Towards the end of the novel, Thérèse and Laurent become so tightly bound together in their fear that their silent but penetrating stares actually take on a literal narrative role to match that of the narrator, for they retell the whole story of the murder 'in the language of the eyes' (p. 121), without uttering a word (though Zola, of course, is obliged to spell out their mutual accusations for us). This is perhaps the most extreme moment of the reduction of the mental and intellectual processes to a purely physical manifestation in the whole of the book.

What these examples (and there are many more) have in common is that they provide ways of compensating for the inbuilt limitations of the system of temperaments (of which, originally, there were only four), by establishing complex meta-phorical and symbolic patterns to strengthen and give nuance to the original scheme, while allowing Zola to remain within his self-imposed discipline of physical description. The same may be said, paradoxically perhaps, of the 'supernatural' element in the book, the ghosts and hallucinations, and Laurent's perpetual scar, or stigma, which at first sight would seem more at home in a Gothic horror extravaganza than a Naturalist novel. These apparently highly unrealistic devices actually play a fundamentally realistic role, by acting as graphic materializations, and constant physical reminders, of the terrible event— the murder—which has destabilized the main protagonists. Like the bite, which turns purple whenever he remembers killing Camille, Laurent's hallucinations are literal sensory phenomena (mostly visual, though, when he feels the presence of Thérèse's 'ghost' after their love-making in his garret, it is evoked by her lingering scent in the bedclothes), and as such they provide a very suitable vehicle for representing what another novelist might have portrayed as a mental obsession. Zola is at great pains to prepare the arrival of Camille's ghost in visual terms, by making the portrait, with its greenish complexion like that 'of a drowned man' (p. 34) and its yellow, globular eyes, a literal pre-echo of Camille's rotting corpse at the Morgue, thereby suggesting in addition an unconscious desire to do away with his rival long before plans for the murder are actually hatched. Laurent's repeated dream that he is returning at night through Paris to Thérèse, only to find the door opened not by her but by the corpse, is an elegant and powerful way of making a link between the themes of sex and death. The later reappearance of the portrait to terrify Laurent then allows a transition to the ghost proper, whose clammy presence the murderers feel literally between them in bed, and finally the dissemination of their obsession into other physical manifestations, notably François the cat and the paralysed Mme Raquin. No wonder, then, that it is the terrifying image of Camille which is literally 'engraved' on Laurent's memory (again, a metaphor of visual representation takes the place of any reference to the abstract mental faculty of imagination), causing his 'rebellious nerves and muscles' (p. 153) irresistibly to reproduce the drowned man's features whenever he tries to paint a portrait. Thus, even that most 'unrealistic' element of the book, the supernatural, can actually be seen as a necessary consequence of Zola's extreme materialism.

The same paradoxical tension between material realism and apparently supra-rational symbolism, in which the latter actually works in support of the former, can be seen in Zola's use of setting in *Thérèse Raquin*. Taking up the second aspect of Taine's critical platform, the importance of environment as an influence on characters of differing temperaments, he claims in the preface to have made a dispassionate study of 'the profound modifications brought about in the human organism by the pressure of surroundings and circumstances' (p. 5). The fact that the book is given an almost contemporary setting, in a real part of Paris with which the author was intimately familiar, would seem to lend credibility to this quasi-scientific intention (notice, once again, that it is the 'organisms' of his characters, rather than their minds, that interest Zola). An unprepared reader might well be led to expect a flat, detailed, but 'objective' presentation of the characters' material surroundings and the events which happen to them. Yet despite numerous gestures towards detailed 'local-colour' realism, Zola's evocations of place always carry an additional charge which is anything but straightforwardly realistic. Sainte-Beuve noticed this immediately and accused him of exaggeration, particularly in the way he built up the atmosphere of the Passage du Pont-Neuf.[12] This 'exaggeration', or persistent stress on one particular aspect or connotation of the setting, is in fact a further means by which Zola creates symbolic and metaphorical patterns to support his system of temperaments and dramatize the conflicts between them. It also greatly enhances the impression of deterministic inevitability with which the events of the novel unfold.

All but eleven of the novel's thirty-two chapters are set entirely in the Passage du Pont-Neuf, and nine of those eleven begin or end there; the two exceptions, the Vernon episode in Chapter II (a flashback to Thérèse's early life) and Laurent's gruesome visit to the Morgue in Chapter XIII, hardly serve to relieve the overwhelming feeling of claustrophobia which pervades the novel. This claustrophobia is further strengthened by the layout of the shop and the flat above, cut off from the outside world, in the first case by the glass roof of the

---

[12] See Sainte-Beuve's letter of 10 June 1868, repr. in the Documents Section of the Garnier-Flammarion edn. (pp.48–50). A decade later Zola was (misguidedly) to accept Sainte-Beuve's strictures on this point (see ibid. 51–2).

arcade, and in the second by the sinister black wall which rises to a great height opposite, blocking out the sky. Even the rear staircase from the bedroom only leads back down into the arcade. A number of smaller descriptive touches also reinforce symbolically our certainty that this is, as Chantal Bertrand-Jennings has put it in her study of space in *Thérèse Raquin*, a 'nightmarish labyrinth' from which there can be no escape.[13] The costume jewellery-seller's little ring-boxes, for instance, are enclosed within the cupboard-like wooden structure from which she trades, itself enclosed within the arcade, while in the shop the boxes of haberdashery goods are all shut tightly away, their colourful contents prevented from spilling out and livening the place up. In each case Zola is offering us an implicit image of Thérèse's repressed condition as Camille's wife, sitting in the shop 'silent and immobile' (the phrase becomes a virtual leitmotiv), with her vivacity and energy bottled up within her. The sense of enclosure is increased even more by a pervasive imagery of death and burial, which begins with the three funereal lamps mentioned in the opening pages, and intensifies through the rest of the book. The moment she arrives in the dark, gloomy shop Thérèse feels enclosed in 'the clinging earth of a grave' (p. 19), and Mme Raquin comes to share her sensation of being buried alive, while both Laurent's garret in the Rue Saint-Victor and his top-floor studio, with their single skylight in the roof, are likened to a dank hole in the ground, or grave, in which the characters (and the reader, who adopts their perspective) feel imprisoned.

The dramatic events and moods of the book are supported and heightened by a considerable range of other symbolic and metaphorical patterns, some of which might be mentioned here in passing. The first of these is the weather, which Zola uses in a subtle, but fairly conventional, manner. Whenever the characters step outside their enclosed urban environment, the natural world in which they find themselves always seems to hold up a mirror to their inner sensations and encourage their deep urges (this is the traditional 'pathetic fallacy' technique). The effect is particularly powerful in the Saint-Ouen scene;

[13] Chantal Bertrand-Jennings, *Espaces romanesques: Zola* (Sherbrooke, Naaman, 1987), 25.

as the last warmth of the day gives way to a chill evening, the normally placid Seine rumbles menacingly and the funereal 'shrouds' of darkness fall in anticipation of the murder. The seasons, too, play a discreet supporting role; the murder happens in the autumn, while the fact that Thérèse is remarried in the depths of winter bodes ill for the success of the relationship. Then again, the images of physical sensation which are threaded through the book are also imbued with a symbolic value which both reflects the action and adds to the complexity and richness of the novel's physiological system of motivations. Perhaps the most striking of these extended metaphor sequences involves the imagery of fire, which functions with changing literal, thematic, and metaphorical meanings as the novel progresses. Thérèse spends much of her youth staring into the fire, a practice she and Laurent resume on their wedding-night when the ghost appears; both she and he experience the 'flames' of passion, associated with a 'fire' in their blood. But once they are married, Laurent's first kiss 'burns' Thérèse's cheek; unable to sleep, the lovers toss and turn 'on a bed of burning coals'; she tries to 'cauterize' the 'wound' in their relationship by kissing the scar on his neck, and longs for 'purification' by fire,[14] until in the end they both realize that the fires of hell await them. Here, the same insistent metaphor undergoes a complete inversion of values as the book progresses; having first designated extreme passion, by the end it pitilessly evokes the horror and despair of damnation. This has the effect both of tightly reinforcing the development of the plot, and of bringing in metaphorically a damning verdict of 'guilty' on the characters and their illegitimate passion, a verdict which Zola as narrator deliberately avoids delivering in explicit terms. The same progression towards an implied, but none the less absolute (and ultimately conventional) moral condemnation can be seen in the parallel imagery of the embrace, which begins as a literal act of wild desire, but becomes towards the end a metaphor for the unbreakable and torturing bonds of dependency which link the murderers to each other in their hatred; it is appropriate that Mme Raquin should be 'embraced' by paralysis and have to be carried

[14] Interestingly, Zola uses the same (conventional) image in the preface to defend his book: 'Sincere study, like fire, purifies all' (p. 5).

around by Laurent in a 'foul embrace', for she becomes bound to them by their dreadful revelations and her impotent desire for revenge. Here again, the intensity and complexity of a three-way sado-masochistic relationship is conveyed, not by psychological analysis, but by a recurrent, highly physical metaphor.

The novel's insistent enclosure within a tight spatial and thematic compass, a carefully controlled frame of reference from which external elements are excluded and within which key images recur with changing meanings, is further reinforced by its narrative structure. A number of critics have observed that this structure is dramatic rather than properly novelistic, for we are given little sense of time passing (the events actually take several years) or of the characters developing;[15] instead, an initial unstable situation seems to work itself inexorably out to an inevitable conclusion in the continuous manner of classical tragedy. In other words, the logic of situation is made much stronger and more prominent than any temporal progression of the sort which is usually said to characterize the novel as a genre. The whole book is narrated in an amorphous past tense, as if everything within it, including the flashbacks, were happening on the same level (Zola makes very little use of the pluperfect tense to differentiate between 'zones' of past time), and most of the actions narrated are in fact typical ones which the characters perform day after day. The author has deliberately avoided producing a novel dependent on an eventful plot, with exotic settings and complex characters, choosing instead to construct his work as a 'space' in which the few important events stand out against a background of monotonously repeated actions, and in which meanings gradually circulate and change. An example which illustrates both the tightness of this structure, and the shift of interest from conventional, uni-directional plot to an almost timeless system of symbolic patterning, is the peculiar transference of characteristics which occurs between Thérèse and Mme Raquin. In her early life Thérèse is a passive agent controlled by Mme Raquin,

---

[15] There are in fact a number of inconsistencies in Zola's chronology of events in the book, which suggest that he did not pay particularly close attention to this aspect. A useful study of this problem can be found in Claude Schumacher, *Zola, Thérèse Raquin* (Glasgow, 1990), ch. 4, pp. 61–6.

for all the depth of feeling smouldering away within her; by the end it is Mme Raquin who has been rendered 'silent and immobile' by the paralysis which makes it impossible for her to express her hatred, while Thérèse busies herself about the apartment doing all the things her aunt used to do, although the aftermath of the murder has left her physically old. A similar transference occurs between the carefree and confident Laurent and the weakly, cowardly Camille, for by the end it is the ghost who has become dominant, while Laurent is reduced to a trembling wreck, and even begins to think that he is Camille. Though it is (just) possible to read these developments singly, in conventional 'character' terms, a more satisfactory view is that, taken together, they reflect the altered situation between all the main characters, a situation restructured by the temperamental conflict which both divides them and, as in a Racinian tragedy, binds them inexorably together.

All these features can be summarized by suggesting that *Thérèse Raquin* downplays conventional narrative, while extending to an unusual degree the thematic and symbolic possibilities of description. The backgrounds and settings generally are certainly calculated to appeal primarily to our visual imagination, but at certain key moments in the book Zola goes much further and actually works up his descriptions, including those of the characters, into properly pictorial compositions. Of course, the old idea that a writer must 'paint a picture' of the things and people he describes can never be literally true, since the process of representation works in quite different ways in words and in pictures. However, Zola was deeply interested in and committed to the avant-garde painting of his day, particularly the work of Manet, and certain of the descriptions in *Thérèse Raquin* are clearly designed to echo both the wider aesthetic principles defended by the modern painters, and even individual canvases. During the writing of the novel he was in close contact with a group of painters including Degas, Renoir, Whistler, and Pissaro, whom he met every week at the café Guerbois, and his early journalistic endeavours had shown him to be a sensitive and well-informed art critic. His hard-hitting public defence of Manet, whose 'Déjeuner sur l'herbe' and 'Olympia', in scandals comparable to that of *Thérèse Raquin*, had recently been attacked for 'immorally' flouting the rules of taste in matters of nudity, had earned him the gratitude of the painter. Manet was actually painting a portrait of Zola, showing him in his study, with a number of Manet's own paintings (including 'Olympia') on the wall in the background, during the period when the novel was being written, and Robert Lethbridge has argued very persuasively that a complex thematic and aesthetic interplay can be discerned between 'Olympia' and *Thérèse Raquin*, mediated by this portrait.[16]

Even on the simplest descriptive level it is easy to make comparisons, as contemporary critics immediately did,[17] between Manet's canvas and the coloration and technique of Zola's initial evocation of Thérèse as she sits in the shop, then later as she appears to Laurent, both physically and in his dreams. There is no space here to do full justice to this complex question, which is discussed at length by Lethbridge. However, by linking Thérèse to the provocatively nude courtesan in Manet's painting sufficiently clearly for the connection to be perceived by his contemporaries, Zola was deliberately accentuating both the connotations of immorality and the aesthetically subversive implications carried by his 'portrait' of Thérèse. Conventionally, nudity in painting was always shown in a carefully controlled social or literary–historical context (the artist's studio, or the story of the rape of the Sabine women, for example); the pseudo-classical, academic Bacchante by Laurent's successful painter-friend is clearly in this tradition. Manet's Olympia, with her black servant and cat (an ironic replacement for the lap-dog in Titian's 'Venus of Urbino', of which the painting is a parodic reworking), infringes these controlling social conventions, just as its unacceptably 'modern' execution ('flat' appearance of the figure, 'misuse' of perspective, 'excessive' contrast between dark and light zones) infringed the artistic canons of the time. It might be argued that Zola's deliberately non-psychological, non-judgemental presentation of Thérèse contravenes both the dominant literary conventions and the social morality of his day in a comparable way to Manet's canvas.

[16] See Robert Lethbridge, 'Zola, Manet and *Thérèse Raquin*', *French Studies*, 34 (1980), 278–99.
[17] See ibid. 284.

His use of landscape and other background description also reveals a preoccupation with the techniques, subject-matter, and moods of painting. Particularly significant in this respect is the Saint-Ouen scene, which is strongly reminiscent, in its treatment of the popular holiday theme, of Renoir's 'Le Déjeuner des canotiers' (part of that painting can be seen on the cover of the Garnier paperback edition of *Thérèse Raquin*, though it was actually completed a short time after the novel was published). The reader's attention, like Thérèse's gaze, is drawn from the foreground (the verandah on which she is standing) into the background, following the line of stalls which stretch out to left and right, with small groups of people (such as the dancing prostitutes and student onlookers) picked out here and there at greater and greater distances, as little genre cameos, in a highly pictorial use of receding perspective. The way in which we (and, again, Thérèse) perceive diners in the middle distance, sitting beneath leaf-covered arbours, as flecks of bright colour filtering through the intervening screen of greenery, is a transposition into words of a brush-stroke technique already being developed by a group of artists whom critics would, a few years later, lump together as 'the Impressionists'. In this scene in particular, then, our perceptions (and those of Thérèse) are being deliberately organized in terms of the bright, fresh, colourful, and essentially euphoric techniques of the most advanced painting of Zola's day. However, unlike Renoir and the other Impressionists who painted such popular festivities and crowd-scenes, Zola refuses to 'aestheticize' the people or the place, stressing instead the smells, noise, and general vulgarity of the event, as if to distance us from this mood of excessive gaiety and prepare us for the sinister events to come.

This sensitivity to light and colour can be seen again in the Morgue chapter, where the dead people's bodies and clothes are described as bright patches against the neutral background of the wall, as well as in the opening description of the haberdashery window, where the symbolic pallor of the aged goods is built up from many different shades of white which combine to form an ironic visual 'symphony' *à la* Gautier, or Whistler. Touches such as these, together with his painterly intuition, in setting the scene for the murder, that the colours and lines of the landscape are 'simplified' as dusk falls, are all signs of a sophisticated visual imagination which suggests that Zola was well equipped to understand Impressionist techniques as they were beginning to evolve around him. However, his later claim to have 'translated Impressionism into literature'[18] seems to be a considerable exaggeration, for many of the techniques examined above are not specific to Impressionism. In reality, his pictorial technique, like that of Laurent, is at least as much Romantically as Impressionistically inspired, as indeed is his theory of neurosis as the origin of Laurent's inspiration.

Perhaps the most enlightening comparison between Impressionist painting and Zola's descriptive technique in *Thérèse Raquin* concerns the different ways in which each exploits an aesthetic of surface observation. In a typical Impressionist canvas we are deliberately prevented from penetrating behind the healthy, smiling faces to the underlying thoughts and feelings, but in compensation for this lack of thematic and emotional depth we are given a seductive play of light and colour over the surface of objects and people, which gives the canvas a busy visual texture. In the same way, though in a much less rosy-cheeked vein, Zola depicts his characters and their world in predominantly visual terms, observing the external, physical symptoms of their inner life but refusing to put conventional labels on what is happening inside them. Unlike the Impressionists, however, Zola has not renounced the 'deeper' realms of experience altogether, but merely translated them into unconventional terms; this emerges clearly in his critical discourse in the preface to *Thérèse Raquin*, which uses metaphors of surgery and dissection to show the novelist rummaging about in the depths of the human organism in search of our profound motivations. While some of the resultant physiological imagery may sometimes make us smile today as a hopelessly

[18] In an interview shortly before his death, Zola is reported to have said: 'I did not merely support the Impressionists, I translated them into literature, through the little touches and tones, coloration and palette of my descriptions. In all of my books ... I was in contact and entered into exchanges with the painters ... They helped me to paint in a new, "literary" manner' (H. Hertz, 'Émile Zola, témoin de la vérité', *Europe*, 30 (1952), 32–3; quoted by Lethbridge, 'Zola, Manet, and *Thérèse Raquin*', 278; my translation).

literal way of cutting the Gordian knot of the mind–body problem, it was very much in the positivistic spirit of its time; it was also, of course, completely incompatible with the surface gaiety which is so characteristic of Impressionism.

A much closer similarity of theme and technique exists with the early, pre-Impressionist work of Zola's boyhood friend from Aix, Paul Cézanne (1839–1906), whom Zola had persuaded to move to Paris. While *Thérèse Raquin* was being written, Cézanne was producing violently erotic and morbidly romantic pictures, which consistently failed to gain admission to the Salon. Zola defended his friend's work, but it is clear that despite its echos of his own preoccupations with physiology, he did not really appreciate it, preferring the more naturalistic if equally subversive painting of Manet. His reticence was due in part to the crudeness of Cézanne's early technique: one art critic has written of the 'underlying fury and latent power revealed by the blackish colour and brutal handling' of his canvases.[19] This of course sounds like Zola's own description of the way Camille's murderer paints, and although the similarity was not recognized at the time, modern critics agree that Laurent is in fact a tendencious and critical portrait of Cézanne, on whom the similarity would not have been lost.[20] It seems clear that the triangular conflict explored in *Thérèse Raquin* is a literary re-working of tensions that the novelist felt in his own life, and in particular that Camille is, to some extent, a distorted self-portrait.

In his technical allusions to Manet and early Impressionism and Cézanne, as in his temperamental system of character-drawing and the apparent amoralism of his value-system, Zola was perhaps setting out in *Thérèse Raquin* to appear more of a radical innovator than he really was. His self-presentation as an 'experimental moralist' exploring extreme states of mind in a new way was clearly hyperbolic, doubtless in part from a desire for self-publicity, but also because an overstatement of his case was the best way to counter the hostility and incomprehension of his critics. While it would obviously be wrong to

[19] Erle Loran, *Cézanne's Composition* (Berkeley, 1947), 133.

[20] Zola was to create another, more fully developed portrait of Cézanne in the figure of Claude Lantier, painter-hero of his 1886 Rougon-Macquart novel *L'Œuvre* (*The Masterpiece*, Oxford World's Classics).

take everything he says in his theoretical writings at face value, however, it would be equally incorrect to dismiss his arguments out of hand as mere 'mystifications'. We should now be in a position to make a sensible assessment of the 'experimental' status of *Thérèse Raquin*, as well as its significance for the future development of Zola's work. The novel can obviously not be regarded as experimental in the scientific sense; the temperaments theory and conflictual relations between characters reveal no new and unexpected truths about human nature, nor is the theory 'tested' according to any genuinely experimental method, since the outcome of the plot is clearly known to the author and planned in advance (as indeed, by the very conventions of the genre, is the outcome of any novel). The real experiment, of course, is novelistic in nature: temperaments, and the descriptive methods and techniques of symbolic patterning which Zola evolved in support of them, are virtually a literary hypothesis which he implements in order to see how far it is adequate to the task of structuring a novel.

He had clear strategic reasons for pursuing this experiment, the most important of which was a desire to evade the claustrophobic conventions and restrictions imposed by a morally and aesthetically ultra-conservative social establishment. The price which had to be paid was the disruption, even destruction, of conventional novelistic psychology, which Zola felt had become an ally of the censor in imposing normative moral values and behavior-patterns in literature. This in itself seemed shocking to many readers of his day; even now, many critics seem desperate to prove that Zola was unable to avoid resorting to psychology, as if that were somehow the only 'natural' way to write a novel. Like many another novelist before and since, he was unwilling to discuss his deepest motivations openly, for that would have drawn attention to the real mechanisms of his creation; instead, he put a well-reasoned scientific gloss on his intentions, something he was able to do with all the more conviction because of his genuine fascination with scientific ideas and scientific rationalism.

As to the ultimate success of Zola's experiment, critical opinion has long been divided. There is no doubt that some of the techniques which he developed in *Thérèse Raquin*, such as the symbolic interweaving of setting and motivation to form apparently non-rational but potently suggestive thematic patterns, continued to serve him well in the great novels of his Rougon-Macquart cycle (one only need think of the devouring mine of *Germinal,* or the evil alembic in *L'Assommoir*). However, the temperaments theory is by no means so prominent in these later works, no doubt because it functions best in the context of a small-scale novel. In fact, this shows up one of the main limitations of *Thérèse Raquin,* one of which Zola was doubtless aware (and which he turned to considerable advantage in reinforcing the book's powerful atmosphere of menace and inevitability): its inward-looking, even claustrophobic construction. It was part of Zola's aim, as we have seen, to 'imprison' his characters metaphorically within their temperaments, just as they are imprisoned literally, for most of the novel, within the Passage du Pont-Neuf. The stultifying environment which pitilessly mirrors Thérèse's and Laurent's loathsome sensations of guilt and drives them inevitably towards death, interacts with their temperaments in a reinforcing, circular way, as the theories of Taine suggested that it should. But the technical circularity of the novel's construction, so necessary for the satisfactory working-out of the system of temperaments, in a sense also traps and imprisons the reader, who is unable to break out of the concentrated, highly directive manner in which plot, character-drawing, and setting are handled by Zola. Every aspect of the book's tightly constrained novelistic structure carries an authorially imposed meaning which guides our reading in a particular direction, leaving little room for those subtle ambiguities of interpretation which, in a conventional psychological novel, often provide so much of our pleasure. While there is no doubt, however, that the claustrophobia felt by the characters occasionally rubs off on the reader, this is more than compensated for by the book's extraordinary intensity and tension. And it is of course ultimately on this qualitative reading experience, rather than on Zola's historically fascinating but no longer very credible scientific theories, that *Thérèse Raquin's* high reputation in our own day still rests. But then again, without the theories, it would have been quite a different novel.

TRANSLATOR'S NOTE

THE manuscript of *Thérèse Raquin* is lost. The story was serialized in *L'Artiste* between August and October 1867, before being published in volume form in December. The standard text has become that of the second edition, published with an additional preface by Lacroix and Verboeckhoven in April 1868. The present translation is based on this version, as reprinted in the Garnier-Flammarion paperback edition of 1970, edited by Henri Mitterrand.

Thérèse Raquin is a gripping story, but most readers would agree that the novel is not perfect on a technical level, and it is some of its less successful features that make it at times an awkward work to translate. This is particularly true of the numerous repetitions ('the former haberdasher', 'the drowned man', 'silent and immobile', etc.), which come back with the insistence of leitmotifs; where these were felt to be just too clumsy or obtrusive in English, they have been rephrased. Zola is not particularly concerned to modulate some of the climaxes in the book: extreme vocabulary (of horror, terror, loathing, etc.) is used early on (we are told in Chapter III, for instance, that Thérèse 'shivered with fear' and was 'frozen with horror' on her first visit to the shop!), so that subsequent intensification can be achieved only by accumulation and repetition. It is clearly not part of a translator's job to try to 'correct' such pervasive stylistic features, so they have been left as they stand. The opposite problem affects much of Zola's quasi-medical vocabulary: in the absence of more precise medical knowledge, phrases such as 'nervous attack', 'irritation of the nerves', etc., were used in his day to designate quite serious and specific disorders, mental and/or physical in origin (the vague terminology reflected the doctors' uncertainty as to the real nature of such conditions). Nowadays these terms have lost their scientific overtones, and survive only in much weaker, popular senses, which might lead modern readers to under value the seriousness of the mental breakdown which afflicts Thérèse and Laurent; again, however, it did not seem appropriate to try to intensify further the symptoms Zola describes, or to convey them in more modern clinical terms. Nor has any attempt been made to rectify or reconcile apparent errors of chronology made by Zola, which can probably be put down simply to carelessness. Some alterations have however been made to the tense-sequences in certain passages (notably in 'flashbacks', where he tends to use the imperfect when a pluperfect might be expected), in order to bring out more clearly in English the relationships between distant and more recent narrative time-frames. It also proved necessary on occasion to decide between frequentative and narrative uses of the French imperfect tense, a distinction which Zola deliberately blurs in order to convey the monotony of the life led by the Raquin household, but which can lead to apparent temporal contradictions in English.

I should like to take this opportunity to thank Hilary Walford for her skilful and sensitive copy-editing of the typescript. I owe an even greater debt of gratitude to my wife, Siân, for putting up with my work schedule during the book's gestation, and still having the courage to read and criticize the result when it was finished.

I should like to thank Adrienne Lee, Melissa Wells, and Sam Rose, members of my 1997–8 MA translation group, for their invaluable comments and suggestions on the translation as it was being revised

A. R.

Leeds
28 May 1998

SELECT BIBLIOGRAPHY

THE text used for the present translation of *Thérèse Raquin* is that of the second edition, published in Paris by Lacroix and Verboeckhoven in April 1868. The following books and articles on Zola have been found to be the most informative on *Thérèse Raquin*:

Bertrand-Jennings, Chantal, *Espaces romanesques: Zola* (Sherbrooke, Naaman, 1987).

Best, Janice, *Expérimentation et adaptation: Essai sur la méthode naturaliste d'Émile Zola* (Paris, Corti, 1986).

Hemmings, F. W. J., 'The Origins of the Terms *Naturalisme, Naturaliste*', *French Studies*, 8 (1954), 109–21.

——*Émile Zola* (2nd edn., Oxford, Clarendon Press, 1966).

Hillairet, Jacques, *Dictionnaire historique des rues de Paris* (2nd edn., 2 vols.; Paris, Minuit, 1964).

Lapp, John C., *Zola before the Rougon-Macquart* (Toronto, University of Toronto Press, 1964).

Lethbridge, Robert, 'Zola, Manet and *Thérèse Raquin*', *French Studies*, 34 (1980), 278–99.

Mitterrand, Henri, Introduction to *Thérèse Raquin* (Paris, Garnier-Flammarion, 1970), 11–34.

——*Le Discours du roman* (Paris, Presses Universitaires de France, 1980).

——*Zola et le Naturalisme* (Paris, Presses Universitaires de France, (Que sais-je?), 1986).

Schumacher, Claude, *Zola, Thérèse Raquin* (Glasgow Introductory Guides to French Literature, 11; Glasgow, University of Glasgow French and German Publications, 1990).

Woollen, Geoff, 'How Streetwise was Zola?', *Bulletin of the Émile Zola Society* 16 (September 1997), 24–8.

Other writings by Zola of special relevance to *Thérèse Raquin* and Naturalism include *Mes Haines* (1866) for an article on Taine, *Mon Salon* (1866) for an article on Manet, and *Le Roman expérimental* (1881); all are to be found in the fifteen-volume *Œuvres complétes* edited by Henri Mitterrand (Paris, Cercle du Livre précieux, 1966–70). In addition, Henri Mitterrand's paperback edition of *Thérèse Raquin* (Paris, Garnier-Flammarion, 1970), contains a useful dossier on the critical storm caused by the novel (pp. 35–54), including the texts of 'Un mariage d'amour' (the first sketch for *Thérèse Raquin*) and the hostile article by 'Ferragus', the supportive letters of Sainte-Beuve and Taine, and Zola's reply to the former (pp. 35–54).

A CHRONOLOGY OF
ÉMILE ZOLA

1840   (2 Apr.) : Birth of Émile Zola in Paris.

1843   Family moves to Aix, where Zola's civil engineer father François is to build a canal.

1847   Death of François Zola.

1852–7   Secondary schooling in Aix. Wins school prizes, writes verse. Friendship with Paul Cézanne.

1858   Goes to live in Paris with mother; enters Lycée Saint-Louis.

1859   Fails *baccalauréat*; two years of relative inactivity and increasing poverty follow. Reads French Romantic novelists, writes poetry.

1862   Starts work for Hachette booksellers and publishers; quickly rises to be head of advertising department.

1863   Begins writing literary reviews for regional newspapers.

1864   *Contes à Ninon* published.

1865   Publishes enthusiastic review of *Germinie Lacerteux*, by the brothers Goncourt. *La Confession de Claude*.

1866   Leaves Hachette to write regular column of literary and art criticism for *L'Événement*. Article in praise (and defence) of Manet. *Le Voeu d'une morte*. 'Un mariage d'amour', short story and sketch for *Thérèse Raquin*, published in *Le Figaro* (24 Dec.).

1867   First two volumes of *Les Mystères de Marseille*, pot-boiler originally serialized in *Le Messager de Provence*. *Thérèse Raquin* (first published in three monthly instalments as *Un mariage d'amour* in Arsène Houssaye's *L'Artiste*).

1868   Polemic with 'Ferragus' over *Thérèse Raquin* in *Le Figaro*; second edition, with preface. Third volume of *Les Mystères de Marseille*. *Madeleine Férat*. Friendship with the Goncourts.

1869–93   Twenty-volume novel-cycle Les Rougon-Macquart, the 'natural history' of a Second Empire family, and Zola's masterpiece. First volume (*La Fortune des Rougon*) published Oct. 1871. Other notable titles include *Le Ventre de Paris* (1873), *L'Assommoir* (1877), which brought him fame and fortune, *Nana* (1880), *Germinal* (1885), and *La Bête humaine* (1890).

1869–71   Writes for republican opposition press.

1870   Marries his mistress, Gabrielle-Alexandrine Meley.

1873   Stage version of *Thérèse Raquin* flops at Théâtre de la Renaissance. Other plays and writings on theatre follow.

1874   *Nouveaux Contes à Ninon.*

1878   Buys house in Médan, where Huysmans, Maupassant, and other Naturalist writers become frequent guests.

1880   Death of Zola's mother. *Le Roman expérimental*, collection of critical and theoretical studies published in newspapers and reviews over preceding five years. Launches campaign in support of Naturalism.

1881   Further collections of literary writings. Abandons journalism.

1885   Campaign against theatrical censorship.

1888   Meets Jeanne Rozerot, who becomes his mistress.

1891   Elected President of the Société des Gens de lettres.

1893   Awarded the *Légion d'honneur* on completion of Les Rougon-Macquart.

1894–8   *Les Trois Villes* (*Lourdes*, 1894; *Rome*, 1896; *Paris*, 1898).

1897   Articles in *Le Figaro* in support of Captain Alfred Dreyfus.

1898   *J'Accuse* published in *L'Aurore* (January). Zola condemned to one year in prison and a fine of 3,000 francs for his role in the Dreyfus affair; flees to England.

1899   Dreyfus pardoned, thanks in part to Zola's campaign. Zola returns to France (June). *Fécondité* (first of *Les Quatre Évangiles*).

1901   *Travail.*

1902   Death of Zola from carbon monoxide poisoning at his Paris home.

1903   *Vérité.* Only fragmentary notes remain of *Justice*, last of the *Quatre Évangiles*.

1906   Dreyfus's name cleared.

1908   Zola's ashes transferred to the Panthéon.

PREFACE TO THE SECOND EDITION

I HAD believed, naïvely, that this novel might do without a preface. It being my habit to say loudly and clearly what I think, and to emphasize even the smallest details of what I write, I had hoped to be understood and judged without need of prior explanation. It would seem that I was wrong.

The critics have given this book a hostile and indignant reception. Certain righteous individuals, writing in no less righteous newspapers, have picked it up between thumb and forefinger, screwed up their faces in disgust, and thrown it on the fire. Even the little literary rags, those same papers which every evening retail the latest gossip from bedrooms and private chambers, spoke of filth and stench and held their noses. I make no complaint about this reception; on the contrary, I am charmed to observe that my fellow-writers have the sensitive nerves of young girls. It is quite evident that my work belongs to my judges, and that they may find it nauseating without my having any right to object. I do, however, resent the fact that not one of the bashful journalists who have blushed whilst reading *Thérèse Raquin* seems to me to have understood the novel. If they had, they might well have blushed deeper, but at least I would now be enjoying the private satisfaction of seeing them disgusted for the right reasons. Nothing is more irritating than to hear honest writers loudly denouncing depravity when one is firmly persuaded they are doing so without knowing what it is they are calling depraved.

It is, therefore, necessary for me to introduce my work to my judges. I shall do so in a few lines only, and for the sole purpose of avoiding misunderstandings in the future.

In *Thérèse Raquin* I set out to study, not characters, but temperaments. Therein lies the whole essence of the book. I chose to portray individuals existing under the sovereign dominion of their nerves and their blood, devoid of free will and drawn into every act of their lives by the inescapable promptings of their flesh. Thérèse and Laurent are human animals nothing more. In these animals I set out to trace, step by step, the hidden workings of the passions, the urges of instinct, and the derangements of the brain which follow on from a nervous crisis. Love, for my two heroes, is the satisfaction of a physical need; the murder they commit is a consequence of their adultery, a consequence they accept as wolves accept the slaughter of sheep; and last, what I have been obliged to call their remorse consists simply in an organic disorder, the revolt of a nervous system stretched to breaking point. There is a total absence of soul, as I will readily admit, for such was my intention.

I hope it is now becoming clear that my objective was first and foremost a scientific one. When I was creating my two characters, Thérèse and Laurent, I set myself a number of problems and then solved them for the interest of it: I tried, for instance, to explain the strange union that can come about between two different temperaments, and to show the profound disorders wrought in a sanguine nature through contact with a nervous one. If the novel is read with care it will be seen that each chapter is the study of a curious physiological case. In a word, I had only one aim, which was: given a powerful man and an unsatisfied woman, to seek within them the animal, and even to see in them only the animal, to plunge them together into a violent drama and then take scrupulous note of their sensations and their actions. I simply carried out on two living bodies the same analytical examination that surgeons perform on corpses.

You will agree that when one emerges from such a labour, still deeply absorbed in the earnest satisfactions of the quest for truth, it is indeed hard to bear accusations that one's only aim was to paint obscene pictures. I found myself in the same position as those artists who copy the nude body without feeling the least stirring of desire, and are completely taken aback when a critic declares himself scandalized by the living flesh depicted in their work. While I was writing *Thérèse Raquin* I was lost to the world, completely engrossed in my exact and meticulous copying of real life and my analysis of the human mechanism, and I assure you that the cruel sexual passion of Thérèse and Laurent had for me nothing immoral about it, nothing which might excite unacceptable desires in others.

The humanity of the models disappeared for me as it does for the artist who has a naked woman stretched out before him, and whose only thought is to put down on his canvas the truth of her form and coloration. Great, therefore, was my surprise when I heard my work called a cesspit of blood and filth, a stinking sewer, an abomination, and I forget what else. I know the delightful rules of the critical game, and have even played it myself; but I admit that I was somewhat disconcerted by the unanimity of the attack. Was there not a single one of my fellow-writers prepared at least to explain my book, if not actually to defend it? Among the chorus of voices crying out, 'the author of *Thésèse Raquin* is a wretched hysteric who delights in flaunting his pornography in public', I waited in vain for someone to say: 'No, you are wrong, this writer is just an analyst, one who may perhaps have become engrossed in human rottenness, but only in the same way as a doctor lecturing to students about disease.'

Note that I am in no way asking the press to respond favourably to a work which, so they claim, their delicate senses find repugnant. I cannot aspire so high. I am merely astonished that my fellow-writers, whose practised eye ought to let them recognize a novelist's intentions within the first ten pages, should have made of me a sort of literary sewer-worker, and I am content to beg them humbly in the future to be good enough to see me as I am, and discuss my work for what it is.

Yet it would have been so easy to understand *Thérèse Raquin*, to observe and analyse the book and point out to me its real faults, without immediately picking up a handful of mud to fling in my face in the name of morality. What was required was a little intelligence and a few real critical ideas. Accusations of immorality, in the field of science, prove absolutely nothing. I do not know whether my novel is immoral; I admit that I never worried about making it more or less chaste. What I do know is that I never for one minute set out to put in the filth that moral people are now discovering in it; that I wrote every scene, even the most torrid ones, with the sole curiosity of the scientist; and that I defy my judges to find in it a single genuinely licentious page, of the kind enjoyed by readers of those titillating little novels which peddle the indiscretions of boudoir and back stage, sell ten thousand copies, and are warmly recommended by the same newspapers nauseated by the truths I have presented in *Thérèse Raquin*.

A few insults and many fatuous remarks are, therefore, all that I have read to date about my work. I say this quite calmly, as I would to a friend who had asked me privately what I thought about the critics' attitude towards me. A highly talented writer to whom I was complaining about the lack of understanding I had received gave me this profound reply: 'You have one tremendous failing which will close everyone's door to you: you are unable to talk to an idiot for two minutes without letting him know that you consider him such.' That cannot be helped; I know the disservice I am doing myself by accusing the critics of lacking intelligence, and yet I am unable to prevent myself from showing the contempt I feel for their narrow outlook and their blind, completely unsystematic way of judging. I am, of course, speaking here of critics in the popular press, who judge with all the literary prejudices of fools, incapable as they are of adopting the broader human perspective required to understand a truly human work. Never have I witnessed such incompetence. The few blows these petty critics aimed at me when *Thérèse Raquin* came out struck, as always, only thin air. Their judgement is always wide of the mark; they are capable of applauding the pirouettes of some heavily powdered actress one moment and screaming about the immorality of a study in physiology the next; they understand nothing, want to understand nothing, and are forever lashing out at the first target put up by their panicky stupidity. It is exasperating to be punished for a crime of which one is absolutely innocent. There are moments when I actually regret not having put in a few obscenities; I would almost be happier with a well-deserved thrashing than see these stupid attacks continue to rain down about my head like tiles off a roof, without knowing why.

In our age there are scarcely two or three men capable of reading, understanding, and judging a book.* From them I am prepared to hear criticism, convinced as I am that they will not speak without having understood my intentions and weighed the results of my efforts. They would certainly refrain from using those great empty words morality and literary modesty; they would recognize my right, in these times of freedom in the arts, to choose those subjects I see fit, demanding only that the resulting works be produced in good conscience, and knowing that stupidity alone is damaging to the dignity of literature. They would certainly not be surprised by the scientific analysis that I have attempted to apply in *Thérèse Raquin*; they would see it as an example of the modern method, an application of the universal investigative tool which our century is using with such passion to lay bare the secrets of the future. Whatever might be their conclusions, they would accept my starting-point, the study of the temperaments and the profound modifications brought about in the human organism by the pressure of surroundings and circumstances. I should be facing true judges, men seeking the truth in good faith, with no puerility or false shame, and no thought of having to feign disgust before naked, living, anatomical specimens. Sincere study, like fire, purifies all. Of course, my work would stand most humbly before the court which I now have the pleasure of imagining; I would call down on it the full severity of the critics, I would wish it to emerge black with crossings-out. But at least I would have known the profound joy of being criticized for what I had attempted to achieve, and not for something I had not done.

I seem already to hear the verdict of the great critics, those of the methodical, Naturalist school which has brought about the renewal of the sciences, history, and literature: '*Thérèse Raquin* is the study of too exceptional a case; the drama of modern life is more various than this, not limited to the horror and madness portrayed here. Cases of this sort belong more in the background of the book. The desire not to let any of his observations go to waste has led the author to stress each tiny detail, and over-do the tension and harshness of the work as a whole. Moreover, the style does not have the simplicity necessary in a work of analysis. In short, if the author now wishes to write a good novel, he should try to take a broader view of society, to depict it in its many and varied aspects, and above all to write in a more precise, natural manner.'*

My intention was to make a brief reply to certain attacks irritating in their bad faith, and I see that I am now beginning to debate with myself, as I always do when I keep pen in hand for too long. I know how much that annoys readers, so I shall stop. If I had the will and the leisure to write a manifesto, I would perhaps have tried to defend what one journalist, writing about *Thérèse Raquin*, has called 'putrid literature'* of this type. Then again, why should I bother? The group of Naturalist writers to which I have the honour of belonging is courageous and active enough to produce powerful works containing within them their own defence. It takes all the blind prejudice a certain brand of criticism can muster to force a novelist into writing a preface. Since from a simple love of accuracy I have committed the error of doing so, I beg to be excused by intelligent people who, in order to see clearly, do not need to have a lantern lit for them in broad daylight.

Émile Zola

15 April 1868

I

AT the end of the Rue Guénégaud, coming up from the river, can be found the Passage du Pont-Neuf,* a sort of dark, narrow corridor running between the Rue Mazarine and the Rue de Seine. This arcade is some thirty paces long and no more than two wide; it is paved with yellowish flagstones, worn, uneven, permanently exuding an acrid-smelling damp, and is covered by a right-angled glass roof black with grime.

On fine summer days when the sun beats oppressively down on the streets outside, a pallid light filters in through the filthy panes and lingers miserably in the passage. On foul winter days or on foggy mornings, the glass casts nothing but darkness on the sticky flags beneath, a vile and murky darkness.

Let into the wall on the left there are a number of shops, dark, low, and cramped, from which chill draughts emerge as if from a vault. These shops sell second-hand books, children's toys, and stationery, and their grey, dust-laden displays doze dimly in the gloom; the windows, a mass of tiny panes, mottle the merchandise inside with strange greenish reflections, while, in the shadowy and lugubrious depths beyond, strange shapes can be seen moving.

All along the right-hand wall of the passage, stall-holders have fixed shallow cupboards in which nameless objects, goods forgotten since they were put there twenty years before, lie strewn along flimsy shelves painted an ugly brown colour. From one such cupboard a woman plies her trade in costume jewellery, selling cheap rings delicately laid out on blue velvet cushions in mahogany boxes.

Above the glazed roof the wall rises towards the sky, black and coarsely rendered, as if covered with leprous sores and zigzagged with scars.

The Passage du Pont-Neuf is not a place where people go for a stroll. It is a short cut, a way of saving a few minutes. Those who pass through it are busy people whose sole concern is to get where they are going as quickly as possible. There

are apprentices in their labourers' aprons, seamstresses returning work they have finished, men and women with parcels
under their arms; old men dragging themselves along in the
dismal half-light which filters through the glass roof, and bands
of children who come there after school to lark about, running
up and down the flagstones in a clatter of clogs. All day long
there can be heard the same irritatingly irregular patter of footsteps hurrying along the passage; nobody ever stops to talk;
everyone goes quickly about his or her business, head down,
at a brisk pace, without so much as a glance at the shops.
The shopkeepers look anxiously at any passer-by who, by some
miracle, happens to stop in front of their window.

   In the evening the arcade is lit by three heavy, square-shaped
gas lanterns hanging down from the glazed roof, on which
they cast lurid patches of light, while only a pale glow falls
on the pavement below in dim, flickering pools which sometimes disappear almost completely. This gives the arcade the
menacing feel of a cut-throats' alley; long shadows slide along
the flags, damp draughts come in off the street, and the whole
place feels like some underground gallery dimly lit by three
funeral lamps. The shopkeepers make do with the feeble rays
which come in through their windows, lighting only one shaded
lamp for the shop, which they place on the corner of the counter; this allows passers-by to make out what there is in the
depths of these warrens where darkness is at home in the middle
of the day. Along the gloomy line of shop-fronts the stationer's
windows are a blaze of light, as two shale-oil lamps pierce
the shadows with their yellow flames. And on the other side
a candle, stuck in the middle of a lamp-glass, spangles the
box of costume jewellery with reflections, while its proprietress
dozes at the back of her stall, her hands hidden under a shawl.

   A few years ago there stood opposite this stall a shop whose
bottle-green woodwork exuded damp from all its cracks. Its
sign was a long, narrow plank which bore the word HABERDASH-
ERY in black letters, and on one of the glass panes of the door
a woman's name was painted, in red: THÉRÈSE RAQUIN. The
deep recesses of the windows to left and right were laid out
with blue paper.

   During the day, only the window display itself could be
made out in the hazy half-light.

On one side there were items of clothing: fluted tulle bonnets at two or three francs apiece, muslin collars and cuffs, woollen cardigans, stockings, socks, and braces. Each item, yellowed and creased, hung pathetically from a little wire hook, filling the window from top to bottom with whitish odds and ends which took on a lugubrious appearance in the transparent gloom. The new bonnets, of a brighter white, stood out starkly against the blue paper which covered the boards, while coloured socks, hanging down from a horizontal wire, sounded a darker note amid the wan, indistinct blankness of the muslin.

In the narrower window on the other side were shelves covered in fat skeins of green wool, black buttons sewn on to white card, boxes of all sizes and colours, hairnets with steel beads laid out on circles of bluish paper, fan-shaped arrays of knitting needles, tapestry patterns, spools of ribbon, heaps of dull and faded objects which had doubtless lain dormant in the same place for the last five or six years. Everything in this display case decaying with dust and damp had turned the same shade of dirty grey.

Near noon in summer, when the sun's glaring rays burned down on the squares and streets outside, one could discern, behind the bonnets of the first window, the pale, serious profile of a young woman, outlined vaguely against the dark shadows which filled the shop. Jutting from beneath the low, steeply sloping brow was a long, narrow, pointed nose; the lips were two thin, pale-pink lines and the chin, short and nervous, was joined to the neck by a broad, supple curve. The body blended into the shadows and could not be seen; all that was visible was the dim whiteness of the profile, with the black hole of a wide-open eye in the middle and a dark mass of hair piled up on top. There it remained, peaceful and unmoving for hours on end, between two bonnets on which the damp metal runner had left a rusty stripe.

In the evening, once the lamp had been lit, the interior of the shop could be seen. It was wider than it was deep; at one end stood a small counter; at the other, a spiral staircase led up to the bedrooms on the first floor. All around the walls were display cases, cupboards, and rows of boxes; four tables and chairs made up the rest of the furniture. The room had a bare, chill appearance; the stock was not allowed to lie about in a riot of gay colours, but was all carefully parcelled up and packed away in corners.

There were usually two women sitting behind the counter: the young one with the serious profile and an old lady who sat dozing with a smile on her face. The latter was around sixty years old; her placid, fleshy face looked white in the lamplight. A large tabby cat sat perched on the corner of the counter, watching her as she slept.

In front of the high counter a man of about thirty would sit reading or talking in a low voice to the young woman. He was short, puny and of languid appearance; with his dull blond hair, sparse beard, and heavily freckled face he looked like a spoilt, sickly child.

Shortly before ten o'clock the old lady would wake up. The shop was shut, and then the whole family went upstairs to bed. The tabby cat followed its owners, purring and rubbing its head against each banister as it went.

Upstairs there were three rooms. The staircase led up to a dining-room which was also used as a living-room. To the left, a porcelain stove stood in an alcove; opposite it was a sideboard; chairs were lined up along the walls and a folding circular table occupied the middle of the room. At one end, behind a glass partition, was a dark kitchen. On either side of the dining-room there was a bedroom.

After kissing her son and daughter-in-law good night, the old lady would retire to her room. The cat always fell asleep on a chair in the kitchen. The married couple went into their own room, which had a second door leading out on to a back staircase, from the bottom of which a dark, narrow passage led back into the arcade.

The husband, who was perpetually shivering with fever, would go to bed, while the young wife opened the window to close the shutters. She would stand there for a few minutes, facing the great black, coarsely rendered wall which reached high up into the sky above the roof of the arcade. After gazing vacantly at the wall she too would go to bed, with an expression of disdain and indifference on her face.

II

MADAME Raquin was a former haberdasher from Vernon,*
where for nearly twenty-five years she had run a small shop.
A few years after the death of her husband she had become
tired of the business and sold off her stock. Her savings, combined with the proceeds of the sale, left her with a capital
of forty thousand francs, which she invested, giving her a pension of two thousand a year. This sum was more than adequate
for her needs. She lived the life of a recluse, untouched by
the poignant joys and sorrows of the world; she had made
for herself an existence full of peace and happy tranquillity.

For four hundred francs a month she rented a small house
with a garden running down to the banks of the Seine. It was
a private, enclosed retreat with a vague scent of the nunnery
about it, surrounded by broad meadows and approached by
a narrow path; the windows of the building looked out over
the river and the deserted little hills on the other bank. The
good lady, now past fifty, buried herself away in this solitude,
living a life of serene contentment in the company of her son
Camille and her niece Thérèse.

By then Camille was twenty. His mother still treated him
like a spoilt little boy. She adored him because she had struggled to keep him alive through a youth full of pain and sickness.
The child had had every imaginable type of fever and illness,
one after the other, and Madame Raquin had put up a fifteen-
year fight against the sequence of fearful maladies which had
threatened to snatch her son from her. She had overcome
them all with her patience, care, and adoring devotion.

When Camille grew up his life was no longer in danger,
but the repeated onslaught of illness and pain had left his
body in a delicate state. His growth had been stunted, so that
he remained small and sickly looking; the movements of his
skinny limbs were slow and tired. His mother loved him all
the more for his weakness and debilitation. She looked on
his poor, pale little face with triumphant tenderness and

thought how she had given him life at least a dozen times over.

During his rare periods of respite from illness, the child had attended classes at a commercial school in Vernon, where he was taught spelling and arithmetic. His entire learning consisted of basic sums and a very superficial grasp of grammar. Later on, he took lessons in bookkeeping and accounting. Whenever Madame Raquin was advised to send her son away to boarding school, she began to shake with fear: she knew that he would die away from her, and always said that books would kill him. Camille remained ignorant, and his ignorance was just one more weakness in him.

At the age of eighteen, at a loss for what to do with himself and bored to death by the protective atmosphere with which his mother surrounded him, he went to work as a cloth merchant's clerk at sixty francs a month. His restless nature made idleness unbearable to him, and he felt much better, much calmer, toiling away like a brute in the office, craning his neck over bills all day long and picking his way meticulously through great lists of figures to be added up. In the evenings, worn out and with his mind a complete blank, he would savour with infinite pleasure the vacant feeling which took possession of him. He had had to argue with his mother about the job; she wanted to keep him for ever by her side, wrapped up in blankets and well away from life's accidents. So he spoke to her with a voice of authority, demanding work as other children demand toys, not out of duty but instinctively, as a natural need. His mother's devotion and tenderness had made him fiercely egotistical; he thought he loved the people who pitied him and were nice to him, but in fact he lived a life apart, shut up in himself, loving only his own well-being and seeking, by all possible means, to increase his own pleasures. Once Madame Raquin's tender-hearted doting had begun to revolt him, he had thrown himself joyfully into a stupid occupation which allowed him to escape from her constant round of medicines and herbal infusions. Then, in the evenings, when he came home from the office, he would run down to the banks of the Seine with his cousin Thérèse.

Thérèse was almost eighteen. One day sixteen years before, when Madame Raquin was still working as a haberdasher,

her brother, Captain Degans, had brought a little girl to her in his arms. He had just arrived back from Algeria.

'You are this child's aunt,' he told her with a smile. 'Her mother is dead ... I don't know what to do with her. You can have her.'

The haberdasher took the child, smiling at her and kissing her pink cheeks. Degans stayed a week at Vernon. His sister asked him scarcely anything about the little girl he had given her. She was told vaguely that the dear little thing was born at Oran and that her mother was a native woman of great beauty. An hour before leaving, the Captain gave her a birth certificate on which the child was recognized as his and bore his name. He left and was never seen again; a few years later he was killed in Africa.

Thérèse grew up sleeping in the same bed as Camille and enveloped in her aunt's clinging devotion to him. Although she was strong and healthy she was looked after like a sickly child, sharing the medicines which her cousin had to take, and obliged to spend her time in the overheated atmosphere of the bedroom where the sick boy lived. For hours on end she would squat pensively in front of the fire, staring straight into the flames without blinking. This life of enforced convalescence made her turn in on herself; she developed a habit of speaking in an undertone, walking about the house without making any noise, and sitting silent and motionless on a chair with a vacant look in her eyes. Yet whenever she lifted an arm or moved a foot forward, it was apparent that she had all the litheness of a cat, with taut, powerful muscles and a store of passion and energy which lay dormant in her inert body. One day her cousin had an attack of dizziness and fell over; in one quick movement she picked him up and carried him back, and this sudden exertion brought a great warm flush to her cheeks. The cloistered life that she led and the debilitating regime to which she was subjected were not able to weaken her tough, resilient frame, but her face had taken on a pale, slightly yellowish complexion and when the light was low she could look almost ugly. Sometimes she would go to the window and stare out at the houses opposite, bathed in golden sunlight.

When Madame Raquin sold up her business and retired

to the little house by the river, Thérèse's heart secretly jumped
for joy. Her aunt had so often told her: 'Sit still, don't make
a noise,' that she always took care to keep the impetuous side
of her nature hidden away deep within her. She possessed
supreme self-control, and an apparent calmness which concealed a tendency to terrible fits of passion. She felt penned
in her cousin's room the whole time, looking after a child
constantly at death's door, and she had the careful movements,
placid, silent air, and halting speech of an old woman. When
she saw the garden, the white river, and the expanse of green
hills rolling away to the horizon, she was seized by a wild
urge to shout and run about; she felt her heart throbbing harder
in her breast, but not a muscle moved in her face, and when
her aunt asked whether she liked their new home, all she did
was smile.

From then on, life improved for her. She kept her lithe
appearance and calm, indifferent expression, and she remained
the child who had been brought up sleeping in an invalid's
bed; but inside herself she could begin living her own burning
and passionate existence. When she was down by the water's
edge on her own she would lie full-length in the grass like
an animal, her black eyes wide open, her body twisted in readi-
ness to pounce. And there she would stay for hours, thinking
about nothing in particular, feeling the bite of the sun's rays
on her body, happy just to dig her fingers into the earth. She
dreamed crazy dreams; she would stare defiantly at the rumbling river and imagine that the water was about to leap up
and attack her; then she would stiffen into a defensive posture,
asking herself furiously how the waters could be tamed.

In the evenings Thérèse, calm and silent again, would sit
by her aunt and do needlework, seeming to doze, with her
face lit by the soft glow from the lamp, while Camille, slumped
deep in an armchair, meditated about his ledgers. The occasional word spoken in a low voice was all that disturbed the
peace of this sleepy interior scene.

Madame Raquin looked on her children with serene benevolence. She had resolved to pair them off in marriage. She still
treated her son as if he were at death's door, and trembled
whenever the thought struck her that one day she would die,
leaving him ill and alone. In her mind she always counted

on Thérèse, telling herself that the girl would be a watchful nurse at Camille's side. Her niece, with her air of calm and uncomplaining devotion, inspired unbounded confidence in her. She had seen her at work, and wanted to give her to her son as his guardian angel. Their marriage was a foregone conclusion.

As children they had known for a long time that one day they were to wed each other. They had grown up with this idea, which had become natural and familiar to them. In the family, the match was spoken of as something necessary and inevitable. Madame Raquin had said: 'We shall wait until Thérèse is twenty-one.' And they waited patiently, without blushes or excitement.

Camille, whose illness had impoverished his blood, knew nothing of the keen desires of adolescence. He still behaved like a little boy towards his cousin, kissing her in the same way as he kissed his mother, purely from habit, never losing his self-centred calm. He regarded her as a playmate who stopped him from getting too bored, and who would sometimes make his herbal tea for him. When he played with her and held her in his arms, he thought he was holding another boy, and felt no stirrings of the flesh. At such moments, it never occurred to him to kiss Thérèse on her warm lips, while she struggled beneath him, laughing nervously.

The girl, too, seemed always to remain cold and indifferent. Sometimes she would fix her large eyes on Camille and stare at him for several minutes with supreme unconcern, only her lips making almost imperceptible movements. No feelings could be read in this inscrutable face, on which a constantly gentle and attentive expression was maintained by an implacable will. Whenever her marriage was mentioned, Thérèse would look grave and simply nod in agreement with everything that Madame Raquin said. Camille would go to sleep.

On summer evenings the two young people would run off down to the water's edge. Camille was irritated by his mother's constant fussing; he had rebellious moments when he wanted to rush about and make himself ill, just to escape from her cloying attentions which were starting to make him feel sick. Then he would drag Thérèse off and challenge her to wrestle with him in the grass. One day he gave his cousin a push and she fell over; she leapt up at once like a wild animal, with her cheeks red and eyes blazing with anger, and threw herself on him with both fists raised. Camille slid to the ground. He was scared.

Months, years passed. The day fixed for the wedding arrived. Madame Raquin took Thérèse to one side and told her about her father and mother, and the whole story of her birth. The girl listened to what her aunt had to say, then kissed her without uttering a word.

That night, instead of going into her own bedroom, which was on the left at the top of the stairs, she went into her cousin's, on the right. That was the only change in her life. The following morning when the young couple came downstairs, Camille still had the same sickly languor about him and the same egotistical tranquillity of mind, while Thérèse had lost neither her mild indifference nor her restrained, frighteningly calm expression.

III

A WEEK after his wedding Camille informed his mother bluntly that he intended to leave Vernon and go to live in Paris. Madame Raquin would not hear of it; she had her existence all planned out, and she absolutely refused to change the least detail of it. Her son threw a tantrum and threatened to make himself ill unless she gave in to his whim.

'I never stood in the way of your plans,' he told her. 'I married my cousin and took all the medicines you gave me. Now that I want to do something of my own, the least you can do is agree with me . . . We leave at the end of the month.'

That night, Madame Raquin did not sleep a wink. Camille's decision had turned her whole life upside down and she was looking desperately for a way of putting it back together again. Gradually she calmed down. It occurred to her that the young couple might have children, and that her little fortune would then no longer be enough. She would have to earn more money, go back into business, and find some well-paid occupation for Thérèse. By the next day she had grown used to the idea, and made plans for a new life.

At lunch she was full of enthusiasm.

'Here's what we'll do', she said to her children. 'I'll go to Paris tomorrow and look for a little haberdashery business, and Thérèse and I will set ourselves up again selling needles and thread. That will keep us out of mischief. You, Camille, can do whatever you want—stroll about in the sunshine, or find yourself a job.'

'I shall find a job,' replied the young man.

The truth was that only stupid ambition had driven Camille to think of leaving. He wanted to be an employee in some large administration, and would go pink with pleasure at the thought of himself sitting in the middle of a huge office, wearing shiny artificial cuffs and with a quill pen tucked behind his ear.

Thérèse was not consulted. She had always shown such pas-

Yikes

sive obedience that her mother and her husband no longer
took the trouble to ask her opinion. She went wherever they
went and did what they did without complaint or reproach,
and without even seeming to notice that she was going somewhere else.

Madame Raquin went to Paris and headed straight for the
Passage du Pont-Neuf. An elderly spinster from Vernon had
given her the address of a relative there who ran a haberdashery
business which she was intending to sell. Madame Raquin
found the shop rather small and dark, but while crossing Paris
she had been frightened by the noise and bustle in the streets
and the luxurious shops, and this narrow arcade with its modest
window displays reminded her of the premises she had had
before, so quiet and peaceful. She felt as though she were
still in the provinces; she breathed freely again at the thought
that her children would be happy in this forgotten corner of
Paris. The modest price of the stock made her mind up for
her: they were asking two thousand francs. The rent for the
shop and the flat above was only twelve hundred a year. As
she had almost four thousand francs in savings, she calculated
that she could buy the stock and pay the first year's rent without
eating into her capital. Camille's salary and the profits from
the haberdashery business would suffice for their everyday
needs, she reckoned, so that she would no longer need to draw
her pension, which could be laid down as capital to increase
her grandchildren's inheritance.

She returned to Vernon in a glow of satisfaction, telling
everyone what a pearl of a place she had found, a perfect spot
right in the middle of Paris. Gradually, during her evening
conversations over the next few days, the damp and dingy
shop in the arcade turned into a palace; she saw it in her mind's
eye as convenient, spacious, and quiet, with a thousand
inestimable advantages.

'Oh my dear Thérèse,' she exclaimed, 'we are going to be
happy there, you can be sure of that! There are three fine rooms
upstairs . . . The arcade is full of people . . . We'll make lovely
window displays . . . You'll see, we'll have lots to do!'

She could not stop talking. All her old shopkeeper's instincts
had been reawakened; she began to give Thérèse advice in
advance about buying and selling, and all the little tricks of

running a business. At last it was time for the family to leave the house on the banks of the Seine; that same evening, they moved into the Passage du Pont-Neuf.

When Thérèse walked into the shop which was to be her home from now on, she felt as if she were dropping into the clinging earth of a grave. A sense of revulsion seized her throat and she shivered with fear. She stared at the damp and dirty arcade, examined the shop, went upstairs, looked over each room; the loneliness and dilapidation of this bare, unfurnished apartment was terrifying. The young woman could find nothing to say, not a gesture to make. She was as if frozen with horror. When her aunt and her husband had gone back downstairs, she sat down on a trunk, her hands tensed, half choked by sobs but unable to cry.

Faced with the reality of their situation, Madame Raquin was embarrassed and ashamed of her dreams. She tried to defend her decision, finding a solution to each new difficulty that arose. She explained away the gloom by saying that the sky was overcast, and finished by saying that all that the place needed was a good sweeping out.

'Who cares,' replied Camille, 'it seems quite all right ... Anyway, we'll only be coming up here in the evening. I won't be back before five or six o'clock ... You two will be together; you won't get bored.'

The young man would never have agreed to live in such a squalid hovel if he had not counted on having a snug and comfortable office to work in. He told himself he would be warm there all day long and would go to bed early in the evening.

For a whole week, the shop and the flat above were in a state of chaos. On the very first day Thérèse had sat herself down behind the counter, and there she stayed. Madame Raquin was astonished at her passivity; she had thought that the young woman would try to bring a touch of beauty to her home, putting flowers in the windows and asking for new wallpaper, curtains, and carpets. But whenever she suggested a repair or improvement, her niece would reply calmly:

'Why bother? We are quite all right as we are; we've no need of luxuries.'

It was Madame Raquin who had to arrange the bedrooms

and sort things out in the shop. In the end, the sight of her
constantly running round in circles started to irritate Thérèse;
she took on a cleaning woman and forced her aunt to sit down
by her side.

Camille went for a good month without finding a job. He
strolled about all day long, spending as little time as possible
in the shop. He became so bored that he began to talk of
going back to Vernon. Finally he found a position with the
Orleans Railway,* at one hundred francs per month. His dream
had come true.

He left for work at eight o'clock each morning. After going
down the Rue Guénégaud, he found himself by the river. Then
he would amble along the Seine with his hands in his pockets,
from the Institute* to the Jardin des Plantes.* He never grew
bored of this long walk, which he did twice a day. He would
watch the flow of the current and stop to look at the timber
barges going downstream, thinking about nothing in particular. Often he would stand in front of Notre-Dame and contemplate the scaffolding surrounding the cathedral, for at that time
it was under repair; he liked looking at the thick wooden beams,
without knowing why. Then he would glance at the Port aux
Vins* as he passed, and count the cabs emerging from the
station.* In the evening, worn out and with his head full of
some idiotic story he had been told at work, he would cross
the Jardin des Plantes, stopping to look at the bears if he was
not in too much of a hurry. He would stay leaning over the
edge of the pit for half an hour at a time, watching the great
beasts lumbering about; their ponderous gait amused him; as
he examined their movements, open-mouthed and with his
eyes popping out of his head, he was filled with a kind of
imbecilic joy. At last he would make up his mind to set off
home, dragging his feet and staring curiously at passers-by,
carriages, and shops as he went.

As soon as he got home he would eat and start reading.
He had bought the complete works of Buffon* and every evening he set himself to read twenty or thirty pages, although
he found it very boring. He also read the *History of the Consulate
and Empire* by Thiers* and Lamartine's *History of the Girondins*,* as well as works of popularized science, all of which
he bought in penny instalments. He thought he was working

to improve his education. Sometimes he would force his wife to listen as he read out particular pages or anecdotes. He was very surprised to find that Thérèse was able to sit silent and pensive for a whole evening, without feeling any urge to pick up a book, and admitted to himself that his wife was basically not very bright.

Thérèse rejected his books impatiently. She preferred to sit doing nothing, staring into space and letting her mind wander aimlessly. In any event, her mood always remained balanced and amenable; she devoted all her will-power to making herself into a passive instrument, completely acquiescent, a model of abnegation.

Business was slow but steady. The profits were always the same from month to month. The clientele was made up of working women from the neighbourhood. Every five minutes or so a girl would come in and buy a few penceworth of goods. Thérèse served all the customers with the same phrases and her lips wore the same mechanical smile. Madame Raquin was more flexible and chattier, and it was really she who attracted people in and made them into regular customers.

Three years passed in an unchanging sequence of days. Camille never once stayed away from the office; his mother and wife scarcely ever left the shop. Thérèse, living amidst the damp and gloom in an oppressive, dismal silence, saw life stretching out pointlessly ahead of her, with every evening bringing the same cold bed and every morning the same empty day ahead.

IV

ONCE a week, on Thursdays, the Raquins had guests round for the evening. The large lamp would be lit in the dining-room and a kettle put on the fire to make tea. It was all a great carry-on. These Thursday evenings stood out from all the others in the week; they became something of a habit with the family, a kind of entertaining but highly respectable orgy. Everyone stayed up until eleven.

Madame Raquin had discovered that one of her old friends, police superintendent Michaud, was living in Paris; he had been stationed in Vernon for twenty years, and had lodged in the same house as her. For this reason a close friendship had grown up between them; but once the widow had sold her shop and gone to live in the house by the river, they had gradually lost touch with each other. Michaud had moved a few months later from the provinces to Paris, to the Rue de Seine, there to live quietly on the fifteen hundred francs a month of his pension. One day when it was raining, he bumped into his old friend in the Passage du Pont-Neuf, and that same evening he came to dinner with the Raquins.

Such was the origin of the Thursday receptions. The former police superintendent made a habit of calling round regularly once a week. Eventually he brought along his son Olivier, a tall, dry, skinny fellow of thirty who had married a tiny, slow-witted, sickly woman. Olivier had a job at the central police station at three thousand francs a month, something of which Camille was extremely jealous; he was a principal clerk in the Department of Public Order and Security. From the very first day Thérèse hated this stiff, cold man who considered that the arcade should be honoured to see his great lanky figure strutting down it, with the weakly form of his poor little wife by his side.

Camille brought along another guest, an old employee of the Orleans Railway. Grivet had served the company for twenty years; he was a senior clerk and earned two thousand one hundred francs a month. It was he who decided who did what in the office where Camille worked, and Camille held him in a certain awe; he dreamed to himself that one day Grivet would die and he would perhaps come to replace him, after ten years or so. Grivet was delighted with the welcome Madame Raquin gave him, and came back each week with perfect regularity. Six months later his Thursday visit had become a duty; he went to the Passage du Pont-Neuf, in the same way as he went to his office each morning, out of pure animal instinct.

From then on, the Thursday gatherings were a real delight. At seven o'clock Madame Raquin would light the fire, stand the lamp in the middle of the table, place a box of dominoes next to it, and dust the tea service which stood on the sideboard. At exactly eight o'clock old Michaud and Grivet would meet up in front of the shop, the one coming from the Rue de Seine and the other from the Rue Mazarine. They would enter and everyone would go upstairs, sitting down round the table to wait for Olivier and his wife, who always arrived late. When the party was complete, Madame Raquin poured the tea, Camille tipped the dominoes out on to the waxed table-cloth and everyone became engrossed in the game. The clicking of dominoes was the only sound to be heard. After each game the players would argue for two or three minutes, then the dismal silence would descend again, interrupted only by more clicking.

Thérèse played with a lack of interest which Camille found irritating. She would sit with François, the fat tabby cat which Madame Raquin had brought from Vernon, in her lap, stroking him with one hand and laying down the dominoes with the other. Thursday evenings were a torture to her; often she would complain that she felt unwell, or had a bad migraine, so that she could avoid playing and sit there doing nothing, half asleep. With one elbow on the table, her cheek propped against the palm of her hand, she would look at the guests her aunt and her husband had invited, through the yellow, smoky fog given off by the lamp. All their ugly faces filled her with exasperation. She glanced from one to the other with deep disgust and sullen irritation. Old Michaud's face was pallid and covered with red blotches, the lifeless face of an old man in his dotage;

Grivet had the narrow features, round eyes, and pinched lips of a cretin; Olivier, whose bones seemed almost to stick through his cheeks, carried his stiff and insignificant head solemnly on top of a ridiculous body; as for Suzanne, Olivier's wife, her soft face was utterly blanched, with dull eyes and white lips. Among these grotesque, sinister creatures in whose company she was shut up, Thérèse could find not one real human being; at times she was overcome by the hallucination of being immured deep in a burial vault in the company of mechanical corpses, which nodded their heads and moved their arms and legs about whenever their strings were pulled. She could hardly breathe in the oppressive atmosphere of the dining-room, and the eerie silence and yellowish glow of the lamp filled her with a vague and unspeakable terror.

Down in the shop, a doorbell had been fitted which gave a high-pitched tinkle when customers came in. Thérèse listened out for this ringing and whenever she heard it she would rush downstairs, happy and relieved to escape from the dining-room. She always took her time serving the customer. Then, once she was alone, she would sit down behind the counter and stay there as long as possible, fearful of going back up, and thoroughly pleased at not having Grivet and Olivier in front of her any more. The damp air in the shop took away the feverish pricking sensation in her hands, and she lapsed back into her customary state of solemn abstraction.

But she could never remain there for long. Camille would grow angry at her absence, unable to understand how anyone could prefer the shop to the dining-room, and on a Thursday evening at that! He would lean over the banister, looking for his wife.

'Well,' he would shout, 'and what do you think you're doing down there? Why don't you come back up? . . . Grivet's having the luck of the devil tonight, he's just won again!'

The young woman would get reluctantly to her feet and go back to her place opposite old Michaud, whose drooping lips would twist into a repulsive smile. And until eleven o'clock she would stay slumped in her chair, holding François in her arms and staring down at him so as not to have to look at the cardboard dolls grimacing all around her.

V

ONE Thursday, when Camille came home from the office, he brought with him a tall, square-shouldered fellow whom he pushed through the door with a friendly shove.

'Mother', he asked Madame Raquin, pointing to him, 'do you recognize this gentleman?'

The old woman stared at the tall fellow, searched through her memory, and drew a blank. Thérèse looked on placidly throughout the whole scene.

'What!' continued Camille. 'You mean you don't recognize Laurent, little Laurent, the son of old Laurent who had such excellent fields of wheat, over Jeufosse way? ... Don't you remember? ... I used to go to school with him; he'd come round to fetch me every morning from his uncle's house nearby, and you always gave him bread and jam.'

Madame Raquin did suddenly remember little Laurent, though it seemed to her that he had grown rather a lot. It was a good twenty years since she had last seen him. She tried to make up for not having recognized him sooner with a flood of recollections and motherly endearments. Laurent had sat down, smiling gently, answering in a clear voice, and looking around him calmly, quite at his ease.

'Would you believe it,' said Camille; 'this character has been working at the Orleans station for the past eighteen months, and we only recognized each other for the first time this evening? It just goes to show what a big, important company it is!'

As he said this, the young man widened his eyes and pursed his lips, as proud as could be that he was a small cog in such a big machine. He went on, shaking his head:

'Of course, he's doing all right, he is, he's got qualifications; he's already getting fifteen hundred a month. His father sent him to college to do law, and he's even learned how to paint. That's right isn't it, Laurent? ... You'll stay to dinner, won't you?'

'All right,' replied Laurent, making no attempt to decline.

He put down his hat and made himself at home in the shop. Madame Raquin hurried off to look after things in the kitchen. Thérèse, who had not yet said a word, looked at the newcomer. She had never seen a real man before. Laurent, tall, strong, and fresh-faced, filled her with astonishment. She stared with a kind of wonder at the low forehead, from which sprung black bushy hair, the full cheeks, red lips, and regular features which made up his handsome, full-blooded face. Her gaze lingered for a while on his neck, which was broad and short, thick and powerful. Then she became lost in contemplation of the huge hands, which he kept spread across his knees as he sat there; their fingers were square and his clenched fist must be enormous, capable of felling an ox. Laurent was of true farming stock; he had a rather heavy, stooping gait, his movements were slow and careful, and his face wore a calm, stubborn expression. Beneath his clothes you could make out the well-developed, bulging muscles and the firm, solid flesh of his body. Thérèse looked him up and down with great curiosity, from his fists to his face, and a little shiver ran through her when her glance settled on his bull's neck.

Camille got out his volumes of Buffon and his penny instalments, to show his friend that he too was studying. Then, as if in reply to a question he had been asking himself for some time, he said to Laurent:

'By the way, you do know my wife, don't you? You remember my little cousin who used to play with us at Vernon?'

'Of course. I recognized Madame at once,' replied Laurent, looking Thérèse straight in the eye.

This direct gaze, which seemed to pierce her to the core, made the young woman feel almost unwell. She gave a forced smile and exchanged a few words with Laurent and her husband, before hurrying off to help her aunt. She was quite unsettled.

They sat down to eat. As soon as the soup was served, Camille thought he ought to make conversation with his friend.

'How's your father getting on?' he asked.

'I've no idea,' said Laurent. 'We've fallen out. We haven't written to each other in the last five years.'

'Well blow me down!' exclaimed the clerk, astonished that such monstrous things could happen.

'Yes indeed, the dear man has all sorts of odd ideas … He's continually ending up in court with the neighbours, so he sent me away to college in the hope that I'd become a lawyer and win all his cases for him. Not one for frivolous ambitions, my old man; even his craziest ideas are calculated to bring him some advantage.'

'And you didn't want to be a lawyer?' said Camille, astonished.

'Certainly not!' continued his friend with a laugh. 'For two years I pretended to go to lectures so that I could keep drawing the twelve hundred francs allowance from my father. I was sharing a place with a college friend who is a painter, and I started painting too. I enjoyed it; it's good fun, not hard work at all. We used to smoke and lark about all day long …'

The Raquin family's eyes widened in astonishment.

'Unfortunately,' continued Laurent, 'it was all too good to last. Dad found out that I'd been lying to him. He cut off my hundred francs a month at a stroke and invited me to go back and till the soil with him. I tried to get by, painting religious pictures, but there's no money in it. Once I realized that I was clearly going to die of hunger, I decided to chuck it in and look around for a job. The old man will pop off one of these days, and I'll just have to wait till then to live the idle life.'

Laurent spoke quite unemotionally. In a few words, he had just told a story which summed him up perfectly. He was basically lazy by temperament, with full-blooded appetites and a pronounced desire for easy and long-lasting pleasures. His great body asked for no more than to do nothing but lounge about all day long in idleness and contentment. He would have been happy just eating and sleeping well, and giving full rein to his passions, without having to lift a finger or risk tiring himself in any way.

The legal profession had filled him with horror, and he shuddered at the idea of tilling the soil. He had thrown himself into art in the hope of making an easy living; he found using a paintbrush light work, and he thought that success was easily

come by. He dreamed of a life of cheap delights, a splendid
life full of women, with much lounging around on divans and
orgies of food and drink. The dream continued as long as
Laurent senior kept sending the money. But once the young
man, who was already thirty, saw starvation looming on the
horizon, he began to think seriously; he did not have the courage to face privation, and would never have gone a day without
bread for the greater glory of art. So, as he said, he had chucked
painting to the devil when he realized it would never satisfy
his broad appetites. His first attempts had never even reached
the level of mediocrity; with his farmer's eye, he had a clumsy
and messy view of nature, and his canvases, muddy-looking,
ill-composed, and grimacing, defied all critical appreciation.
In any case, he was not particularly vain as an artist, and was
not excessively depressed when he was forced to lay down
his brushes. The only thing he really missed was his school
friend's spacious studio, in which he had been able to laze
about so enjoyably for four or five years. He also missed the
women who used to come and model, whose favours were
within the reach of his purse; the brutish pleasures he had
discovered in this world had left him with compelling needs
of the flesh. Still, he felt quite at home working as an office
employee; he enjoyed the regular life, the daily round of drud-
gery, which did not tire him out physically but sent his mind
to sleep. Only two things irritated him: there were no women,
and the food in the eighteen sous restaurants did not satisfy
his stomach's gluttonous cravings.

   Camille listened, staring at him in doltish astonishment.
This weakling, whose soft and puny body had never once felt
a tremor of desire, began to picture in a childish way the studio
life which his friend was telling him about. He imagined the
women exhibiting their bare flesh; he questioned Laurent
further.

   'You mean', he said, 'there were women who actually took
their clothes off, in front of you?

   'Certainly,' replied Laurent with a smile, looking at Thérèse,
who had turned very pale.

   'That must make you feel rather ... funny,' continued
Camille with a giggle. 'I'd have been all embarrassed ... The
first time, I suppose you didn't know where to look.'

Laurent had spread out one of his great hands and was staring closely at the palm. His fingers trembled slightly and his
cheeks flushed pink.

'The first time', he went on as if speaking to himself, 'I
think I found it quite natural ... It's great fun, this whole
art business, it's just that you can't make a penny at it ...
I had one model, an adorable red-head, with firm white skin,
superb breasts and hips as broad as ...'

Laurent looked up and saw Thérèse in front of him, silent
and motionless. The young woman was looking at him with
a fixed and burning gaze. Her eyes, dull black, were like two
bottomless shafts, and between her half-open lips could be
seen the pink highlights of her mouth. She was sitting hunched
up and withdrawn, but she was listening.

The one-time painter looked across from Thérèse to Camille
and had to hold back a smile. He completed his sentence with
a rounded, voluptuous movement of the hand which Thérèse
followed with her eyes. They had got round to dessert, and
Madame Raquin had just gone down to serve a customer.

When the table-cloth was removed, Laurent, who had been
lost in thought for some minutes, suddenly turned to Camille
and said:

'You know, I really should paint your portrait.'

This idea delighted Madame Raquin and her son. Thérèse
remained silent.

'It's summer now', continued Laurent, 'and since we get
out of the office at four, I can come round here and have
you sit for me for a couple of hours in the evening. A week's
all it will take.'

'That's fine', said Camille, pink with pleasure, 'and you
can stay for dinner! I'll have my hair curled, and put on my
black coat.'

The clock struck eight. Grivet and Michaud made their
entrance. Olivier and Suzanne arrived behind them.

Camille introduced his friend to the gathering. Grivet pursed
his lips with disapproval. He disliked Laurent, because he considered that he had been promoted too quickly. In any case,
bringing in a new face was not something to be undertaken
lightly, and Madame Raquin's guests could not accept a
stranger without a show of coldness.

Laurent was on his best behaviour. He understood the situation and did his utmost to please and gain acceptance straightaway. He told jokes, his loud laughter livened up the whole evening, and he even won the friendship of Grivet himself.

That evening Thérèse did not look for excuses to go down to the shop. She stayed in her seat until eleven, playing games and chatting and avoiding catching Laurent's eye; he in any case paid no attention to her. The man's full-blooded temperament, his powerful voice and rich laugh, and the bitter, pungent aroma given off by his whole person, disturbed the young woman and plunged her into a state of nervous anxiety.

VI

FROM that day on Laurent came round to see the Raquins almost every evening. He lived in the Rue Saint-Victor,* opposite the Port aux Vins, in a tiny furnished garret at eighteen francs a month; this room, with a skylight in the sloping ceiling which opened to reveal nothing but a narrow slit of sky, was scarcely six square metres in size. Laurent always went back to this hovel as late as possible. Before he had met Camille, as he did not have the money to go hanging around in cafés, he used to linger in the little eating place where he took his evening meal, smoking one pipe after another while he drank a rum coffee which cost three sous. Then he would make his way slowly back to the Rue Saint-Victor, strolling along the river and stopping to sit on benches when the weather was warm.

He came to regard the shop in the Passage du Pont-Neuf as a charming retreat, warm, peaceful, and full of pleasant chatter and friendly attentions. He saved the three sous from his rum coffee and enjoyed drinking Madame Raquin's excellent tea instead. There he would stay, dozing, letting his meal go down and feeling very much at home, until ten o'clock, and he would leave only after helping Camille to lock up the shop.

One evening he brought along his easel and box of paints, as he was planning to begin Camille's portrait the next day. A canvas was bought and minute preparations made. Finally the artist set to work in the couple's bedroom, where, as he said, the light was better.

It took him three evenings to draw the head. He dragged the charcoal laboriously across the canvas in small, inhibited strokes; his stiff, lifeless technique was a grotesque parody of the primitive masters. He copied Camille's features like a student drawing from the nude, with a hesitant hand and a clumsy accuracy which gave the face a sullen expression. On the fourth day he put some tiny blobs of colour onto his palette and began to paint, using the very tips of his brushes; he applied the colour in messy dabs and short, closely hatched lines, rather as if he had been using a pencil.

At the end of each sitting Madame Raquin and Camille were always in ecstasies. Laurent said that they must wait, it would soon start to be more of a likeness.

Since work had begun on the portrait, Thérèse had been spending all her time in the bedroom-turned-studio. She left her aunt alone behind the counter and went upstairs on the slightest pretext to watch Laurent paint, oblivious of everything else.

As serious and subdued as ever, but even paler and more silent, she would sit down and follow the movement of the brushes. Not that she seemed to derive much enjoyment from watching; she came as if attracted by a strange force, and there she stayed, unable to tear herself away. Occasionally Laurent would turn round, smile at her, and ask whether she liked the portrait. She scarcely spoke in reply, but quivered and resumed her fascinated contemplation.

On his way back to the Rue Saint-Victor in the evening, Laurent's mind was full of debate as he argued with himself whether or not he should become Thérèse's lover.

'Now there's one little lady who will be my mistress whenever I like,' he said to himself. 'She's forever there at my back, examining me, taking my measure, weighing me up . . . She's always quivering and she has a funny expression, quiet but passionate. One thing's for sure, she needs a lover; you can see it in her eyes . . . And it must be said, Camille's a pretty poor substitute.'

Laurent laughed to himself at the memory of his friend's puny, pallid form. Then he went on:

'She's bored to death in that shop . . . I only go there because I've got nothing better to do. Otherwise, you wouldn't catch me anywhere near the Passage du Pont-Neuf! It's so damp and dismal. It must be death to a woman like her . . . She finds me attractive, I'm sure of that, so why not me rather than someone else?'

He kept halting as his mind filled with ridiculous imaginings, and stood watching the Seine flow by with a preoccupied air.

'May as well, and why not?!' he exclaimed; 'I'll give her a kiss at the first opportunity . . . I bet she'll fall straight into my arms!'

As he set off again, he was overcome once more by uncertainty.

'The thing is,' he thought to himself, 'she's really very plain; she's got a long nose and a big mouth. Anyway, I don't love her the slightest bit. And it could well get me into some unpleasantness. I'll have to think hard about it.'

Laurent, who was very prudent, turned these thoughts over in his mind for a whole week. He calculated everything that might happen if he started an affair with Thérèse, and only resolved to try it when he was certain in his own mind that he really had something to gain.

It is true that he found Thérèse plain and did not love her, but then she would not cost him anything; the women he usually picked up cheaply were certainly no prettier, nor any better loved. On grounds of economy alone, it was a good idea to take his friend's wife. Besides, it was a long time since he had last satisfied his appetites; when money was short he stinted the flesh, and he certainly did not want to miss an opportunity of indulging it a bit now. Then again, when he came to think about it, an affair like this could hardly lead to any trouble: it would be in Thérèse's interests to cover it up, and he could easily jilt her when he felt like it; even if Camille did find out and get annoyed, he would just thump him if he started to throw his weight around. Whichever way he looked at it, the prospect seemed an easy and alluring one to Laurent.

From then on he lived in a pleasantly confident frame of mind, waiting his moment. He had made up his mind to act directly, at the first opportunity. He foresaw cosy evenings ahead; all the Raquins would be working for his greater enjoyment, with Thérèse soothing his heated passions, Madame Raquin covering him in motherly attentions, and Camille chatting to him of an evening in the shop so that he would not get too bored.

The portrait was nearly finished and still no opportunity had presented itself. Thérèse was there all the time, anxious and subdued, but Camille never left the bedroom and Laurent began to despair of ever getting him out of the way for an hour or so. Eventually he was obliged to announce that the portrait would be finished the next day. Madame Raquin

declared that they would all dine together in celebration of
the painter's work.

The following day, when Laurent had put the finishing
touches to his canvas, the whole family gathered round to
exclaim at the likeness. It was a vile portrait, dirty grey with
great purplish blotches. Laurent was incapable of using any
of the brighter colours without making them dull and muddy;
he had unwittingly exaggerated the pallid skin-tones of his
model, and Camille's face had the greenish hue of a drowned
man; the features were twisted and contorted by the grimacing way in which they were drawn, which actually made the
sinister resemblance even more striking. But Camille was
delighted; he said that the picture had an air of distinction.

When he had finished admiring his own face, he declared
that he was going to fetch two bottles of champagne. Madame
Raquin went back down to the shop. The artist was left alone
with Thérèse.

The young woman had remained crouching there, staring
absently in front of her. She was quivering, and seemed to
be waiting for something. Laurent hesitated; he examined the
canvas, and played with his brushes. Time was slipping away,
Camille might come back, there might never be another opportunity. Suddenly, the painter turned round and found himself
face to face with Thérèse. They looked intently at each other
for a few seconds.

Then in a violent movement Laurent bent down, took the
young woman in his arms, and pressed her against his chest.
He pushed her head back and crushed her lips beneath his
own. She made one wild, instinctive attempt to fight him off,
then suddenly her resistance ceased and she slid down on to
the floor. They did not exchange a word. Their act was silent
and brutal.

VII

FROM the beginning, the lovers felt their affair to be something necessary, inevitable, and utterly natural. At their first meeting they spoke familiarly and kissed without any blushing or embarrassment, as if their intimacy had already been going on for a number of years. They were quite calm and at ease in their new situation, and they lived completely without shame.

They worked out how they would meet. As Thérèse could not go out, it was decided that Laurent would come round to her. In a clear and confident voice she explained to him the arrangement she had thought up. They would see each other in the bedroom. Her lover would come up the side passage which led off the arcade, and she would let him in through the door at the top of the stairs. Meanwhile, Camille would be at his office and Madame Raquin downstairs in the shop. Such a bold plan could scarcely fail.

Laurent agreed. For all his prudence, he had a kind of animal daring, the daring of a man with huge fists. His mistress's calm, serious air was strong encouragement to come and taste of a passion so daringly offered. He picked an excuse, his boss gave him two hours off, and he hastened round to the Passage du Pont-Neuf.

As soon as he set foot in the arcade, he felt a strong tingle of anticipation. The woman who sold costume jewellery was sitting right opposite the door to the side passage. He had to wait until she was busy, selling a brass ring or some earrings to a young working woman. Then he slipped quickly into the passage and climbed the dark, narrow staircase, pressing against the damp, sticky walls. Every time he stumbled on one of the stone steps, the noise gave him a burning sensation in the chest. A door opened, and there on the threshold, dazzling in the white glow of the lamp, he saw Thérèse in her camisole and petticoat, her hair tied up tight in a bun. She shut the door and flung her arms round his neck; she had a warm scent of white linen and newly washed flesh.

Laurent was astonished at how beautiful he found his mistress. He had never before seen this woman as she really was. Thérèse, lithe and strong, hugged him and threw back her head, her face lit up by smiles in which passion burned. It was as if her features had been transfigured by love; her expression was wild but caressing, her lips moist and her eyes shining; she was radiant with joy. With her body wound sinuously around his, she was beautiful with the strange beauty of complete abandon. It was as if her face had been illuminated from within and flames were leaping from her flesh; and the fire in her blood and the tautness of her muscles filled the air around her with warm exhalations, bitter and penetrating.

From the first kiss, she showed an instinctive skill in the arts of love. Her hungry body threw itself into the experience of pleasure with total abandon. She was emerging from a dream and awakening to passion, and passing from the feeble arms of Camille into the muscular embrace of Laurent. This approach of a powerful man was like a sudden jolt which had shocked her body out of its slumber. All the instincts of a highly strung woman now burst to the fore with incomparable violence, as her mother's blood, that African blood which burned in her veins, began to pulse furiously through her slight, still almost virginal body. She offered herself to him with a total absence of shame, and she was racked from head to toe by long drawn-out spasms.

Laurent had never known a woman like this, and it disconcerted him, made him ill at ease. He did not normally receive such a passionate welcome from his mistresses; he was used to cold, indifferent kisses and tired, satiated love-making. Thérèse's moans and fits almost frightened him, while at the same time stimulating his sensual curiosity. When he left her he was tottering like a drunkard. The next day, once he had regained his caution and his rather forced composure, he asked himself whether or not to go back to this lover whose kisses so inflamed his passions. At first he firmly resolved to stay at home. Then he began to weaken. He wanted to forget Thérèse, the sight of her naked body and her sweet but brutal caresses, yet there she still was, implacable, holding her arms out to him. The physical pain which this vision caused him soon became unbearable.

He gave in, arranged another meeting, and returned to the Passage du Pont-Neuf.

From that day on Thérèse became a part of his life. He did not yet accept her, but bowed to her will. There were hours when he was filled with horror, and moments when all his caution came back, and all in all the affair was an unpleasant disruption; but his fears and misgivings always gave way before his desire. One assignation was followed by another, then many more.

Thérèse had no such doubts. She gave herself to him unsparingly, going straight where her passion led. This woman, who had been bowed down by circumstances and was finally standing up for herself, laid bare her whole being, and explained to him her past life.

Sometimes she would put her arms around Laurent's neck, pull herself up along his chest, and say to him in a voice still breathless with passion:

'Oh, if only you knew how much I have suffered! I was brought up in the clammy heat of a sick-room. I had to sleep next to Camille; at night I tried to move away from him to escape the disgusting stale smell of his body. He was tetchy and stubborn; he refused to take his medicines unless I shared them with him, so to please my aunt I had to drink all sorts of potions. I don't know how it didn't kill me . . . They have made me ugly, my poor darling, they've stolen everything I had, so you can never love me as much as I love you.'

She wept and she kissed Laurent, then went on with hatred smouldering in her voice:

'I don't wish them any harm. They brought me up, took me in and protected me from destitution . . . But I would have preferred abandonment to their hospitality. I had a desperate need for wide-open spaces; as a little girl, I dreamt of roaming barefoot along dusty roads, begging alms and living the life of a gypsy. I was told that my mother was the daughter of a tribal chief in Africa; I often thought of her, and how close I am to her in my blood and my instincts; I wished I had never had to leave her, and that she might still have been carrying me across the desert on her back . . . Ah! What a way to grow up! Thinking about the long days which I spent in that bedroom with Camille coughing and groaning still fills me with disgust and anger. I used to squat in front of the fire, mindlessly watching his infusions boil and feeling my limbs grow stiff. I couldn't even move around; my aunt used to scold me whenever I made a noise ... Later on I did have a taste of real joy, in the little house by the river, but by then I had already been too much repressed; I could hardly walk and I fell over whenever I tried to run. Then they buried me alive in this awful shop.'

Thérèse breathed heavily as she squeezed her lover in her arms; she was taking her revenge, and her delicate, supple nostrils quivered nervously.

'You wouldn't believe how vicious they've made me,' she went on. 'They've made me into a hypocrite and a liar ... They so smothered me in their bourgeois comforts that I can't understand how there can still be blood in my veins ... I looked down at the ground and put on the same dismal, stupid expression, and lived the same dead life, as them. When you first saw me, I looked just like some dumb animal, didn't I? Gloomy, cast down, all passive? I had no hope left, I was thinking of throwing myself in the Seine one day ... But before I reached that state of dejection, how many nights of rage I spent! Back in my cold room in Vernon, I used to bite my pillow to stifle my shouts, and hit myself and call myself a coward; my blood was on fire and I could almost have torn my body to pieces with rage. Twice I wanted to run away and just keep going, out into the sunshine, but my courage failed me; they had turned me into a docile pet with their flabby benevolence and revolting affection. So I lied and kept on lying; I stayed put, all sweetness and silence, when I really wanted to hit out and bite back.'

The young woman stopped, wiping her moist lips on Laurent's neck. After a moment's silence, she added:

'I don't know any more why I agreed to marry Camille. I didn't protest, out of a sort of disdainful indifference. I took pity on the poor child. When I used to play with him, I felt my fingers sinking into his limbs as if they were made of clay. I took him because my aunt offered him to me, and because I had no intention of putting myself out for him. And in my husband I found that same poorly little boy next to whom I'd already had to sleep from the age of six. He was just as frail and complaining, and he had the same stale, sickly smell which had so nauseated me all those years ago ... I'm telling you all this so that you won't be jealous ... I felt a kind of disgust rising in my throat; I remembered all the potions I had drunk, and I moved away from him; I had some dreadful nights. But you, you ...'

And Thérèse lifted her upper body, arching her back, with her fingers caught in Laurent's strong hands, looking down at his broad shoulders and enormous neck.

'I love *you*, I have done since the day Camille first pushed you into the shop. You may not respect me, because I gave myself to you all at once, everything ... Truly, I don't know how it happened. I am proud, I'm impetuous too, and I felt like hitting you that first day, when you kissed me and threw me to the floor here in this bedroom ... I don't know how I can have loved you; actually, it was more like hate. The sight of you irritated me, I couldn't stand it; when you were there, my nerves were stretched to breaking-point, my mind went blank, and I saw red. Oh, how I suffered! Yet I wanted my suffering and longed for you to come; as I moved round and round your chair I sensed your breath on my body and felt my clothes brush against yours. It was as if your blood were radiating warmth as I passed, and it was this burning aura surrounding you that attracted me and held me close to you, despite my inner urge to rebel ... You remember when you were doing the painting here? An irresistible force attracted me to your side, made me breathe in your atmosphere with painful delight. I realized that I seemed to be begging for kisses and I was ashamed to be so enslaved; I knew I should fall if you only touched me. But I gave in to my weakness, shivering with cold while I waited for you to deign to take me in your arms.'

Then Thérèse fell silent, still quivering, proud and avenged. She held Laurent, drunk with passion, to her breast, and in that bare and freezing bedroom there were enacted scenes of fiery passion, sinister and brutish. Each new meeting brought still more violent ecstasies.

The young woman seemed to thrive on her daring and impudent behaviour. She never hesitated or showed any fear. She threw herself into adultery with a sort of frantic energy, facing

danger with alacrity and taking pride in doing so. Whenever
her lover was due to come round, her only precaution was
to warn her aunt that she was going upstairs for a rest; while
he was there, she would walk about, talk, and do everything
with no attempt at concealment, without ever worrying about
making a noise. Sometimes, in the early days, this scared
Laurent.

'For heaven's sake,' he would whisper to Thérèse, 'don't
make such a racket; Madame Raquin will be coming up.'

'It's all right!' she laughed. 'You are a real worrier. She's
stuck behind her counter; what do you think she'd come up
here for? She'd be too afraid of the till being robbed . . . Anyway, let her come up if she wants to. You can always hide. I
don't give a damn about her. I love you.'

Laurent was scarcely reassured by her words. His sneaking
peasant's caution had not been entirely stifled by passion.
Soon, however, by force of habit, he came to accept without
undue terror the difficulties of these assignations in broad daylight, in Camille's own bedroom, only feet from the old haberdasher. His mistress kept explaining to him that danger spares
the bold, and she was right. The lovers could not have found
a safer place than this room where nobody would ever come
looking for them. Incredibly, they were able to satisfy their
desires there quite undisturbed.

One day, however, Madame Raquin did come up, fearing
that her niece might be ill. The young woman had been upstairs
for nearly three hours, and she had now taken her daring to
the point of not even bolting the door between the bedroom
and the dining-room.

When Laurent heard the old woman's heavy tread coming
up the wooden stairs, he snatched up his waistcoat and hat
in a panic. Thérèse began to laugh at his peculiar expression.
She grabbed him forcefully by the arm, made him bend down
at the head of the bed, in a corner, and said to him in a quiet,
self-possessed voice:

'Stay there . . . don't move.'

She threw on top of him all the men's clothes that were
lying about, and over the whole pile she spread a white petticoat
which she had taken off. She did all this with swift, accurate
movements, without becoming at all flustered. Then she lay

down, her hair in disorder, half naked, still flushed and quivering from their embrace.

Madame Raquin opened the door quietly and crept on tiptoe towards the bed. Thérèse pretended to be asleep. Laurent was sweating beneath the petticoat.

'Thérèse, my dear,' asked the haberdasher with concern, 'aren't you feeling well?'

Thérèse opened her eyes, yawned, turned over, and replied in plaintive tones that she had a terrible headache. She begged her aunt to let her go back to sleep. The old woman went away just as she had come, without making any noise.

Silently laughing, the two lovers kissed each other with violence and passion.

'You see,' said Thérèse triumphantly; 'we have nothing to fear here. All these people are blind, they aren't in love.'

Another day, the young woman had an odd idea. She could behave at times as if she were quite crazy, her mind wandering.

François the tabby cat was sitting upright in the middle of the room. Solemn and motionless, he stared at the two lovers with his big round eyes. He seemed to be scrutinizing them unblinkingly, lost in some devilish reverie.

'Just look at François,' said Thérèse to Laurent. 'He looks as if he understands what's going on, and he's going to tell Camille all about it this evening ... Wouldn't it be funny if he suddenly started to talk in the shop one of these days? He'd have some fine tales to tell about us.'

Thérèse found the idea of François starting to speak extremely amusing. Laurent looked at the cat's big green eyes and felt a shiver run down his spine.

'Here's what he'd do,' Thérèse went on. 'He'd stand up, point at you with one paw and me with the other, and shout out: "Monsieur and Madame get up to all sorts of naughty things together in the bedroom; they take no notice of me, but since their illicit affair makes me sick, please put them both in prison so they won't disturb my nap in future."'

Thérèse joked about like a child, imitating the cat by stretching out her fingers into claws and rolling her shoulders in feline undulations. François, still sitting perfectly still, watched her all the time; only his eyes seemed to be alive, while two deep wrinkles at the corners of his mouth put a laughing expression on his stuffed-animal face.

Laurent felt a chill in his bones. He thought Thérèse's fooling around was ridiculous. He stood up and put the cat out of the door. The truth was that he was afraid. His mistress had not yet taken him over altogether; deep down there still lingered a little of the unease he had felt when Thérèse had first kissed him.

VIII

IN the shop, of an evening, Laurent was utterly happy. He generally came back from the office with Camille. Madame Raquin had taken a maternal liking to him; she knew he was penniless, that he did not eat well and slept in an attic, and she had told him once and for all that there would always be a place for him at their table. She felt the same garrulous affection for him which many old women have for people from the same part of the world as themselves, who bring with them memories of the past.

The young man availed himself freely of their hospitality. After the office, before going home, he would take a little turn along the river with Camille; this intimacy suited them both as a way of avoiding boredom, for they chatted as they strolled along. Then they would decide to go home and eat the meal Madame Raquin had prepared. Laurent would open the door of the shop as if he owned the place, sitting on the chairs back to front, smoking and spitting, as if he were in his own home.

He was not in the least put out by the presence of Thérèse. He behaved towards her in an open, friendly manner, making jokes and addressing perfectly ordinary pleasantries to her without his expression giving anything away. Camille would laugh, and, since his wife only responded to his friend in monosyllables, he was firmly of the belief that they could not stand each other. One day he even reproached Thérèse for what he called her coldness towards Laurent.

Laurent had really struck gold: he had become the wife's lover, the husband's friend, and the mother's spoilt child, all at once. He had never before experienced such complete satisfaction of his appetites. He basked in the infinite gratification provided by the Raquin family. Moreover, he found his position among them quite natural. He spoke familiarly to Camille, with neither anger nor remorse in his voice. So sure was he of his own caution and self-control that he did not even watch his words and actions; the single-mindedness with which he revelled in his good fortune protected him from mistakes. In the shop his mistress became a woman like any other, whom he must not kiss or find attractive. The only thing that prevented him from kissing her in front of everyone else was his fear of being told not to come back. Otherwise, he could not have cared less about how it would hurt Camille and his mother. The consequences that the discovery of their affair might bring never entered his head. He regarded himself simply as behaving like a poor man without enough to eat, as anyone else might have done in his place. Hence his unthinking complacency, his cautious daring, his detached and ironic attitude.

Thérèse, more nervous and highly-strung than he, was compelled to act out her role. She did it to perfection, thanks to the skill in hypocrisy which her upbringing had given her. For close on fifteen years she had lived a lie, stifling her passionate impulses and bending her implacable will to the task of appearing dull and passive. Now it cost her but little to adopt a chill, lifeless mask which froze her features. Whenever Laurent entered he found her wearing a serious, reserved expression which made her nose seem longer and her lips thinner. She was ugly, bad-tempered, and unapproachable. Nor did she overdo things, but simply played her old character, without any sudden change which might awaken suspicion. She took a keen pleasure in deceiving Camille and Madame Raquin; she was not like Laurent, simply wallowing in the satisfaction of his fleshly desires, with no thought of right and wrong; she knew what harm she was doing, and she was seized by fierce urges to get up from the table and kiss Laurent full on the mouth, just to show her husband and aunt that she was not some tame lap-dog, but had a lover.

At times, a warm flush of joy went to her head; then, however good an actress she might be, she could not stop herself from singing, as long as her lover was not there and she had no fear of betraying him. Madame Raquin was delighted with these sudden outbursts of gaiety, for she normally reproached her niece for being too serious. The young woman bought pots of flowers to put in the bedroom window; then she had new wallpaper put up, and wanted a carpet, curtains, rosewood furniture. All this luxury was for Laurent.

⌐Nature and circumstance⌐seemed to have made the two of
them for each other, and pushed them together. This nervous,
insincere woman and this man of full-blooded temperament
and animal instincts made up a powerfully bonded couple.
They complemented each other and were mutually protective.
In the evening, as they sat at the table in the pale lamplight,
the strength of their union could be seen in the solid, smiling
face of Laurent opposite the mute, impenetrable mask of
Thérèse.

These were quiet, pleasant evenings. Friendly words broke
the silence in the warm, transparent shadows. They squeezed
closer together around the table after dessert and chatted about
the hundred little details of the day, with recollections of the
day before and plans for the morrow. Camille liked Laurent
as much as he could like anyone, in his smug, egotistical way,
and Laurent seemed to return his affection; they exchanged
protestations of loyalty, kindly gestures, and considerate
glances. Madame Raquin, with her placid expression, spread
her own peace of mind around her children, in the calm air
they breathed. It was like a meeting of very old friends who
knew each other's every feeling and had complete trust in the
strength of their friendship.

Thérèse, calm and unmoving like the others, looked on at
their complacent relaxation, their bourgeois pleasures, and
deep down she was filled with savage laughter; her whole being
jeered at them while her face retained its cold rigidity. She
reminded herself with exquisite delight that only a few hours
earlier she had been in the bedroom next door, half naked,
her hair undone, lying on Laurent's chest; she recalled every
detail of their afternoon of mad passion, running over each
one in her memory and comparing that earlier steamy scene
with the deathly picture which she now had before her eyes.
Oh! how she was deceiving these good people, and how happy
she was to deceive them in such a triumphant and insolent
way! It was there, only a few feet away, behind a flimsy partition, that she regularly entertained a man, wallowing in the
bitter-sweet pleasures of adultery. But for now, her lover had
to be a person whom she no longer knew, her husband's friend,
a kind of foolish interloper of whom she had no need to take
any notice. This dreadful play-acting, this life of deception,

the comparison between the burning embraces of the day and the pretended indifference of the evening, sent the blood coursing through her veins with a new ardour.

Whenever Madame Raquin and Camille happened to go downstairs, Thérèse would leap up and silently, but with brutal energy, crush her lips against those of her lover, staying in that position, panting and hardly able to breathe, until she heard the wooden stairs creak again. Then she would slip quickly back to her place and put on her sullen frown, while Laurent calmly took up his chit-chat with Camille where they had left off. It was like a lightning flash of passion, quick and blinding, in a deadened sky.

Thursday evenings were a little more lively. Laurent, bored to death by the proceedings, nevertheless made it his duty not to miss a single one; as a precaution, he wanted to be known and respected by Camille's friends. He had to sit and listen to the ramblings of Grivet and old Michaud. Michaud always told the same old stories of murder and theft, while Grivet talked about his subordinates and his superiors and his department, all mixed up together. The young man took refuge in the company of Olivier and Suzanne, who seemed less overwhelmingly stupid; he was also quick to call for a game of dominoes.

It was on Thursday evenings that Thérèse would fix the day and the time of their assignations. In the confusion as the guests left, while Madame Raquin and Camille were showing them out by the door into the arcade, she would go up to Laurent, whisper to him, and squeeze his hand. Sometimes, when everyone's back was turned, she would even kiss him, out of bravado.

This life of alternating tension and release lasted for eight months. The lovers lived in utter contentment; Thérèse no longer felt boredom or longing, while Laurent, satiated, cosseted, and looking even better fed, feared only one thing: that this delightful existence might one day come to an end.

IX

ONE afternoon, as Laurent was about to leave the office to go running into the waiting arms of Thérèse, his boss sent for him and told him firmly that in future he was forbidden to take time off. He had taken unfair advantage, and now the administration had resolved to dismiss him if he left his post one more time.

He sat there in desperation until the evening. He had to earn a living, he could not risk the sack. That evening the look of annoyance on Thérèse's face was a torture to him. He did not know how to explain to his mistress why he had gone back on his word. While Camille was shutting up the shop, he went quickly over to her:

'We can't see each other any more,' he whispered; 'my boss has refused to let me have any more time off.'

Camille was coming back. Laurent had to go without giving any more details, leaving Thérèse to face the shock of this brusque declaration. Frustrated, and refusing to accept that her pleasure could be disturbed in this way, she spent a sleepless night turning unlikely plans for assignations over in her mind. The following Thursday she spoke to Laurent for a minute at the most. Their anxiety was all the greater as they had nowhere to meet to talk things over and decide what to do. Thérèse arranged another time with her lover, but once more he failed to turn up. From then on she was obsessed with a single idea: to see him at all costs.

For a fortnight Laurent had been unable to get near Thérèse. He now realized how badly he needed her; the regular satisfaction of his desires had given him sharp, imperative new appetites. He no longer felt the least unease when embracing his mistress, but sought her embrace with the obstinacy of a starving animal. A surging passion had been building up in his body, and, now that his lover had been taken away from him, this passion burst out in blind rage; he was in love to the point of fury. Everything about his flourishing animal make-up seemed to be unconscious; he obeyed his instincts and allowed himself to be dictated to by the will of his organism. A year earlier he would have greeted with scathing laughter any suggestion that he would ever be enslaved by a woman to the point where his whole peace of mind was undermined. But, unbeknown to him, desire had worked away deep inside him until it had finally delivered him, bound hand and foot, into the wild embrace of Thérèse. Now he was afraid he would cast prudence aside altogether, and did not dare go to the Passage du Pont-Neuf of an evening for fear of committing some act of folly. He was no longer in control of his actions; his mistress, with her cat-like suppleness and nervous sensitivity, had slowly insinuated herself into every fibre of his body. He needed this woman to live, as one needs food and drink.

He would certainly have done something stupid if he had not received a letter from Thérèse telling him to stay in the next evening; she promised to come and see him around eight o'clock.

As he left the office he got rid of Camille by saying that he was tired and wanted to go straight to bed. Thérèse, after dinner, also acted out her role; she mentioned a customer who had moved without paying her bill, played the determined creditor, and declared that she was going to demand her money. The customer lived in the Batignolles district.* Madame Raquin and Camille thought this was a long way to go and doubted whether she would succeed, but they were not overly surprised and let her set off without suspecting anything.

She ran to the Port aux Vins, slipping on the greasy cobbles and bumping into passers-by in her haste to get there. Her face became beaded with sweat, her hands were burning, and she felt drunk. She ran quickly up the lodging-house stairs. On the sixth floor, quite out of breath and with her eyes swimming, she saw Laurent leaning over the bannister, waiting for her.

She went into his attic room, which was so cramped that there was hardly space for her wide skirts. She tore off her hat with one hand and leaned against the bed in a faint . . .

The wide-open skylight brought a flood of cool evening air down on to the burning hot bed. The lovers stayed for a long time in this garret, as though buried deep in a cave. Suddenly, Thérèse heard the clock of the Pitié hospital* strike ten. She wished she did not have to listen to it; she stood up unwillingly and, for the first time, looked round the room. Then she found her hat, tied the ribbons, and sat down, saying slowly:

'I have to go now.'

Laurent had come to kneel down in front of her. He took her hands in his.

'See you again one day,' she went on, without moving.

'Not just one day,' he exclaimed; 'that's too uncertain. Which day will you come back?'

She looked him in the eye.

'Do you want me to tell you the truth?' she said. 'Well then, the truth is, I don't think I ever will come back. I've got no more excuses, and I can't invent any.'

'So, it's farewell, then?'

'No! I won't let it be!'

She spoke these words in an angry and horrified voice. Then she added more quietly, not knowing what she was saying and without moving from her chair:

'I'm going to go now.'

Laurent was deep in thought. He was thinking about Camille.

'I've got nothing against him,' he said eventually, without speaking his name. 'But he really is starting to be too much of a nuisance ... Couldn't you get rid of him somehow, send him off on a journey, anywhere, a long way away?'

'Oh sure!' Thérèse nodded ironically. 'You really think he's the sort to go on a long journey? There's only one journey you don't come back from. But he'll see us all in the grave first. People like him spend their lives at death's door without actually dying.'

There was a moment's silence. Laurent shuffled closer on his knees, hugging his mistress to him, his head resting on her bosom.

'I had a dream,' he said; 'I wanted to spend a whole night with you, fall asleep in your arms and wake up the next morning to feel your kisses ... I want to be your husband ... Do you understand?'

'Oh yes!' replied Thérèse with a shudder.

And she suddenly bent over Laurent's face and covered it in kisses. Her hat-strings caught on the young man's rough beard; she had forgotten that she was fully dressed and that her clothes would be creased. She was sobbing, and she panted as she repeated through her tears:

'Don't say such things, or I'll stay here and never have the strength to leave you! Give me courage instead, tell me that we will see each other again ... You need me, don't you, and some day we will find a way of living together?'

'So come back, come back tomorrow,' replied Laurent, running his shaking hands up her body.

'But I can't ... I've told you, I haven't got an excuse!'

She was wringing her hands. She went on:

'Oh, I'm not afraid of the scandal; if you like, when I get home I'll tell Camille that you are my lover and I'll come back here for the night. It's you I'm afraid for; I don't want to ruin your life, I just want to make you happy.'

The young man's instinct for prudence was reawakened.

'You are right,' he said; 'we mustn't act like children. Oh! if only your husband were to die!'

'If my husband were to die ...' Thérèse repeated slowly.

'We could get married, we'd have nothing more to fear, we could enjoy each other to the full ... What a lovely, pleasant life it would be!'

The young woman leapt to her feet. Her cheeks went pale, she stared at her lover with a sombre look in her eye, and her lips began to twitch.

'People do sometimes die,' she murmured eventually. 'Only, it's dangerous for those who are left behind.'

Laurent made no reply.

'The thing is,' she went on, 'none of the well-known methods is any good.'

'That's not what I meant,' he said. 'I'm no fool, I want to love you in peace and quiet. I was just thinking that accidents happen every day; it's easy for a foot to slip or a tile to slide off a roof ... See what I mean? If that happens, only the wind is to blame.'

His voice sounded strange. He smiled, then added caressingly:

'Now don't you worry, we shall love each other all right, and live happily ... Since you can't come to me, I'll sort it all out. If we have to go for months without seeing each other, don't forget me, remember that I'm working away for our happiness.'

He caught Thérèse up in his arms as she was opening the door to leave.

'You are all mine, aren't you?' he went on. 'Swear that you'll give yourself to me, completely, whenever I want.'

'Yes,' she exclaimed, 'I belong to you, do with me what you will.'

They stayed there for a moment, defiant and silent. Then Thérèse tore herself away and, without looking back, ran out of the room and down the stairs. Laurent listened as the sound of her footsteps grew fainter.

When he could no longer hear anything, he went back in and lay down. The sheets were warm. He felt stifled in this pit that Thérèse had left full of the heat of her passion. It was as if he were still breathing something of her presence; she had been there, filling the room with her penetrating scent of violets, and now his arms could embrace nothing more than the intangible ghost of his mistress which hovered all around him. He was smitten with renewed and unsatisfied desire. He left the window open. Lying on his back, with bare arms and open hands, hoping for some cool air, he began to think things over, staring at the dark blue square of sky framed by the skylight.

Until daybreak the same idea went round and round in his head. Before Thérèse had come he had not had any thought of murdering Camille; then, under the pressure of events and in exasperation at the thought that he would not see his lover ever again, he had talked of his death. Thus a new corner of his unconscious nature had revealed itself: carried away by his adultery, he had started dreaming of murder.

Now, in a calmer frame of mind and alone in the peaceful night, he studied the problem of murder; the idea of death, first uttered in despair between two kisses, kept returning with piercing and implacable clarity. Laurent, constantly jolted by insomnia and set on edge by the musky scent which Thérèse had left behind, laid traps in his mind, calculated the risk of things going wrong, and went over the advantages that becoming a murderer would bring.

In every way it was definitely in his interests to contemplate committing the crime. He told himself that his father, the farmer from Jeufosse, was going to hang on for ever; he might have to stay an office clerk for another ten years, taking his meals in cheap eating houses and living in a garret, with no wife of his own. The prospect filled him with immense frustration. With Camille dead, on the other hand, he'd marry Thérèse, inherit Madame Raquin's money, resign from his job, and be free to stroll about in the sunshine. Thereupon, he began to dream of the lazy life he would lead, doing nothing but eating, sleeping, and waiting patiently for his father to die. And when reality reared its head in the middle of his dream, the obstacle was always Camille; he clenched his fists as though to strike him down.

Laurent wanted Thérèse; he wanted her to be entirely his own and always close at hand. If he did not get rid of the husband, the wife would elude him. As she had said, she could not come back to see him. He might easily have kidnapped her and taken her off somewhere, but then they would both have starved to death. There was less risk in killing the husband; it would not create a scandal, he would just be pushing one man out of the way and taking his place. With his brutal peasant's logic he found this an excellent and natural expedient. In fact, even his innate prudence encouraged him to take the quick way out.

He lay sprawled on his bed, in a sweat, his damp face buried in the pillow where Thérése's hair had lain. He took the material repeatedly between his parched lips, drinking in the delicate perfumes it contained, and lay there breathless and gasping for air, while bands of flame flickered across his closed eyelids, wondering how on earth he could kill Camille. Then, when he had no breath left, he would turn over in one bound on to his back and, his eyes wide open and with the cold draught from the window playing full on his face, would search among the stars in the bluish square of sky for some advice on how to kill, some plan of murder.

No ideas came to him. As he had said to his mistress, he was not a child, or a fool; he wanted nothing to do with daggers or poison. What he needed was some underhand method, to be employed without danger, a sort of sinister suffocation with no cries or terror, where the victim simply disappeared. How-

ever strongly he was pushed on and encouraged by his passion,
his whole being called imperiously for caution. He was too
cowardly, too much of a sensualist, to put his quiet life at
risk. He was going to kill, but only in order to live a happy,
peaceful existence.

Gradually he was overtaken by sleep. The cold air had
chased away from the attic the warm, scented ghost of Thérèse.
Laurent, worn out but calmer, felt himself succumbing to a
vague, pleasant feeling of numbness. As he was nodding off
he made up his mind to wait for a favourable opportunity,
and then, with consciousness slipping away, he was lulled by
the murmuring thought: 'I'll kill him, I'll kill him.' Five
minutes later he was asleep, his breathing serene and regular.

Thérèse had reached home at around eleven, quite unaware
of how she had got back to the Passage du Pont-Neuf, for
her head was on fire and her mind racing. Her ears were still
so full of the things she had heard that she felt as if she had
only just come down from Laurent's room. She found Madame
Raquin and Camille anxious and concerned; she gave curt
replies to their questions, saying that it had been a wasted
errand and that she had stood for an hour on the pavement
waiting for an omnibus.

When she climbed into bed, the sheets felt cold and clammy.
Her limbs, still burning, shivered with repugnance. Camille
soon went off to sleep, and for a long time Thérèse looked
at his pasty face resting stupidly on the pillow, his mouth open.
Then she drew away from him, feeling a sudden urge to thrust
her clenched fist into his mouth.

X

NEARLY three weeks passed. Laurent went back to the shop each evening; he looked tired and unwell, there were slight bluish circles around his eyes, and his lips had become pale and cracked. Otherwise, he still had the same heavy calm about him, continuing to look Camille in the eye and behaving towards him in the same open, friendly way. Madame Raquin had begun to make an even greater fuss of this friend of the family since she had seen him sinking into a sort of dull fever.

Thérèse had resumed her usual dumb, sullen expression, and was more unmoving, inscrutable, and impassive than ever. It was as if for her Laurent did not exist; she scarcely gave him a glance, spoke to him only occasionally, and treated him with complete indifference. Madame Raquin, whose kind heart was offended by this attitude, sometimes said to the young man: 'Take no notice of my niece's coolness. I know her; her face seems cold, but her heart is warm, full of affection and devotion.'

The two lovers had no more assignations; since that night in the Rue Saint-Victor they had had no time alone together. Whenever they found themselves face to face of an evening and behaved with feigned indifference, like strangers, there were storms of passion, horror, and desire raging beneath the surface tranquillity of their faces. Thérèse went through bouts of anger, fits of cowardice and sarcasm; Laurent's mind was full of dark and brutal thoughts, and agonizing indecision. Neither dared examine the depths of his or her own being, and a disturbing fever filled their brains with a kind of dense, acrid vapour.

Whenever they could, behind a door, without speaking, they would clasp each other's hands almost to breaking-point in a rough and short-lived embrace, as if they wanted to tear strips from each other's flesh with their fingers. This was the only way they had of appeasing their desire; they put their whole bodies into it, and asked each other for nothing more. They were waiting.

One Thursday evening, before they settled down to a game of dominoes, Madame Raquin's guests were having their usual little chat. One of the great topics of conversation was always old Michaud's career in the police, and the strange and sinister adventures in which they supposed he had been involved. Grivet and Camille would listen open-mouthed to the ex-superintendent's stories, with the terrified expressions of little children listening to tales of *Bluebeard* or *Tom Thumb*. They found them frightening and entertaining at the same time.

That particular evening Michaud had just been relating a horrible murder, with details which had sent a shiver down his audience's spine, when he added with a shake of his head:

'But we don't know the half of it . . . How many crimes remain undiscovered! How many murderers escape human justice!'

'What!' exclaimed Grivet in astonishment. 'You mean, out there, in the street, there are still murdererous swines walking about who haven't been arrested?'

Olivier smiled disdainfully.

'My dear sir,' he replied in a crushing voice, 'if they haven't been arrested, it's because nobody knows they are murderers.'

His reasoning did not seem to convince Grivet. Camille came to his aid.

'For my part, I think the same as Monsieur Grivet,' he said pompously. 'I like to believe that the police are doing a good job, and that I will never have to rub shoulders with a murderer as I walk along the pavement.'

Olivier took his words as a personal afront.

'Of course the police are doing a good job,' he exclaimed with annoyance. 'But we can't do the impossible. There are some real villains around who learn their trade from the devil himself, and they would escape even from God. Isn't that so, father?'

'Yes indeed,' agreed old Michaud. 'For example, when I was at Vernon—perhaps you'll remember this, Madame Raquin—a wagoner was done in on the main road. The body was found hacked to pieces at the bottom of a ditch. The guilty party was never caught. He may still be alive today; perhaps he's a neighbour of ours, and perhaps Monsieur Grivet will bump into him on his way home.'

Grivet went as white as a sheet, scared to look round for fear that the wagoner's murderer was standing behind him. But in fact, he was quite enjoying his fright.

'No, really, no,' he stammered, not knowing what he was saying, 'no, I can't believe all that. I know another story: once upon a time a servant girl was sent to prison for stealing some of her employer's silver. Two months later, as they were felling a tree, they found the cutlery in a magpie's nest. The thief was this magpie. The girl was released. So you see,' he ended triumphantly, 'the guilty do always get their just deserts after all.'

Olivier sneered. 'So I suppose', he said, 'they locked up the magpie?'

'That's not what Monsieur Grivet meant,' said Camille, annoyed at seeing his superior made fun of. 'Mother, let's have the dominoes . . . '

While Madame Raquin went off to fetch the box, the young man went on, addressing himself to Michaud:

'So you admit, do you, that the police are powerless, and that there are still murderers walking around in broad daylight?'

'I'm afraid so, unfortunately,' replied Michaud.

'It isn't right!' concluded Grivet.

During this conversation Thérèse and Laurent had remained silent, not even smiling at Grivet's foolish tale. They sat with their elbows on the table, slightly pale-faced and with a distant look in their eyes, both listening intently. Just for a moment their eyes met, dark and burning. Little beads of sweat began to form at the roots of Thérèse's hair, and a chill draught sent an imperceptible shiver across Laurent's skin.

XI

SOMETIMES on Sundays, when the weather was fine, Camille
would make Thérèse go out with him for a stroll along the
Champs-Elysées. She would always have preferred to stay in
the dank and gloomy atmosphere of the shop; she quickly grew
tired and bored of trailing along the pavements on her husband's arm, stopping outside shops and having to listen to
his imbecilic comments and exclamations of surprise, or put
up with his stupid silence. But Camille would not hear of
it; he enjoyed showing off his wife, and whenever he met one
of his colleagues, and especially one of his superiors, he was
full of pride at being able to exchange salutations in the company of Madame. Apart from that, he walked simply for walking's sake, almost without uttering a word, stiff and unnatural
in his Sunday best, loitering along with a doltish, self-important
expression on his face. For Thérèse, it was a real trial to be
arm in arm with such a man.

On such outing days Madame Raquin would accompany
her children as far as the end of the arcade, before kissing
them goodbye as if they were setting off on a long journey,
with endless advice and urgent pleas for care:

'Whatever you do, beware of accidents,' she would say to
them. 'There is so much traffic here in Paris! Do promise
me you won't go near the crowds.'

Eventually she would allow them to start on their way,
watching them for a long time before going back into the shop.
The heaviness in her legs prevented her from walking any great
distance.

On other, less frequent occasions the couple would go outside Paris, to Saint-Ouen or Asnières,* where they would eat
a fried lunch in one of the riverside restaurants. These were
rare and festive outings which were discussed a good month
in advance. Thérèse was much happier, almost joyful even,
about such expeditions, which kept her out in the open air
until ten or eleven at night. Saint-Ouen and its green islands

reminded her of Vernon; when she was there, all the wild affection she had felt for the Seine as a young girl was reawakened
within her. She would sit on the gravel and dip her hands
in the water, feeling herself coming alive in the hot sunshine,
tempered by a cool, shady breeze. While she would happily
sit on stones or muddy earth, not caring if her dress got dirty
or torn, Camille would carefully unfold his handkerchief and
squat down beside her with infinite care. Lately, the young
couple had almost invariably invited Laurent along with them,
and he livened up their walks with his laughter and peasant's
vitality.

One Sunday, Camille, Thérèse, and Laurent set out for
Saint-Ouen at about eleven, after breakfast. This outing, which
had been planned for a long time, was to be the last one of
the season. Autumn was coming and chill winds were already
starting to send a shiver through the air in the evenings.

That morning, the sky was still as serene and blue as ever,
and it was hot in the sun and warm in the shade. They decided
that they must take advantage of the last rays of summer.

The three trippers climbed into a cab, accompanied by
effusions of anxiety and regret from the old haberdasher. They
crossed Paris and left the cab by the fortifications,* then took
the road to Saint-Ouen on foot. It was noon. In the brilliant
sunlight the dusty road had the blinding whiteness of snow.
The air was scorching hot, heavy and acrid. Thérèse dallied
along on Camille's arm, hiding beneath her sunshade, while
her husband fanned his face with a voluminous handkerchief.
Laurent came along behind them, with the sun burning down
on the back of his neck, although he did not seem to notice;
he whistled and kicked stones, and from time to time a wild
expression came into his eyes as he stared at his mistress's
swaying hips.

As soon as they arrived in Saint-Ouen, they began to look
for a clump of trees with a carpet of shady green grass. They
crossed on to an island and plunged into a thicket. A reddish
layer of fallen leaves covered the ground, rustling and crackling
underfoot. The innumerable tree trunks went straight up, like
clusters of Gothic columns, and the branches came down to
head-height, so that the strollers' horizon was hemmed in by
a copper-coloured vault of dying leaves, and the black and

white shafts of the oaks and aspens. In this wild, remote place they found a small, deserted clearing, a melancholy retreat where everything was cool and quiet. All around them they could hear the rumbling of the Seine.

Laurent picked a dry spot, lifted the tails of his coat, and sat down. Thérèse flung herself down among the leaves in a great rustling of skirts; she was half buried in the folds of her dress, which had ridden up around her, laying one leg bare to the knee. Laurent, lying on his front with his chin on the ground, contemplated this leg while listening to his friend attacking the government for not turning all the little islands in the Seine into parks, with benches, gravelled walks, and well-pruned trees, as in the Tuilerie gardens.*

They stayed there in the clearing for nearly three hours, waiting for the sun's heat to diminish so that they could go for a longer walk in the country before dinner. Camille talked about work, and told inane stories; then, worn out, he lay back and fell asleep, after covering his eyes with his hat. Thérèse, her eyes closed, had already been pretending to doze for a long time.

Now, Laurent began to slide slowly towards her until, stretching forward with his lips, he deposited a kiss first on her shoe, then on her ankle. As he did so, the leather and the white stocking seemed to burn his mouth. The heady smell of the earth, mingled with Thérèse's delicate fragrance, went to his head, setting his blood on fire and his nerves on edge. For a month he had been living in a state of frustrated chastity. The walk along the road to Saint-Ouen in the full sun had set him aflame. Now there he was, hidden away in an isolated retreat, amid the sensual shade and the silence, yet unable to take into his arms the woman who already belonged to him. Her husband might wake up and see them, then all their precautions would be in vain. That man was always getting in the way. And the lover, stretched out on the ground, hiding behind his mistress's skirts, trembling with frustration, pressed silent kisses on her shoe and her stocking. Thérèse, playing dead, did not move a muscle; Laurent thought she was asleep.

He stood up, as his back had started aching, and leaned against a tree. Then he saw that she was actually staring up into the air, her eyes shining and wide open. Her face, framed between her raised arms, was dull and pallid, with a cold rigidity about it. She was deep in thought. Her unblinking eyes were like a dark chasm in which nothing could be seen but black night. She lay there motionless, without turning to look at Laurent as he stood behind her.

Her lover studied her, almost frightened to see her so motionless and unresponsive to his caresses. This deathly white face, drowning in the folds of her skirts, filled him with a mixture of fear and sharp desire. He wanted to lean forwards and kiss her staring eyes shut. But Camille was also there asleep, lying almost on her petticoats. This pathetic creature, his skinny body slumped awkwardly on the ground, was snoring gently; beneath the hat which half covered his face, his mouth gaped open, twisted by sleep into a foolish grimace; the pasty flesh of his scraggy chin was sullied here and there by little reddish hairs, and with his head tipped backwards his wrinkled, scrawny neck could be seen, in the middle of which his prominent, brick-red Adam's apple bobbed up and down with every snore. Sprawled thus in sleep, Camille was an exasperating and unprepossessing sight.

Laurent, who was watching him, suddenly raised his heel in the air; he was going to stamp on Camille's face once and for all.

Thérèse stifled a cry, went white, and shut her eyes. She turned her head away as if to avoid being spattered with blood.

And, for a few seconds, Laurent's foot hovered above the sleeping Camille's face. Then, slowly, he brought his leg down and moved a few paces further away. He had realized that to murder him like that would be utterly stupid; if he stove in Camille's head, he would soon have the whole police force after him. He only wanted to get rid of him in order to marry Thérèse, and he intended to live it up after the crime, like whoever it was who had murdered the wagoner in the story old Michaud had told them.

He went down to the water's edge and watched the river flowing by with a vacant expression on his face. Then, suddenly, he plunged back into the copse; at last he had hit on a plan, a convenient murder that would not put him in any danger.

He woke up the sleeping man by tickling his nose with a

straw. Camille sneezed and got up, remarking on what a fine joke it was. He liked Laurent for his pranks, which always made him laugh. Then he shook his wife as she had kept her eyes tight shut; when Thérèse had stood up and shaken out her skirts, which were all creased and covered in dead leaves, they made their way out of the clearing, snapping off any twigs in their path.

They left the island and set off, along tracks and paths thick with groups of people in their Sunday best. Girls in bright-coloured dresses ran about among the hedges; a crew of oars-men sang as they went by; strings of well-off and respectable couples, elderly people, office workers out with their wives, all sauntered along beside the ditches. Every path was like a crowded and noisy street. Only the sun maintained its aloof calm; as it declined towards the horizon, it cast immense pools of pale brightness on the reddening trees and white roads. A penetrating chill was beginning to settle out of the quivering sky.

Camille no longer had Thérèse on his arm; he was chatting with Laurent and laughing at his friend's jokes and amazing feats, as he jumped ditches and lifted huge boulders. Thérèse walked along on the other side of the road with head bent, occasionally stooping to pick a blade of grass. When she had fallen some way behind, she stopped and watched her lover and her husband from a distance.

'Come on, aren't you hungry?' Camille eventually called back to her.

'Of course!' she replied.

'Well get a move on, then!'

Thérèse was not hungry, but she was tired and anxious. She did not know what Laurent was up to, though she was so ap-prehensive that her legs were trembling beneath her.

The three came back down to the river bank to look for a restaurant. They sat down at a table on a sort of wooden verandah outside a cheap eating house which stank of grease and wine. The place was full of shouting and singing and the clatter of crockery; in all the private alcoves, and larger rooms too, there were parties of trippers talking in loud voices, and the thin partitions made the din even louder with their vibration. The staircase shook as the waiters ran up it.

Up there on the verandah the greasy odours were wafted away by the breeze from the river. Thérèse leaned against the balustrade and looked along the riverbank. To the left and the right stretched a double row of bars and fairground stalls; beneath arbours and through the last of the yellowish leaves of the trees she could see white table-cloths, black coats, and the bright colours of women's dresses; people were coming and going, bare-headed, running around and laughing; and to the raucous din of the crowd were added the dismal tones of barrel organs. A smell of fried food and dust lingered in the still air.

Down below Thérèse, some tarts from the Latin Quarter were dancing in a circle on a patch of worn grass, chanting a children's rhyme. With their hats tipped back on their shoulders and their hair loose, they were holding hands and playing like little girls. They had rediscovered something of their childish voices, and their pale faces, bruised by brutal caresses, had taken on a delicately virginal blush; an occasional emotional tear came into the corner of their wide-open, brazen eyes. Some students sat watching them dance, smoking clay pipes and making lewd remarks at their expense.

Further away, the serenity of evening was falling on the river and the little hills beyond, as the air filled with vague bluish vapours which drowned the trees in a transparent mist.

'Hey, waiter!' Laurent shouted down the staircase, leaning over the banister, 'what about our dinner?'

Then, seeming to change his mind, he went on:

'I say, Camille, how about going out in a boat before we settle down to eat? It will give them time to roast our chicken for us. Otherwise we'll get bored stiff hanging around for an hour.'

'If you like,' replied Camille without enthusiasm. 'But Thérèse is hungry.'

'No, no, I can wait,' Thérèse hastened to reply, as Laurent gave her a meaningful look.

They all went back down. As they passed the counter they reserved a table and decided on what to eat, saying they would be back in an hour. Since the restaurant owner also hired out boats, they asked him to come and untie one for them. Laurent selected a narrow skiff whose flimsiness frightened Camille.

'Good grief!' he exclaimed, 'we'll have to keep pretty still in that, or we'll be in for an early bath!'

The truth was that he was horribly afraid of water. When he was a child at Vernon his sickly state prevented him from splashing about in the Seine, and, while his school friends ran down to the river and dived straight in, he always stayed wrapped up in warm blankets at home. Whereas Laurent had become an intrepid swimmer and indefatigable oarsman, Camille had never lost that terror women and children have of deep water. He prodded the end of the little boat with his toe as if to convince himself it was strong enough.

'Come on then, in you get,' shouted Laurent with a laugh. 'You're always a bundle of nerves!'

Camille stepped over the side and wobbled his way to the stern, where he sat down. When he felt the wooden seat beneath him, he spread himself out and cracked a joke, to show his bravery.

Thérèse had stayed on the bank, solemn and unmoving, standing next to her lover who was holding the mooring rope. He bent down and said to her in an urgent whisper:

'Watch out, I'm going to throw him in ... Just do as I say ... I'll take care of everything.'

She went horribly pale, standing as if rooted to the spot; her body stiffened and her eyes widened.

'Go on, get in the boat,' whispered Laurent.

She did not make a move. A terrible struggle was taking place within her and she had to stretch her will-power to breaking-point to avoid bursting into tears and collapsing on the ground.

'Ha, ha!' exclaimed Camille. 'Laurent, look at Thérèse. She's the one who's scared! Will she, won't she ... ?'

He was lying sprawled on the seat in the stern with his elbows propped on either side of the boat, putting on a show of bravado. Thérèse gave him a peculiar look; his sneering jibes were like a whiplash which compelled her to act. Suddenly, she jumped in. She stayed up at the prow. Laurent took the oars. The boat left the bank and headed slowly out towards the islands.

Dusk was falling. The trees were casting long shadows and the water along the edges of the river was black; in the middle there were wide streaks of pale silver. Soon the boat was right out in mid-Seine. Now all the noises of the riverside were muted; by the time it reached them, the singing and shouting sounded muted and melancholy, sad and languid. The smell of fried food and dust had gone; there was a freshness in the air, and it now felt chilly.

Laurent stopped rowing and let the little boat drift downstream.

In front of them there rose the great russet mass of the islands. The two banks, dark brown speckled with grey, stretched away like two broad bands converging at the distant horizon. Water and sky seemed to have been cut out of the same whitish cloth. Nothing has quite the sorrowful calm of an autumn evening; the light seems pale in the quivering air and the trees shed their old leaves. The whole countryside, burnt up by the fiery rays of summer, feels death approaching with the first chill winds, and the skies fill with their plaintive and despairing gusts. Night descends, bearing shrouds in its shadow.

The three kept silent. Sitting in the boat as it drifted with the current, they watched the last glimmer of light depart from the tops of the trees. They were getting near the islands. The great russet masses were now darker; the whole landscape was becoming simplified in the half-light; the Seine, the sky, the islands, and the little hills were no more than brown and grey patches fading into a milky mist.

Camille, who had ended up lying on his stomach with his head hanging out over the side, dipped his hands in the water.

'Golly, it isn't half cold!' he exclaimed. 'It wouldn't be much fun taking a nose-dive into that!'

Laurent made no reply. For a while now he had been anxiously scrutinizing both banks; he began sliding his great hands along towards his knees, and his lips tightened. Thérèse, sitting stiff and motionless, her head tilted slightly back, waited.

The boat was about to move into a dark, narrow channel between two islands. From the far side of one of them could be heard the muffled song of a crew of oarsmen who must be rowing back up the Seine. In the distance upstream the river was empty.

Then Laurent stood up and seized Camille around his waist. The clerk burst out laughing.

'No, stop it, you're tickling me!' he said. 'Now that's enough larking about! Come on, stop it or you'll make me fall in!'

Laurent squeezed harder and gave a heave. Camille turned round and saw the terrifying, contorted expression on his friend's face. He did not understand, but was seized by an obscure dread. He tried to cry out but felt a rough hand grab him round the throat. Instinctively, like an animal defending itself, he pulled himself up on to his knees, clutching at the side of the boat. He struggled like that for a few seconds.

'Thérèse! Thérèse!' he called out in a stifled, rasping voice.

The young woman looked on, holding on to one of the seats with both hands as the boat creaked and danced on the river. She was unable to close her eyes, for a fearful muscular contraction kept them wide open, riveted on the horrific spectacle of the struggle. She was rigid and speechless.

'Thérèse! Thérèse!' the unfortunate Camille called again, now at his last gasp.

At this final appeal for help Thérèse burst into tears. Her nerve had broken, and the crisis that she had been dreading flung her trembling into the bottom of the boat. There she lay, collapsed in a heap and half dead.

Laurent was still shaking Camille and squeezing him by the throat. He eventually managed to wrench him away from the boat with his other hand, and held him up in the air like a child in his powerful, outstretched arms. As his head was thrown back and the neck unprotected, his victim, crazed with rage and terror, twisted round and sank his teeth into it. Then the murderer, stifling a howl of pain, flung the clerk into the river, but the teeth took with them a lump of his flesh.

Camille fell into the water with a scream. He came back to the surface two or three times, and his cries became more muffled each time.

Laurent did not lose a second. First, he turned up the collar of his jacket to conceal his wounds. Then he seized hold of Thérèse, who had passed out, flipped the boat over with a twist of his feet, and, still holding his mistress, dropped into the Seine. He held her up above water, calling piteously for help.

The oarsmen whose singing he had heard from the far side

of the island rowed energetically over towards them. They realized that something unfortunate had just happened; they res-
cued Thérèse, whom they laid on a seat, and Laurent, who
began to lament at the death of his friend. He threw himself
back into the water and looked for Camille in all the places
where he could not possibly be, and returned in tears, wringing his hands and tearing his hair. The rowers tried to pacify
and console him.

'It's all my fault,' he shouted; 'I should never have let the
poor fellow dance about like that in the boat. At one point
we must all have been on the same side, then we capsized.
As he went in, he shouted to me to save his wife.'

As always happens in such cases, two or three of the young
oarsmen claimed to have witnessed the accident.

'Yes, we saw you all right,' they said. 'God knows, when
you're in a rowing boat you can't just jump about as if you
were on dry land. Oh! the poor little thing, what a terrible
awakening she's in for!'

They took up their oars again, towed the boat back, and
led Thérèse and Laurent to the restaurant, where their dinner
was ready. News of the accident went all round Saint-Ouen
in a few minutes. The rowing crew told the story of what had
happened as if they had seen it all with their own eyes. A
crowd of sympathizers took up station outside.

The proprietor and his wife were good people, who placed
their wardrobes at the disposal of the shipwrecked pair. When
Thérèse came round from her faint, she had a fit of hysterics
and burst out in heart-rending sobs; she had to be put to bed.
Thus nature made its own contribution to the sinister per-
formance which had just been played out.

When she had calmed down, Laurent placed her in the safe
keeping of the restaurant owners, saying that he wanted to
return to Paris alone in order to break the appalling news to
Madame Raquin as tactfully as possible. The truth was that
he was afraid of what Thérèse would do in her overwrought
nervous state. He preferred to give her time to think things
over and learn her part.

It was the boating crew who ate Camille's dinner.

XII

IN a dark corner of the public omnibus which brought him back to Paris, Laurent put the finishing touches to his plan. He was almost certain he would get away with it. His heart was filled with the anxious, grim joy of a crime accomplished. When he arrived at the Clichy barrier,* he took a cab to where old Michaud lived, in the Rue de Seine. It was nine in the evening.

He found the former police superintendent sitting down to eat, in the company of Olivier and Suzanne. He had decided to go there to cover himself in case anyone should suspect him, and to avoid having to break the dreadful news to Madame Raquin in person. That was something he felt peculiarly loath to do, for he fully expected her to be so grief-stricken that he would be unable to summon sufficient tears to act his own part credibly; moreover, he found the thought of her maternal anguish oppressive, although he didn't really care about it otherwise.

When Michaud saw him come in wearing scruffy clothes that were too small for him, he looked at him quizzically. Laurent related the accident in a broken voice, as if hardly able to speak with grief and fatigue.

'So I came to find you,' he said in conclusion, 'because I didn't know what to do about those two poor women who have been so cruelly struck down. I just didn't have the courage to go and see his mother on my own. Please, will you come with me?'

While he was speaking, Olivier stared at him with a fixity which filled him with terror. The murderer had thrown himself headlong into this police lair in an act of daring calculated to save him. But he could not prevent himself from trembling as he felt the scrutiny of their gaze, and saw suspicion where there was really only incredulity and pity. Suzanne, turning pale, looked more fragile than ever, and close to fainting. Olivier, afraid of the idea of death but otherwise absolutely unmoved by the story, took on an expression of grief and suprise as he examined Laurent's face, purely out of habit and without in the least suspecting the sinister truth. As for old Michaud, he uttered exclamations of shock, sympathy, and astonishment, shuffling around on his chair, clasping his hands together and raising his eyes to heaven.

'Oh! my God', he said in a half-choking voice, 'Oh! my God, what an appalling thing! You have only to go out of the house and suddenly, you're dead, just like that. It's horrible! And poor Madame Raquin, his dear mother—whatever are we to tell her? Yes, indeed, you were quite right to come to us . . . We'll certainly go with you.'

He stood up and shuffled up and down the room, looking everywhere for his hat and stick, all the time making Laurent go back over the details of the catastrophe and exclaiming anew at each sentence.

They all four went downstairs. At the entrance to the Passage du Pont-Neuf Michaud stopped Laurent.

'Don't come up,' he said to him. 'Your presence would give the game away that something awful has happened. His unfortunate mother will suspect the worst and make us come out with the truth before we are ready. You wait here for us.'

This arrangement was a relief to the murderer, who was trembling at the thought of going into the arcade. His composure returned and he began to walk up and down the pavement, in perfect peace of mind. At times he quite forgot the turn of events, and started looking into shop windows and whistling between his teeth, or turned round to eye up women who brushed past him. He stayed there in the street for a good half hour, feeling more and more his usual self.

He had not had anything to eat since the morning so, overcome by hunger, he went into a *pâtisserie* and stuffed himself with cakes.

Meanwhile, in the shop in the Passage du Pont-Neuf, a heart-rending scene was going on. Despite all Michaud's precautions and his affectionate and considerate words, the moment came when Madame Raquin realized that something dreadful had happened to her son. At once she demanded to know the truth, with such despairing insistence and such wailing and floods of tears that her old friend gave way. When she was finally told, her grief was tragic to behold. She went utterly to pieces, her whole body racked by stifled sobs of horror and despair which jolted her backwards and left her hardly able to breathe, while from time to time a shrill shriek welled up from the bleak depths of her grief. She would have grovelled on the floor if Suzanne had not put her arms round her waist and shed tears on her knees, lifting her white face up to look at her. Olivier and his father stood there in awkward silence, looking away, disagreeably affected by a scene which could so upset their manly self-esteem.

The poor mother had visions of her son tumbling about in the rough waters of the Seine, his body horribly stiff and bloated; and at the same time she saw him as a little baby in his cradle and herself chasing away the figure of death as it hovered over him. She had brought him back into the world at least a dozen times; she loved him for all the love she had shown him over thirty years. And now he had died far away from her, all of a sudden, in the cold dirty water, like a dog. Then she remembered the warm blankets in which she used to envelop him. Such lavish care, such a warm, cosy childhood, such coaxing and outpourings of affection, all to see him wretchedly drowned like that! At these thoughts, Madame Raquin felt a great lump rise in her throat; she hoped she would die, suffocated by her despair.

Leaving Suzanne with the old lady, Michaud and Olivier hurried outside to find Laurent, and set off with all speed back to Saint-Ouen.

Scarcely a word was exchanged between them on the way. Each had buried himself in a corner of the cab which jolted them along through cobbled streets, and they sat silent and motionless in the gloom. From time to time a gas light would cast its bright but fleeting glow on their faces. They were enveloped in a lugubrious cloud of despondency by the sinister event which had brought them together.

When they eventually arrived at the riverside café, they found Thérèse lying in bed, her hands and face burning hot. The proprietor told them in low tones that the young lady had a temperature. The truth was that Thérèse, feeling weak and lacking courage, and fearing that she might own up about the murder in a fit of nerves, had decided to feign illness.

So she stayed grimly silent, keeping her eyes and lips tight shut and refusing to see anyone in case she said too much. With the sheets pulled up to her chin and her face half hidden in the pillow, she made herself as small as possible and listened anxiously to what was being said around her. And amid the reddish glow which filtered through her closed eyelids, she kept seeing Camille and Laurent struggling on one side of the boat, followed by her husband's form, wan, horrific, and larger than life, rising straight out of the muddy waters of the river. This relentlessly returning vision stoked up the fever in her blood.

Old Michaud attempted to speak to her and console her. With a gesture of impatience she turned over and started sobbing again.

'Leave her alone, Sir,' said the café owner, 'the slightest noise starts her trembling. What she needs, you know, is rest.'

Down below, in the main dining-room, a policeman was taking details of the accident. Michaud and his son went downstairs, followed by Laurent. Once Olivier had made it known that he was a senior official at the Prefecture, the whole business was over in ten minutes. The rowers were still there, recounting the drowning in minute detail, describing how the three had fallen into the water and generally presenting themselves as eye-witnesses. If Olivier and his father had been in the slightest bit suspicious, their fears would have been utterly allayed. But they had never doubted the truth of Laurent's story for an instant; on the contrary, they introduced him to the policeman as the victim's best friend, and they made sure that he noted in his report the fact that the young man had plunged into the water to save Camille Raquin. The following day the accident was reported in the newspapers with a great wealth of detail. The unfortunate mother, the inconsolable widow, the brave and noble friend—the story had everything, and it soon went the rounds of the Parisian press, before being picked up by the provincial rags, where it finally faded from view.

When the policeman had finished taking statements, Laurent felt a hot surge of joy run through his body, putting new life into him. Since the moment when his victim had sunk his teeth into his neck, he had as it were stiffened himself, acting mechanically according to a plan worked out long in advance. Every action, word, and gesture had been dictated solely by an instinct for self-preservation. Now that he was sure he was not going to be found out, his blood began to course regularly and pleasantly again through his veins. The police had passed close to his crime and seen nothing; they had been fooled into believing him innocent. He was safe. This thought sent a delicious sweat of relief running down his body, filling him with a warm glow which restored his suppleness of limb and quickness of mind. He carried on playing the part of a grief-stricken friend with incomparable skill and self-possession. In fact, though, he was enjoying a purely animal satisfaction; and he was thinking about Thérèse, lying upstairs in the bedroom.

'We can't leave this unfortunate young woman here,' he said to Michaud. 'She may be on the verge of a serious illness; we absolutely have to take her back to Paris. Come on, we must convince her to come with us.'

Upstairs, he spoke to Thérèse himself, begging her to get up and let them take her back to the Passage du Pont-Neuf. When she heard the sound of his voice she shuddered, opened her eyes wide, and looked at him. She was dazed and trembling; with great difficulty she sat up but did not reply. The men went out of the room, leaving her alone with the proprietor's wife. When she had dressed, she went shakily downstairs and was helped into the cab by Olivier.

The journey passed in silence. With consummate impudence and daring Laurent slid his hand across Thérèse's skirt until he could hold her fingers. He was sitting opposite her in the shifting shadows; as she kept her head bowed he could not see her face. Having grasped her hand, he squeezed it firmly in his own all the way back to the Rue Mazarine. He could feel it trembling, but it was not drawn back; instead, from time to time it gave a sudden squeeze of its own. And the two hands were burning hot, their palms damp and sticky and their tightly interlaced fingers squashed together at every jolt. It seemed to Laurent and Thérèse that their blood was circulating through their joined hands and round each other's hearts, so that their hands became the fiery focus of all their bubbling life-force. In the dark of the night and the desolate silence which hung everywhere, this frantic hand-clasp was like a crushing weight heaped on to Camille's head to keep him underwater.

When the cab came to a halt, Michaud and his son got out first. Laurent leaned over to his mistress and whispered:

'Be strong, Thérèse. We have a long time to wait. Don't forget . . . '

The young woman had still not spoken. Now she opened her lips for the first time since the death of her husband.

'Oh! I shan't forget,' she said with a shudder, in a voice hardly louder than a breath.

Olivier held out his hand, offering to help her down. This time Laurent went into the shop. Madame Raquin was lying down, suffering from a serious attack of delirium. Thérèse dragged herself to her bed and Suzanne scarcely had time to undress her. Reassured that everything was turning out for the best, Laurent withdrew and walked slowly back to his squalid quarters in the Rue Saint-Victor.

It was now past midnight. A cool breeze was blowing through the silent, deserted streets, and the young man could hear only the regular sound of his own footsteps on the pavement. The cool air filled him with a sense of well-being, the silence and the shadows gave him momentary sensations of pleasure. He slowed to a stroll.

He was relieved to have committed his crime at last. He had killed Camille and now the whole thing was over and done with; nothing more would ever be said. From now on he was going to live in peace and quiet, until it was time to take possession of Thérèse. The thought of committing a murder had choked him at times with panic; now that he had succeeded, a weight had been lifted from his chest, he could breathe easily again, and he was free of the anxiety which fear and hesitation had inflicted.

He was actually in rather a dazed state, and his limbs and his thoughts were weighed down by tiredness. He went home and fell into a deep sleep, but, while he slept, slight nervous twitchings passed across his face.

XIII

THE next morning Laurent awoke feeling refreshed and in good spirits. He had slept well. The cold air coming in through the window quickened his sluggish blood. He scarcely remembered the events of the day before; were it not for the burning sensation in his neck, he might have thought he had gone to bed at ten after an uneventful evening. But Camille's deep bite was like the burn of a red-hot iron on his skin, and, whenever the pain of the injury intruded upon his thoughts, it hurt him most cruelly. It felt like a dozen needles slowly penetrating his flesh.

He turned down his shirt-collar and studied the wound in a cheap, tarnished mirror on the wall. It was a red gash the size of a two-soùs coin; the skin had been torn away to expose the pinkish flesh, which had black spots in it; trickles of blood had run down as far as the shoulder, leaving congealed trails which were now flaking off. Against the white of the neck, the bite stood out a deep and powerful brown; it was on the right, below the ear. Laurent stooped forward and stretched his neck out to see, and the greenish mirror distorted his expression into an atrocious grimace.

He washed thoroughly, satisfied with his examination and telling himself that the wound would heal over in a few days. Then he dressed and went quietly to the office, as usual. There he told the story of the accident with emotion in his voice. When his colleagues read the reports that were going round in the papers, he became a real hero. For a week all the employees of the Orleans Railway had just one topic of conversation; they were all proud that one of their number had been drowned. Grivet waxed lyrical on the imprudence of venturing out into the middle of the Seine when it is so easy to watch the river flowing by from a bridge.

But Laurent still had one nagging worry. They had not been able to record Camille's death officially. Thérèse's husband was certainly dead, but the murderer would have preferred his body to be found so that a formal certificate could be issued. The day after the accident a fruitless search had been made for the drowned man's body; it was thought that it had probably become wedged in some hole in the bank of one of the islands. There were scavengers actively scouring the Seine in the hope of claiming the reward.

Laurent gave himself the task of dropping in at the Morgue* every morning on his way to work. He had sworn to make sure of everything himself. Although it made him feel sick with repugnance and occasionally sent shivers down his spine, he went there regularly for over a week to examine the faces of all the people who had drowned, laid out on the slabs.

When he went in, a stale, sickly smell turned his stomach, the smell of scrubbed flesh, and chill draughts made his skin prickle; the dampness of the walls seemed to weigh down his clothes at the shoulders. He went straight over to the glass screen which separated the onlookers from the corpses, pressed his pale face up against the glass, and looked in. Rows of grey slabs stretched out in front of him. Here and there naked bodies stood out in patches of colour, green and yellow, white and red, against the slabs; some of them had kept their flesh intact in the rigidity of death, while others looked like heaps of bloody, rotting meat. At the back, hanging against the wall, were pathetic rags of trousers and skirts grimly contorted against the bare plaster. At first Laurent saw only the greyish background of stones and walls and the blotches of red and black made by the clothes and the corpses. There was a tinkling of running water.

Gradually he began to make out individual bodies; then he went along from one to another. He was only interested in those who had drowned; if there were several corpses swollen and blue from the water, he would examine them avidly in the hope of recognizing Camille. Often, the flesh of their faces would be peeling off in strips, with bones poking through the softened skin, so that the whole thing looked mushy and formless. Laurent hesitated, studying each body and trying to see in it the skinny frame of his victim. But drowned corpses are always bloated; he saw enormous bellies, bulging thighs, and rounded, powerful arms. Unable to decide, he stood shivering in front of these greenish hunks of meat, which seemed to be mocking him with their leering grimaces.

One morning he had a terrible fright. He had been looking at one drowned man, small and horribly disfigured, for a number of minutes. His flesh was so softened and decomposed that the water running over the corpse was washing it away scrap by scrap. The jet playing on the face was digging a hole to the left of the nose. All of a sudden the nose collapsed and the lips came away, showing the white teeth below, and the drowned head split itself with grim laughter.

Each time he thought he had recognized Camille, Laurent felt a burning in his heart. He desperately wanted to find his victim's body, but whenever he imagined that it was indeed there in front of him his courage failed him. His visits to the Morgue gave him nightmares and fits of shuddering which left him panting for breath. He shook off his fears and told himself not to act like a child; he wanted to be strong, but, despite himself, his body refused, and his whole being was overcome by revulsion and horror as soon as he found himself in the damp, sickly-smelling atmosphere of the mortuary.

Sometimes he reached the last row of slabs and there were no drowning cases, so he breathed more easily and his repugnance diminished somewhat. Then he became simply a curious visitor, taking a strange pleasure in looking violent death in the face and seeing the lugubriously bizarre and grotesque attitudes in which it takes people. He found such sights entertaining, particularly when there were women there with their bare breasts showing. Such brutal displays of nudity, the bodies spattered with blood and sometimes even with holes in them, attracted him and held him spellbound. On one occasion he saw a young woman of twenty, a working-class girl, strong and buxom, who seemed to be lying asleep on the stone. Her plump, fresh body had gone an extremely soft and delicate shade of white; she was half smiling, her head tipped gently to one side, and was provocatively offering her bosom to his gaze. She would have looked just like a harlot stretched out on a bed, were it not for the black stripe around her neck which gave her a sort of shadowy necklace; in fact, she was an ordinary girl who had hanged herself out of unrequited love. Laurent looked at her for a long time, running his eyes all over her body, absorbed in a kind of fearful lust.

Every morning while he was there he could hear the public coming and going behind him.

The Morgue is a show within the reach of every purse, something which passers-by, rich or poor, can enjoy for nothing. The door is open; anyone who wishes to walk in can do so. There are connoisseurs who go out of their way not to miss a single one of these morbid spectacles. When the slabs are bare, people go away disappointed, feeling they have been swindled and muttering between their teeth. When they are well covered with a fine display of human flesh, the visitors jostle each other for cheap thrills, exclaiming in horror and joking, applauding, or whistling as if they were at the theatre, and go away well satisfied, declaring that the Morgue has certainly put on a good show that day.

Laurent soon began to recognize the regulars, a disparate mixture of people who all came to weep or cackle in each other's company. Some were labourers on the way to work, carrying their tools and a loaf of bread under their arm; they always thought death was terribly funny. Among them were apprentice wags who made the onlookers smile by passing some droll comment on each corpse's particular grimace; they called those who had died in fires coal-men; the hanged, the murdered, the drowned, and bodies which had been crushed or mutilated, stimulated them to particular feats of wit, and in somewhat tremulous voices they stammered out their comic remarks in the shivering silence of the mortuary. Then there were thin, dessicated old men of the better-off sort, out for a stroll and with nothing better to do, who looked at the bodies with the foolish distaste of refined and peaceable citizens. There were also great numbers of women: young working-girls with pink complexions, in white linen and clean skirts, who slipped nimbly along from one end of the glass screen to the other, their eyes wide open and attentive as if they were staring in the window of a fashion store; poor women, with stunned expressions on their faces and a pitiful air, and fashionably dressed ladies swishing nonchalantly past in their silk dresses.

One day Laurent saw one of these ladies standing transfixed a few steps back from the glass screen, holding a cambric handkerchief up to her nose. She was wearing a gorgeous grey

silk skirt and a cape of black lace; her face was partly covered by a veil, and her gloved hands looked tiny and extremely
slender. Around her there lingered the sweet perfume of violets. She was staring at a corpse. A few feet away, stretched
out on a slab, lay the body of a strapping young man, a
mason who had just fallen to his death from a scaffolding;
he had a powerful chest, his muscles were taut and prominent,
and his flesh white and well nourished; death had turned him
into a marble statue. The lady carried on examining him, turning him over, as it were, and weighing him with her gaze.
The sight of this man completely enthralled her. She lifted
a corner of her veil and looked once more, then went away.

Occasionally gangs of boys would turn up, mere children
between twelve and fifteen years old, who would run the length
of the screen, stopping only in front of female corpses. They
pushed their hands against the glass and stared impudently
at the bared breasts. They dug each other in the ribs and made
lewd remarks, learning about vice at the school of death;
the Morgue is where many a young lout makes the acquain-
tance of his first mistress.

After a week of this Laurent felt heartily sick. At night he
had nightmares about the corpses he had seen in the morning.
Eventually, the loathsome and disgusting daily round into
which he had forced himself began to disturb him so much
that he resolved to go only twice more. The next day, on enter-
ing the Morgue, he received a violent blow to the heart: there
in front of him, laid out on a slab on his back, with his head
raised and his eyes half open, was Camille, staring up at him.

The murderer walked slowly over to the glass screen as
though drawn by a strange attraction, unable to take his eyes
off his victim. He felt no pain, only a sensation of deep cold
inside and a slight pricking of the skin. He would have expected
to be shaking more than he was. He stayed stock still for five
long minutes, lost in unconscious contemplation, engraving in
his memory, in spite of himself, each horrible line and each
foul colour of the picture which he had before his eyes.

Camille was a revolting sight. He had been in the water
for a fortnight. His face still looked firm and stiff; his features
had been preserved, only the skin had taken on a yellowish,
muddy hue. The head, thin, bony, and slightly puffy, was

grimacing; it was at a slight angle, the hair was plastered against the temples, and the eyelids were up, revealing the globular whites of the eyes; the lips were twisted down at one corner in a horrible sneer; the blackish tip of the tongue was poking out between the white teeth. This head, stretched and tanned like leather, was all the more shocking in its expression of pain and terror for having kept a human appearance. The body had been horribly battered and looked like a heap of decomposing flesh. It was clear that hardly anything was holding the arms on any more, for the shoulder-blades protruded through the skin of the shoulders. The ribs made black stripes across the greenish chest, and the left side of the body had burst open, leaving a hole with jagged, dark red edges. The whole torso was rotten. The legs were more solid and stretched straight out, but were covered in disgusting blotches. The feet were falling off.

Laurent looked hard at Camille. He had never before seen such a horrific case of drowning. On top of everything else the corpse had taken on a shrunken appearance; it looked scrawny and pathetic, all huddled up into a tiny heap as it rotted away. Anyone would have guessed straightaway that he was only a twelve-hundred-franc employee, sickly and stupid, whose mother had fed him on herbal infusions. This poor body which had grown up wrapped in warm blankets now lay shivering on a cold slab.

When Laurent finally managed to tear himself away from the sight before which a harrowing curiosity held him gaping and motionless, he went outside and began walking quickly along the embankment. And as he walked he said to himself over and over again: 'That's what I've done to him; he looks disgusting.' He felt sure he was being followed around by a pungent smell, the smell which the putrefying body would now be giving off.

He went to find old Michaud and told him that he had just recognized Camille's body on a slab at the Morgue. The formalities were duly completed, the drowned man was buried, and a death certificate issued. Laurent, certain now that he was safe, threw himself luxuriously into the task of forgetting his crime, and the irritating and distressing scenes which had followed the murder.

XIV

THE shop in the Passage du Pont-Neuf remained closed for three days. When it opened again, it seemed even damper and more gloomy. The stock on display, yellowed by dust, wore the same air of mourning as the rest of the household; in the dirty windows things lay about in disorder. Behind the cotton bonnets hanging from rusty rails, Thérèse's face had a duller, more earthy pallor and a sinister, unmoving calm.

All along the arcade the old wives were exchanging pitying comments about what had happened. The woman who sold costume jewellery pointed out to each of her clients how much thinner the young widow's face had become, as if she were some interesting and pitiful curiosity.

For three days Madame Raquin and Thérèse had stayed in their beds, without speaking, without even seeing each other. The old haberdasher, propped up on her pillows, stared straight ahead with an idiot gaze. The death of her son had dealt her a great blow to the head, and she had been knocked senseless. She sat there for hours at a time, calm and motionless, lost in the emptiness of her despair and seized from time to time by fits of weeping, screaming, and delirium. In the neighbouring room Thérèse seemed to be asleep; she had turned to face the wall and pulled the blanket up over her eyes, and there she lay stretched out, stiff and silent, with not a single sob disturbing the bedclothes that covered her. It was as if she were hiding away, in the darkness of the bed, those thoughts which had taken away her power of movement. Suzanne, who was looking after the two women, shuffled quietly from one to the other, bending her waxen face over the two beds, unable either to make Thérèse turn to face her instead of shrugging her off impatiently, or to console Madame Raquin, whose tears began to flow whenever the sound of a voice startled her out of her collapsed state.

On the third day Thérèse threw back the bedclothes and sat up on the edge of the bed with a kind of feverish resolve.

Brushing her hair aside, she sat for a while with her hands on her temples, staring straight ahead and apparently lost in thought. Then she jumped out of bed. Her limbs were red and trembling with fever; her skin, which in places hung in folds as thought empty of flesh, was marbled with great livid blotches. She had suddenly aged.

When she entered the room, Suzanne stood still in surprise at finding her up, and in her placid, languid voice she advised her to go back to bed and rest a little longer. Thérèse took no notice; she was looking for her clothes and putting them on with hurried, trembling movements. When she had dressed she went to look at herself in the mirror, rubbed her eyes, and ran her hands over her face as if to wipe something away. Then, without uttering a word, she walked quickly through the dining-room and went in to see Madame Raquin.

The former haberdasher was in a calm, dazed state. When Thérèse entered she turned her head and watched the young widow cross the room until she stood before her, silent and downcast. The two women looked at each other for a few seconds, the niece with growing anxiety, the aunt making painful efforts to remember. When at last things came back to her, Madame Raquin held out her trembling arms, put them round Thérèse's neck, and cried out:

'My poor child, my poor Camille!'

She wept, and her tears dried on Thérèse's burning skin; Thérèse hid her own dry eyes in the folds of the sheet and stayed bending over the bed, waiting for the old woman to cry herself out. Since the murder, she had been dreading this first encounter; she had stayed in bed so as to delay the moment of its arrival and contemplate, undisturbed, the terrible role she now had to play.

When she saw that Madame Raquin was calmer, she started to fuss around her, advising her to get up and go down to the shop. The old haberdasher had almost regressed into childhood. The appearance of her niece had brought about a sudden improvement, which had now restored her memory and her awareness of things and people around her. She thanked Suzanne for looking after her, began to talk more, and, although very weak, was no longer delirious but overcome with grief, which sometimes made her choke. With occasional outbursts of tears she would watch Thérèse walking around; then she would call her over, put her arms round her once more, and tell her with a catch in her voice that she was all she had left in the world.

That evening she agreed to get up and try to have something to eat. Thérèse was then able to see what a terrible blow her aunt had received. The poor old woman's legs had become so bad that she needed a walking stick to drag herself through into the dining-room, and once she was there she felt as if the walls were swaying around her.

The very next morning, however, she insisted the shop should be opened. She was afraid of going mad if she stayed alone in her bedroom. She moved heavily downstairs, pausing on each step, and went to sit behind the counter, where she remained, serene and sad, from that day on.

By her side stood Thérèse, musing and waiting. The shop resumed its sombre calm.

XV

FROM time to time, every two or three days, Laurent would come round in the evening, stay in the shop for half an hour, chatting with Madame Raquin, then go away again without once having looked directly at Thérèse. The old haberdasher regarded him as her niece's saviour, a noble soul who had done everything in his power to give her back her son. She always welcomed him with affection and kindness.

One Thursday evening Laurent was there when old Michaud and Grivet came in. It was exactly eight o'clock. The employee and the former police chief had each decided independently of the other that they could now resume their pleasant routine without intruding, and they arrived at the very same minute, as if driven by the same mechanism. Behind them, Olivier and Suzanne also made their entrance.

They all went upstairs to the dining-room. Madame Raquin, who was not expecting anyone, hastily lit the lamp and went to make tea. When they were all seated round the table with cups in front of them, and the dominoes had been tipped out of their box, the poor mother, suddenly transported back into the past, looked round at her guests and burst into tears. There was one empty seat, the seat where her son used to sit.

Her despairing outburst plunged the whole company into a chill and awkward silence. Their faces wore an expression of selfish contentment. They felt embarrassed, for they had not kept the slightest memory of Camille alive in their hearts.

'Come now, dear lady,' exclaimed old Michaud a touch impatiently, 'you mustn't upset yourself so, you'll make yourself ill.'

'We're all mortal,' Grivet observed bluntly.

'Crying will never bring your son back,' said Olivier pompously.

'I beg you,' murmured Suzanne, 'don't make us all upset.'

As Madame Raquin only started sobbing louder, unable to staunch her tears, old Michaud went on:

'Come, come, pull yourself together now. We're here to amuse you, you know, so for heaven's sake don't let's all feel sorry for ourselves; try and forget ... We'll play for two sous a game, all right?'

Making a supreme effort, the haberdasher forced back her tears, aware perhaps of her guests' selfish smugness. Still shaking, she dried her eyes; the dominoes rattled in her poor hands and the tears which still clung beneath her eyelids made it difficult for her to see. The game began.

Laurent and Thérèse had watched this brief scene with solemn and impassive expressions. He was delighted to see the Thursday evening gatherings reinstated. That had been his dearest wish, for he knew that he would need them if he was to achieve his goal. Also, though he did not quite know why, he felt more at ease among these few people whom he knew, and could now look Thérèse in the eye again.

Thérèse, dressed all in black and with a pale and distant look, now seemed to him endowed with a beauty which he had not seen before. He was happy when her eyes met his and bravely sustained his gaze. She still belonged to him, body and soul.

XVI

FIFTEEN months went by. The stress of the first hours subsided; each day brought greater tranquility and indifference, and life resumed its normal languid course, slipping into the dull monotony which follows all great crises. And, at the beginning, Laurent and Thérèse fell in willingly with this new existence; but it was changing them, for a hidden process had taken place within them which would have to be analysed with extreme subtlety if one wished to differentiate its various phases.

Soon, Laurent was again dropping round at the shop every evening, as in the past; but he no longer ate there or settled down for the whole evening. He would arrive at half past nine and leave after locking up. It was as if he were fulfilling a duty by helping the two women in this way. If he ever neglected his task, he would apologize the next day with the humility of a servant. On Thursdays he helped Madame Raquin to light the fire and do the honours of the household. She was charmed by his quiet and considerate behaviour.

Thérèse calmly observed him as he busied himself around her. Her face had lost its pallor; she seemed to have softened and become more smiling and healthy. From time to time, however, a nervous contraction would still pinch the corners of her mouth into two deep lines which brought a strangely frightened, pained expression to her face.

The two lovers no longer made any attempt to see each other on their own. They never sought a rendez-vous or exchanged a furtive kiss. For the moment, the murder had as it were smothered the sensual fire in their flesh; by killing Camille, they had managed to assuage those fierce and insatiable desires which had remained unsatisfied while they had lain locked in each other's arms. The crime had given them a feeling of acute pleasure which made their embraces seem insipid and loathsome in comparison.

And yet they now had endless opportunities to lead the life

of free love of which they had dreamed and for which they had committed murder. The dazed, invalid Madame Raquin was no obstacle; the house belonged to them and they could come and go just as they wished. But love had lost its appeal, their appetite had disappeared; they stayed there quietly chatting, looking at each other without a blush or a shudder, as if they had forgotten the wild embraces that had bruised their flesh and made their bones crack. They even tried to avoid being alone together, for in such intimacy they could find nothing to say and neither wanted to show too much coldness. Whenever they shook hands, the touching of their skin made them feel slightly queasy.

In any case, they both believed that they knew what had caused the indifference and fear which had come between them. They put their coldness down to prudence, thinking that their calm and celibate behaviour was the product of superior wisdom. They pretended to themselves that this serenity of the flesh and slumber of the heart was what they themselves wanted. Furthermore, they saw the repugnance and unease that they were feeling as indications, left over from the shocking event, of some deep-down fear of punishment. From time to time they would try to renew their hope by force and pick up the thread of their passionate dreams again, but they were always astonished to find their imaginations empty. So they clung desperately to the idea that they would soon be married; when they had reached that goal, when all their fears were past and they belonged entirely to each other, they would rediscover their passion and taste the delights of which they had dreamed. This new hope made them calmer and stopped them from falling further into the void which had opened up within them. They managed to convince themselves that they loved each other as much as before, and awaited the hour which would make their happiness complete by binding them to each other for ever.

Never before had Thérèse known such peace of mind. She was undoubtedly turning into a more likeable person, as the implacable determination which had so governed her character began to relax.

At night, alone in her bed, she was happy; Camille's thin face and scrawny body were no longer there beside her to

frustrate her flesh and fill her with unsatisfied desires. She
felt virginal again, like a little girl, as she lay there peacefully
in the silence and the dark, surrounded by white bed curtains.
She liked her large, rather cold bedroom, with its high ceiling,
dark corners, and convent-like atmosphere. She even came
to regard the great black wall which rose up in front of her
window with affection; throughout one summer, each evening,
she would stand for hours at a time looking at its dark stones
and gazing up at the narrow strip of starry sky outlined by
the chimneys and roof-tops above. She only ever thought
of Laurent when a nightmare jolted her awake; then, sitting
bolt upright with her nightdress clasped round her, shivering
and wide-eyed, she told herself that she would not have such
sudden frights if only there were a man lying by her side. She
thought of her lover as she would a guard-dog, as someone
to protect her; no flutter of desire ran across her cool, calm
skin.

During the day, in the shop, she took more interest in things
and came out of herself, no longer living in a state of inner
revolt, with thoughts of hatred and vengeance bottled up inside
her. Daydreaming now bored her; she needed action, and
things to look at. From dawn to dusk she watched the people
walking through the arcade, finding entertainment in their
comings and goings and the noise they made. She became
curious and talkative and, in short, was now a proper woman,
for until then her actions and ideas had all been those of a
man.

From her observation post she noticed a young man, a student, who lived in furnished lodgings in the vicinity and who
passed by the shop several times a day. He was pale and handsome, with the luxuriant hair of a poet and an officer's mous-
tache. Thérèse found him distinguished looking. She fell in
love with him for a week, just like a schoolgirl. She began
to read novels and compared the young man with Laurent,
whom she found dull and coarse in comparison. Reading
opened up romantic horizons of which she had known nothing
until now; before, she had loved with her blood and her nerves,
but now she began to love with her head. Then one day the
student vanished; he had probably moved. She forgot all about
him in a few hours.

She joined a subscription library and became passionately involved with the heroes of all the novels which came into her hands. This sudden love of reading had a great influence on her temperament; she developed a nervy sensitivity which made her laugh or cry for no reason. The balance which had been developing in her personality was now upset. She fell into a vague, dreamy state out of which she was jolted from time to time by thoughts of Camille; then she would long for Laurent again with a mixture of desire, fear, and misgiving. All this plunged her back into her earlier anxieties; sometimes she tried to work out a way of marrying her lover immediately, while at other times she thought of running away and never seeing him again. The novels she read, which were always about chastity and honour, put up a kind of barrier between her instincts and her will. She was still the fearless creature who had wanted to wrestle with the Seine and had flung herself headlong into adultery, but now she also became aware of what kindness and gentleness meant; she began to understand the meek face and passive attitude of Olivier's wife, and realized that it is possible to be happy without killing one's husband. This prevented her from seeing herself in her true light, and she lived in a cruel state of indecision.

Laurent, for his part, went through various phases of calm and fevered agitation. At first he felt profoundly at peace with himself, as if a great weight had been lifted from his mind. Occasionally he would wonder in astonishment whether it had not all been a bad dream, and whether he really had pushed Camille into the water and seen his body on a slab at the Morgue, after all. Thinking back to his crime, he was filled with a strange sense of astonishment; he would never have believed himself capable of committing a murder. Whenever he reflected that he might have been found out and guillotined, all his caution and cowardice rushed back, making him shudder and bringing a cold sweat to his brow as he felt the icy kiss of the blade on the back of his neck. While he had been busily occupied he had gone straight ahead, with the blind tenacity of a dumb beast. Now, when he looked back at the chasm which he had just crossed, he was overcome by terror and faintness of heart.

'I must really have been drunk,' he thought; 'that woman

must have intoxicated me with her caresses. Good God, what
a crazy fool I've been! To risk the guillotine for something
like that ... It went off all right in the end, but if I had my
time again I wouldn't even consider it.'

Laurent subsided into inactivity and became more cowardly
and cautious than ever. He was getting fat and letting himself go. Looking closely at his great lump of a body, which
seemed to have neither bones nor sinews in it, nobody would
have dreamt of accusing him of violence and cruelty.

He resumed his old life-style. For several months he was
a model employee, fulfilling his allotted task with an exemplary
absence of initiative. In the evenings he would eat in a cheap
restaurant in the Rue Saint-Victor, slicing his bread thinly,
chewing it slowly, and dragging his meal out as long as possible;
then he would lean his chair back against the wall and smoke
his pipe, looking for all the world like a large and jocular
family man. During the day he thought about nothing; at night
he slept heavily, without dreaming. With his pink, fleshy face,
full stomach, and empty head, he was quite happy.

His fleshly appetite seemed to have died and he scarcely
gave a thought to Thérèse, except as one thinks of a woman
whom one will eventually marry, at some indeterminate date
in the future. He awaited the hour of his marriage with
patience, forgetting his wife-to-be but dreaming of the new
position which would then be his: he would resign from the
office, take up painting, and stroll about all day at his leisure.
These hopes brought him back to the shop in the arcade every
evening, despite the vague uneasiness which he felt whenever
he went in.

One Sunday, feeling bored and at a loose end, he called
round on a former school friend, the young painter with whom
he had shared lodgings for a long time. The artist was working
on a painting which he intended to submit to the annual
Salon,* showing a nude Bacchante stretched out on a piece
of drapery. At one end of the studio a model was lying with
her head tilted back, her upper body twisted round, and
one hip raised. Occasionally she would laugh, and stretch
her arms and thrust out her chest to relieve the stiffness. Laurent, who had sat down opposite her, watched her while he
smoked and chatted to his friend. The sight set his heart

thumping and his nerves tingling. He stayed there until the
evening, then took the woman home with him. For nearly
a year he kept her as his mistress. The poor creature found
him a handsome figure of a man and fell in love with him.
She went off each morning and posed all day long, then came
home at the same time each evening. She paid for her own
food, clothes, and upkeep with the money she earned, and
so did not cost Laurent a penny; he was not the slightest
bit concerned about where she came from or what she had
been doing. She brought an added element of balance into
his life; he accepted her as a useful, necessary object which
helped keep his body relaxed and healthy. He never knew
whether he loved her, and the idea that he was being unfaithful to Thérèse never crossed his mind. He felt fatter and
happier. That was all.

Meanwhile, Thérèse had come out of mourning. She was
now wearing light-coloured dresses, and one evening it so
happened that Laurent found her younger and prettier-look-
ing. But he still felt slightly ill at ease in her company, and
for some time now she had seemed to him over-excitable and
strangely capricious, bursting into laughter or tears for no
reason. Her vacillating moods scared him, because he could
guess something of the struggles and storms going on within
her. He began to hesitate, filled with an awful fear of com-
promising his own equanimity; he was living a peaceful life
and satisfying his appetites sensibly, and was afraid of putting
this balanced existence at risk by getting involved once more
with a nervy woman whose passionate nature had already
driven him to distraction. Not that he thought this through
rationally, but he was instinctively aware of the upheaval that
possessing Thérèse would inevitably create.

The first thing which jolted him out of his lethargy was the
thought that the time had finally come to think about his marriage, as Camille had now been dead for almost fifteen months.
For a moment he considered not getting married at all, but
jilting Thérèse and keeping the model instead, since her
compliant and inexpensive affection was all he needed. But
then he told himself that it would be absurd to have killed
a man for nothing; and, as he remembered the crime and the
terrible efforts he had made to gain sole possession of this

woman who now so disturbed him, he felt that the murder
would become pointless and abhorrent if he did not go ahead
and marry her. The idea of pushing a man into the river so
as to make off with his widow, waiting fifteen months, and
then deciding instead to live with a little tart who touted her
body around artists' studios, seemed so ridiculous it made
him smile. Anyway, was he not tied to Thérèse by a bond
of blood and terror? He could dimly feel her crying out and
writhing inside him; he belonged to her. Besides, he was also
afraid of his accomplice; if he did not marry her, perhaps she
would go and tell everything to the courts, out of jealousy
and revenge. These ideas made his head throb and caused
his fever to return.

At this juncture the model suddenly walked out on him.
One Sunday she failed to return home, doubtless having found
a warmer and more comfortable nest elsewhere. Laurent was
moderately distressed; he had got used to having a woman
lying by his side at night, and he felt a sudden gap in his
life. A week later his nerves could stand it no longer. He took
once more to installing himself for whole evenings at a time
in the shop in the arcade, and looking at Thérèse with an
occasional glint in his eye. The young woman, still quivering
from her long hours of reading, took on a languid and provoca-
tive air beneath his gaze.

And so, after a long year of waiting filled with distaste and
indifference, they both found themselves afflicted once more
by the torment of desire. One evening, as he was shutting
up the shop, Laurent held Thérèse back in the arcade.

'Would you like me to come up to your room this evening?'
he asked passionately.

She threw up her hands in horror.

'No, no, let's wait,' she said. 'We must be careful.'

'It seems to me I've already waited long enough,' said Laurent; 'I'm tired of it, I want you now.'

Thérèse gave him a wild look; her hands and face were on
fire. She seemed to hesitate, then said abruptly:

'Let's get married, then I'll be yours.'

XVII

As he left the arcade, Laurent's mind was on edge and his body tense. Thérèse's warm breath, her compliance, had brought back his desires with all their former keenness. He walked along the embankment with his hat in his hand, so he could feel the fresh breeze full on his face.

When he arrived at the door of his lodging-house in the Rue Saint-Victor he suddenly felt afraid of going upstairs and being alone. He was overcome by a childish dread, inexplicable and entirely unexpected, that there might be a man hiding in his attic room. He had never before been subject to such ridiculous imaginings. He did not even try to reason away the strange shudder which came over him; he went into a bar and stayed there for an hour until midnight, sitting motionless and silent at a table and mechanically downing large glasses of wine. His thoughts turned to Thérèse, and he grew angry with her for not letting him into her room that same evening, for he was sure he would not have been afraid in her company.

Closing time came round and he was thrown out. He went back in to ask for some matches. The lodging-house concierge lived on the first floor, so Laurent had to go down a long alleyway and up a number of stairs before he could pick up his candle. The awful darkness in the alley and on the stairs filled him with dread. Normally, he would have crossed this dark area quite light-heartedly. That evening he did not dare ring the bell, telling himself that behind a certain projection by the cellar entrance there might be murderers lurking who would leap at his throat as he went by. In the end, though, he did ring, then lit a match, and made up his mind to venture into the passage. The match went out. He stood stock still, panting, not daring to run away, scraping matches against the damp wall with such panic that his hand shook. He thought he heard voices and footsteps ahead of him. The matches kept snapping in his fingers. He managed to light one. The sulphur started sizzling, setting light to the wood so slowly that it further increased Laurent's alarm; in the flickering shadows cast by the sulphur's pale, bluish glow he thought he could make out monstrous shapes. Then the match caught, and the light became white and much brighter. Greatly relieved, he went cautiously forward, taking care that the match did not go out. When he had to pass by the cellar, he squeezed up against the opposite wall, for there was a pool of shadow there that scared him. Then he scurried up the few stairs which lay between him and the concierge's office, and only when he finally had the candle in his hand did he feel safe. He took his time climbing the rest of the stairs, holding the candle aloft and lighting up all the corners by which he had to pass. The huge, weirdly-shaped shadows, like those which always flit to and fro around anybody carrying a lamp up a staircase, filled him with vague apprehension as they loomed up in front of him, then vanished.

When he arrived at the top of the building, he opened his door and quickly locked himself in. The first thing he did was to look under the bed and give the room a minute inspection, to make sure there was no one hiding in it. He shut the skylight in case anyone should come in that way. Once he had taken these precautions he started to relax, and, as he undressed, he began to be astonished at his own cowardice. Eventually he smiled and told himself he was being childish. He had never been the timorous type and he could not understand this sudden attack of panic.

He went to bed. Once he had got warm between the sheets, his thoughts turned again to Thérèse, whom his fright had made him forget. With his eyes obstinately closed he tried to go to sleep, but his mind began working despite himself, and thoughts took shape and linked themselves together, all showing him how advantageous it would be to him to get married as soon as possible. Now and again he would turn over and say to himself: 'Let's not think about it any more, and go to sleep; I have to get up at eight tomorrow to go to work,' before making another effort to drift off into sleep. But the ideas came back one by one, the hidden reasoning processes started up again, and he soon found himself back in a state of agitated musing which filled his brain with the necessity of getting married, and with all the arguments which his lust and his caution by turns could advance for and against his possessing Thérèse.

Then, when he realized that he could not sleep and that insomnia was keeping his body in an excited state, he turned on to his back, opened his eyes wide, and allowed the memory of her to come flooding into his mind. All equanimity was now lost and he was once more in the grip of the feverish imaginings of days gone by. It occurred to him to get up and go back to the Passage du Pont-Neuf. He would get them to open the gate, go and knock at the side door at the bottom of the stairs, and Thérèse would let him in. At this thought, he felt the blood rush to his neck.

His daydream was astonishingly real. He saw himself walking quickly along various streets, past all the houses, and thought to himself: 'I'll go down this boulevard and across that crossroads, to get there quicker.' Then the gate of the arcade squeaked open and he was walking down the narrow gallery, which was dark and deserted, congratulating himself on being able to go up to Thérèse's room without being seen by the woman who sold costume jewellery. Then he imagined himself in the side passage, going up the narrow stairs as he had done so often in the past. There he felt the same fierce thrill as before, as he remembered all the delicious terrors and the bitter-sweet sensuality of adultery. His memories became realities that impinged directly on all his senses: he could smell the musty reek of the corridor, touch the damp walls, and see the murky gloom which hung everywhere. And he climbed each step, panting and listening intently, beginning already to indulge his lustful fantasies as he timorously approached the woman he desired. Finally, he scratched gently at the door, it opened, and Thérèse was standing there waiting for him, all white in her petticoats.

His imaginings unfolded before him like real events, and as he stared into the darkness he could see everything. When, after racing though the streets, going into the arcade, and climbing the back stairs, he believed he really did see Thérèse, pale and burning with passion, he leaped straight out of bed, muttering: 'I must go, she's waiting for me.' His sudden movement drove away the hallucination; he felt the cold of the floor-tiles and was afraid. He stood still for a while, barefoot, listening. He thought he heard a noise on the landing outside. If he went round to see Thérèse, he would have to go back down past the cellar door; the idea sent a great shiver down his spine. He was overcome once more by dread, an unthinking, overwhelming terror. He looked suspiciously around his room at all the whitish streaks of light, then, quietly but with anxious and hasty precautions, climbed back into bed, where he pulled the covers up over himself and hid from view, as if taking refuge from a knife or some other threatening weapon.

The blood had rushed violently to his neck, which was now burning, and when he touched it he could feel beneath his fingers the scar left by Camille's bite. He had almost forgotten about it; now, when he rediscovered it there on his skin, he was terrified by the feeling that it was eating into his flesh. He had drawn his hand away quickly to avoid touching it, but he could still feel it devouring him, burning a hole in his neck. So he tried to scratch it gently with the tip of a nail; the terrible burning sensation was redoubled. To prevent himself from clawing at his own skin he squeezed both hands tightly between his drawn-up knees. And there he lay, rigid, his nerves on edge, with this gnawing in his neck and his teeth chattering in fear.

Now his thoughts became terrifyingly fixed on Camille. Until then, Laurent's nights had not been disturbed by the drowned man. Now, the thought of Thérèse had ushered in the ghost of her husband. The murderer no longer dared open his eyes for fear of catching sight of his victim in some corner of the bedroom. At one point his bed felt strangely as if it were shaking, and he imagined that Camille was hiding underneath, jerking it up and down and trying to shake him out in order to bite him. Wild-eyed and with his hair standing on end, he clung to his mattress as the shaking grew more and more violent.

Then he realized that the bed was not shaking at all. Relief flooded over him. He sat up, lit his candle, and called himself a fool. To calm his feverish panic he swallowed a large glass of water.

'I shouldn't have stopped off in that bar for a drink,' he thought to himself. 'I don't know what's the matter with me tonight. It's stupid, I'll be flaked out tomorrow at work.

I should have got into bed and gone straight to sleep, instead of turning all sorts of things over in my head; that's what kept me awake ... Anyway, I'll go to sleep now.'

He blew the light out once more and buried his head in the pillow, feeling a little better and determined not to think about anything else, and to stop being afraid. His nerves were beginning to unwind with fatigue.

He did not sleep his usual deep, heavy sleep, but slipped slowly into a vague drowsiness as if he were merely numbed, drifting into a gentle, delectable insensibility. As he dozed he could still feel his body, and his mind remained awake in his deadened flesh. He had chased away the thoughts that had come into his head, and struggled against wakefulness, but when he dropped off and his strength and will-power deserted him, the thoughts slipped back one by one and took possession again of his drifting mind. Then the dreams began afresh. He retraced the path that separated him from Thérèse; he ran down the stairs, past the cellar and out into the open, then along all the same streets as before when he had been dreaming with his eyes open, into the Passage du Pont-Neuf and up the back stairs, until he scratched at the door. But instead of Thérèse, instead of the young woman in her underwear, with her breasts uncovered, it was Camille who opened the door, Camille as he had seen him at the Morgue, greenish and horribly disfigured. The corpse opened its arms to him with a horrible laugh, poking the tip of its blackened tongue out between white teeth.

Laurent screamed and woke up with a start, covered in a cold sweat. He pulled the bedclothes up over his eyes, swearing angrily at himself, and tried to go back to sleep.

He dropped off again as slowly as before. The same heaviness overcame him, and, as soon as his will-power had slipped away in his torpid, semi-conscious state, he started running back to where his obsession led him, to Thérèse, and once again it was the drowned man who opened the door.

Terrified and miserable, Laurent sat up again in bed. He would have given anything in the world to drive away this implacable dream, and wished he could fall into a leaden slumber that would obliterate all his thoughts. While he was awake he had sufficient energy to ward off his victim's ghost, but, as soon as he lost control over his mind, it took him off down a path of erotic imaginings which led to sheer terror.

He made another attempt to sleep, falling into a succession of delicious dozes followed by sudden and painful awakenings. In his furious stubbornness he was constantly rushing towards Thérèse, only to come up against the corpse of Camille. More than ten times he made the same journey, setting off with his flesh on fire, following the same route with minute exactness, feeling the same sensations and performing the same actions, and more than ten times he saw the drowned man offer himself to his embrace when he opened his arms to clasp his mistress to him. This same sinister outcome which woke him up every time, panting and desperate, did not discourage his desire; a few minutes later, as soon as he had fallen asleep again, his lust would forget the repulsive corpse which awaited it and set off once more in search of a woman's warm, lithe body. For an hour Laurent experienced this sequence of nightmares, constantly repeated but always unexpected, which jolted him awake with more acute horror each time.

One such jolt, the last, was so violent and painful that he decided to get up and abandon the struggle. Dawn was approaching and a dismal grey light was coming in through the skylight, which now marked out a whitish, ashen-coloured square of sky.

Laurent dressed slowly and with sullen irritation. He was exasperated at not having slept and at having allowed himself to fall prey to a terror which he now told himself was mere childish stupidity. As he was climbing into his trousers he stretched, rubbed his limbs, and ran his hands over a face which was drawn and puffy from the feverish night he had spent. And he kept telling himself:

'I really shouldn't have been thinking about all those things; I could have gone to sleep and been fresh and wide awake now ... Oh! If only Thérèse had been willing, last night, if only she had slept with me ... '

This idea that Thérèse would have prevented him from being afraid calmed him a little, but what he dreaded most was having to endure other nights like the one he had just been through.

He splashed his face with water and gave his hair a comb. This summary toilet cleared his head and saw off the last of his fears. He began to think cogently, though he still felt a great weariness in his limbs.

'But I'm no coward', he told himself as he finished dressing, 'and I couldn't give a damn about Camille ... It's ridiculous to believe the poor wretch is under my bed; I might start thinking that every night. I really must hurry up and get married. With Thérèse holding me in her arms I shan't have any further thoughts of Camille. She'll kiss my neck and I won't feel the dreadful burning any more. Now, let's just have a look at that bite.'

He went over to his mirror, stuck out his chin, and scrutinized his neck. The scar was light pink. As he made out his victim's tooth-marks, Laurent felt a twinge of anxiety, the blood rushed to his head, and he noticed something strange happening. The rising blood turned the scar a vivid crimson colour, making it stand out starkly against his fleshy white neck. At the same time he felt a sharp pricking sensation, as if needles were being stuck into the wound. He quickly pulled his shirt collar back up.

'Never mind!' he thought to himself, 'Thérèse will make it better. A few kisses will do the trick. What a fool I am to think about things like that!'

He put on his hat and went downstairs. He needed fresh air, and a good walk. As he passed in front of the cellar door he smiled, although he did check that the hook which secured it was firmly in place. Once he was outside he walked slowly along the deserted pavements in the cool morning air. It was about five o'clock.

Laurent had a terrible day. He had to struggle against an overwhelming urge to sleep which came over him at the office during the afternoon. His heavy, throbbing head would begin to nod despite himself, and he would jerk upright again whenever he heard the approaching footsteps of one of his superiors. This struggle, and the repeated disturbance, left his limbs more tired than ever, and filled him with intolerable stress.

That evening, despite his tiredness, he was determined to go and see Thérèse. He found her in a feverish, downcast state, and worn out like himself.

'Poor Thérèse has had a bad night,' Madame Raquin told him after he had sat down. 'She seems to have had nightmares,

and terrible trouble getting back to sleep. I heard her cry out
several times. This morning she was not at all well.'

While her aunt was speaking, Thérèse stared hard at Laurent. They probably each guessed what terrors the other had
been through, for the same nervous tremor ran over both their
faces. They remained sitting opposite each other until ten
o'clock, making banal conversation but reading each other's
thoughts and imploring each other with their eyes to hasten
the moment when they could unite against the drowned man.

XVIII

THÉRÈSE too had been visited by the ghost of Camille during that feverish night.

Laurent's burning plea for a meeting, after more than a year of indifference, had suddenly whipped up her feelings afresh. As she lay alone in bed, her body had begun to tingle at the thought that their marriage would soon take place. Then, as she tossed in insomnia, she had seen the drowned man standing before her; like Laurent, she had been racked by a mixture of terror and desire and, like him, had told herself that she would not be afraid any more, or feel such pain, when she could hold her lover in her arms once again.

At exactly the same time, this woman and this man had both experienced a sort of nervous crisis which threw them back, gasping and terrified, into their monstrous love-affair. A relationship of blood and lust had grown up between them. They both shuddered the same shudders; their hearts, linked by an agonizing fraternity, trembled at the same terrors. They now had but one body and one soul with which to feel pleasure and pain. This common bond, this mutual inter-linking, is a psychological and physiological fact which can often be observed in people thrown violently together by severe nervous shocks.

For more than a year Thérèse and Laurent had borne lightly the chain that bound their limbs to each other with equanimity. In the period of numbness that had come after the acute crisis of the murder, in the feelings of repugnance and the need for peace and forgetfulness which had then followed, these two prisoners had been able to imagine themselves free, no longer linked together by an iron bond. The chain had hung slack on the ground while they rested, and they had fallen into a contented stupor and looked around for love elsewhere, trying to lead a sensible and balanced existence. But the day came when, driven by events, they began once more to exchange words of passion, and the chain snapped taut again, giving them such a jolt that they realized they were now attached to each other for ever.

The very next day Thérèse quietly set to work to bring about her marriage to Laurent. It was a difficult and perilous undertaking. The lovers were terrified of doing anything imprudent and arousing suspicion, of revealing too suddenly why Camille's death had been in their interests. Realizing that they could not mention marriage to anyone, they decided on a most prudent plan which would bring Madame Raquin herself and her Thursday guests to offer them what they did not dare to ask for themselves. All they had to do now was plant the idea of Thérèse getting remarried in the minds of these good people, while making them believe that it had occurred to them first, and was in fact their idea.

It would be a long and delicate piece of play-acting. Thérèse and Laurent had each taken the part that suited them best, and now they moved forward with the utmost care, carefully calculating their slightest gesture or word. In reality they were devoured by an impatience which made them tense and set their nerves on edge. They were living in a state of nervous irritation, and it was only their cowardly fear of the consequences that forced them to appear smiling and calm.

If they were in a hurry to get marriage over with, it was because they could no longer stand being apart and on their own. Every night they were visited by the drowned man, and insomnia laid them on a bed of burning coals, turning them over with red-hot irons. The state of nervous irritation in which they were living still kindled new desires in them each evening, setting atrocious hallucinations before their eyes. Once darkness had fallen, Thérèse no longer dared to go up to her bedroom; she was filled with a dreadful panic whenever she had to stay shut up until morning in that great room, which peopled itself with ghosts and strange gleams of light as soon as she put her candle out. She ended up leaving it lit and preferring not to sleep at all, so that she could keep her eyes wide open. And whenever her eyelids did close with tiredness, she always saw Camille there in the dark and opened them again with a jerk. She would drag herself about the next morning, totally shattered, having slept for only a few hours in the light. As for Laurent, he had become decidedly cowardly

since the night when he had first been afraid of going past
the cellar door. Before then he had lived with a kind of brutish
self-assurance; now, the slightest noise made him quiver and
turn pale, like a little boy. The shudder of terror that had
gone through his limbs then had remained with him. At night
he was in an even worse state than Thérèse, for fear shook
that great soft, cowardly body of his to the core. He would
watch the daylight fade with painful apprehension. Several
times he decided not to go home at all, and spent the whole
night walking round the deserted streets. Once he crouched
under a bridge until morning, frozen to death in the pouring
rain, not daring to get to his feet and walk back up the embankment, and watched the dirty waters flowing past in the grey
shadows for almost six hours; at times, panic made him fling
himself flat on the wet ground, as he imagined he could see
long lines of drowned bodies drifting down on the current,
under the arch. Whenever weariness did drive him back to
his lodgings, he would double-lock his door from the inside
and lie there until dawn, struggling against terrible bouts of
fever. The same nightmare kept recurring time and again,
as he imagined he was falling out of the ardent, passionate
arms of Thérèse into the chill, clammy arms of Camille; one
minute he dreamed that he was being smothered in Thérèse's
hot embrace, and the next that he was being clasped to the
drowned man's decomposing chest in a glacial hug. This sudden alternation of feelings of lust and loathing, this contact
first with a body hot with love, then with cold, slime-softened
flesh, left him shivering, gasping for breath, choking in
terror.

Every day the lovers' panic grew worse, and every day their
nightmares made them more demented and distraught. Their
only hope against insomnia was the kisses that they exchanged,
but out of prudence they did not dare arrange assignations.
So they looked upon their wedding day as their day of salvation,
to be followed by a night of bliss.

Thus they anticipated their union with all the desire they
felt to sleep peacefully again. During their period of indifference they had hesitated, forgetting the selfish and passionate
reasons which had driven them both to commit murder but
had then evaporated once the deed was done. Now that they

were once again burning with lust, they rediscovered in the
depths of their egotistical passion the reasons which had first
made them kill Camille—to enjoy afterwards, as they thought,
the pleasures which a legitimate marriage would bring. And
yet it was with a vague sense of despair that they took the
supreme decision to unite openly. Deep down they were afraid,
and their very desire trembled with apprehension. They had,
as it were, looked deep into each other's natures, as into a
chasm whose horror drew them ever closer to its edge; each
peered down into the other's being, clinging on in silence while
an intense, delicious sensation of vertigo turned their limbs
to water and gave them a crazy urge to plunge into the whirling
void. But, faced with present reality, in which waiting was
filled with anxiety and desire laden with fear, they felt an urgent
need to shut their eyes and dream of a future of amorous
bliss and tranquil fulfilment. The more they trembled at the
sight of each other, the more clearly they saw the abyss into
which they were about to fling themselves, and the more they
tried to make themselves happy promises and list the inescapable reasons which were moving them inevitably towards
marriage.

Thérèse wanted to marry solely because she was afraid, and
her body cried out for the violent caresses of Laurent. She was
in the throes of a nervous crisis which had virtually driven her
mad. The truth was, she scarcely reasoned at all, but threw
herself into her passion with a mind warped by the novels she
had read and a body inflamed by the cruel insomnia that had
kept her awake for several weeks.

Although Laurent, more stolid in temperament, had also
given in to his terror and his desires, he still intended to make
his decision a reasoned one. In order to prove to himself that
his marriage was a necessity and that he was finally going to
be completely happy, and to dispel the vague fears that as-
sailed him, he now went back over all his earlier calculations.
As his father, the peasant from Jeufosse, was stubbornly refusing to die, he told himself that his inheritance could still be
a long time in coming, and even began to fear that it might
escape him entirely and disappear into the pockets of one of
his cousins, a strapping lad who still tilled the soil, much to the
approval of Laurent's father. Then he would stay poor for ever,

living in a garret with no wife, sleeping badly, and eating
still worse. Nor did he plan on working for the rest of his
days; he was beginning to get dreadfully weary of his office,
and even the light work that had been entrusted to him was
becoming too much for his lazy nature. The outcome of his
reflections was always that perfect happiness consisted in doing
nothing. Then he remembered that he had drowned Camille
in order to marry Thérèse and be able to do nothing thereafter.
No doubt the desire to possess his mistress all for himself had
played a large part in his thoughts of crime, but he had perhaps
been led to commit the murder even more by the hope of taking Camille's place, of being looked after like him and enjoying a state of permanent bliss. If he had been driven by passion
alone he would not have acted with such cowardly prudence.
The truth was that he had sought by murder to ensure for
himself a calm life of idleness, and the lasting satisfaction of
his appetites. All these thoughts, whether explicit or unconscious, now came back to him. To keep up his spirits he
kept telling himself that the time had come to profit from
Camille's death in the way he had expected. And he listed
for himself all the advantages and delights of his future existence: he would leave his job and live in delicious idleness;
he would eat, drink, and sleep his fill; he would always have
a passionate woman on hand to restore the balance of his blood
and his nerves; he would soon inherit forty-odd thousand
francs from Madame Raquin, for the poor old girl was now
declining by the day; in short, he would make a life of animal
satisfactions for himself and forget everything else. Laurent
had gone over all this many times since the two of them had
decided on marriage; he kept searching his mind for still more
advantages and was over the moon whenever he thought he
had found, in the depths of his selfishness, a new argument
for marrying the drowned man's widow. But however hard
he pushed himself to hope, however much he dreamed of a
fat future of idleness and pleasure, sudden shivers still chilled
his skin and he still had, at times, a feeling of dread that stifled
the joy in his throat.

XIX

MEANWHILE, the secret efforts of Thérèse and Laurent were beginning to bear fruit. Thérèse had put on a glum, despairing expression which began to worry Madame Raquin after several days. The old haberdasher demanded to know what was making her niece so sad. So the young woman played her part as inconsolable widow with consummate expertise, talking in vague terms of lassitude, depression, and nervous pains, without going into details. When her aunt pressed her with questions, she replied that she was quite well and had no idea why she was feeling so downcast, and did not know what was making her cry. She sighed tearfully the whole time, with wan, sorrowful smiles that gave way to silences heavy with emptiness and despair. Seeing this young woman turned in on herself and apparently wasting away with some unknown ailment finally made Madame Raquin seriously alarmed. She had no one left in the world but her niece, and every evening she prayed God to safeguard her child so that there would be someone to close her eyes when she died. This last love of her old age was therefore mixed with a little selfishness. Once it occurred to her that she might lose Thérèse and have to die all alone in that dank shop in the arcade, she felt that all the slight consolations which had helped her to go on living were suddenly under threat. From then on she never took her eyes off her niece, anxiously studying her airs of sadness and wondering what on earth she could do to cure her of this silent despair.

In circumstances of such gravity she thought she should ask the advice of her old friend Michaud. One Thursday evening she kept him back in the shop and told him her fears.

'It's obvious,' the old fellow replied with the brutal frankness of his former profession; 'I've noticed for some time now that Thérèse has been moping and looking miserable, with that sallow complexion of hers, and I know exactly why.'

'You do?' said Madame Raquin. 'Quick, tell me. If we can only cure her!'

'Oh, the remedy's easy enough,' Michaud continued with a laugh. 'Your niece is fed up because she has been alone at night in her room for close on two years now. She needs a husband, you can see it in her eyes.'

The former superintendent's harsh directness was hurtful to Madame Raquin. She had thought that the deep wound in her which had not ceased bleeding since the dreadful accident at Saint-Ouen must be just as raw, just as cruel, in the heart of the young widow. With her son dead, she felt that there could never be another husband for her niece. Now here was Michaud claiming, with his vulgar laugh, that Thérèse was sickening for a husband.

'Marry her off as soon as you can,' he said as he departed, 'if you don't want her to wither away altogether. That's my view, dear lady, and it's the right one, believe you me.'

At first, Madame Raquin could not get used to the idea that her son had already been forgotten. Old Michaud had not even spoken Camille's name, and he had joked about Thérèse's so-called illness. The unfortunate mother realized that she alone was keeping alive, in the depths of her being, the memory of her dear child. She burst into tears, and it seemed to her that Camille had just died a second time. Then, when she had had a good cry and tired herself out with grief, she began despite herself to think about what Michaud had said, and grew used to the idea of buying a little happiness at the cost of a marriage which, by going against the scruples of her memory, would amount to killing her son all over again. Cowardly impulses overcame her whenever she found herself alone in front of Thérèse, gloomy and downcast, in the glacial silence of the shop. She was not one of those rigid, emotionless individuals who take a perverse pleasure in living in perpetual despair; with the effusive temperament of a nice, affable old lady, she had enough flexibility of mind and commitment to others to want to live a life of active kindness. Since her niece had stopped speaking and was just standing around looking pale and feeble, her existence had become intolerable and the shop had begun to seem like a tomb; she would have liked to be surrounded by life and warmth, caresses and affection, and a gentle, happy atmosphere which would help her to await the coming of death in peace. These unconscious wishes led

her to accept the idea of Thérèse getting married again; she
even forgot her son a little, and a kind of reawakening came
about in the deathly existence she had been leading, with a
new will to do things and fresh occupations for her mind.
Her head now became filled with the need to find a husband
for her niece. The poor old woman took this search very seriously indeed, for she was thinking even more of herself than
of Thérèse; she intended to marry her off in such a way that
she herself would be happy, for she very much feared that
the young woman's new husband might come along and upset
the last days of her old age. The thought of bringing a stranger
into her everyday existence terrified her, and this was the only
thing that held her back from speaking openly to her niece
on the subject.

    While Thérèse was acting out her comedy of listlessness
and depression with the perfect hypocrisy that her upbringing
had given her, Laurent took the part of the sensitive and oblig-
ing man about the house. He was full of little kindnesses for
the two women, especially Madame Raquin, on whom he
showered delicate attentions. Gradually he made himself indis-
pensable in the shop, and he was the only one to bring a bit
of cheerfulness into that dark hole. Whenever he was not there,
in the evenings, the old haberdasher would cast about uneasily
as if there were something missing, almost afraid of having
to face Thérèse and her miseries on her own. In fact, Laurent
only ever stayed away for an evening in order to reinforce
his position of power; normally, he would come round to
the shop from the office every day, and stay until the arcade
was locked up for the night. He would run errands and bring
Madame Raquin various little things that she needed, for she
could only walk with difficulty. Then he would sit down and
make conversation. He had discovered a stage voice, quiet
but penetrating, which he used to charm the ears and heart
of the dear old lady. Above all, he seemed most solicitous
about Thérèse's state of health, as a friend and a sensitive
soul distressed by the pain of others. Several times he took
Madame Raquin to one side and terrified her by appearing
frightened himself of the alterations and ravages which he said
he could see in the young woman's face.

    'We shall lose her before long,' he murmured in a tearful

voice. 'It's no good pretending to ourselves that she isn't seriously ill. Alas for our poor bit of happiness, and our lovely quiet evenings!'

Madame Raquin listened anxiously to what he was saying. Laurent even carried his audacity so far as to talk about Camille.

'You see,' he went on, 'my poor friend's death was a terrible blow to her. She has been wasting away for the last two years, since the tragic day when she lost Camille. Nothing can console her, nothing can cure her now. We must just resign ourselves.'

These impudent lies made the old lady shed hot tears. Her son's memory upset her and blinded her to what was going on. Whenever someone spoke the name of Camille she would burst out sobbing, and so abandon herself to her grief that she could have hugged the person who had used her poor child's name. Laurent had noticed the unsettling effect that this name had on her, and so he was able to make her cry at will and overwhelm her with feelings that stopped her seeing things clearly; he exploited this power in order to keep her grief-stricken and compliant in his hands. Each evening, however much it sickened him, he brought the conversation round to the rare qualities of Camille, his tender heart and fine mind, and sang his victim's praises with complete cynicism. From time to time, when his eyes caught those of Thérèse staring at him in an odd way, he shuddered, realizing that he was beginning to believe all the good things he was saying about the drowned man; then he would stop talking, suddenly overcome with intense jealousy and dread that the young widow might actually love the man he had thrown into the water, and was now praising with such hallucinatory conviction. Throughout the whole conversation Madame Raquin would be in floods of tears, completely oblivious to her surroundings. While she cried, she thought what a loving, generous soul Laurent was, for he alone remembered her son, and he alone still spoke about him in a voice trembling with emotion. As she dried her eyes, she would look at the young man with unstinting affection, loving him like her own son.

One Thursday evening Michaud and Grivet were already in the dining-room when Laurent entered, went over to Thérèse, and asked her, with gentle concern, about her health.

He sat down for a while at her side, acting his part as the affectionate and worried friend for the benefit of those present. As the two young people were sitting together and exchanging a few words, Michaud, who was watching them, leaned over and whispered to the old haberdasher, pointing at Laurent:

'Look, that's the husband your niece needs. Fix the marriage up as quick as you can. We'll help, if needs be.'

Michaud's face wore a knowing smile, for he considered that what Thérèse needed was a powerful man for a husband. Madame Raquin was struck as it were by a sudden illumination, seeing in a flash everything that she herself stood to gain from the marriage of Thérèse and Laurent. It would only serve to strengthen the ties which already linked herself and her niece to that kind-hearted fellow who always came round to cheer them up of an evening. It would also avoid introducing a stranger into her house, so that there would be no risk of upsetting her—quite the opposite, in fact, for, at the same time as providing Thérèse with support, it would bring an additional joy to her old age, as this young man who had treated her with filial affection for the last three years would now be a second son to her. Then she began to think that marrying Laurent would make Thérèse less unfaithful to the memory of Camille. Such are the strange niceties of judgement to which religions of the heart are prone. Madame Raquin, who would have wept to see a stranger kissing the young widow, felt no inner repugnance at the thought of handing her over to the embraces of her son's former best friend. She felt, as the saying goes, that it would be keeping things in the family.

All that evening, while the guests played dominoes, the old haberdasher cast such tender glances at the young couple that he and she both guessed their play-acting had worked and was about to reach its intended conclusion. Before leaving, Michaud had a short talk in undertones with Madame Raquin; then he ostentatiously took Laurent by the arm and declared that he would accompany him a little way home. As he went out, Laurent exchanged a rapid glance with Thérèse, a glance heavy with meaning.

Michaud had taken it upon himself to sound Laurent out. He found him most devoted to the two ladies and extremely surprised at any notion of a marriage between Thérèse and himself. Laurent added in an emotional voice that he loved his poor friend's widow like a sister, and would feel he was committing an act of real sacrilege if he were to marry her. The former police superintendent pressed his case, putting forward a hundred good reasons why Laurent should give his consent, appealing to his dedication and even going so far as to say that his duty required him to give Madame Raquin another son, and Thérèse another husband. Gradually, Laurent allowed himself to be talked round; he pretended to be giving in to his emotions and accepting the idea of marriage as a sudden inspiration from above, dictated by thoughts of duty and devotion, as old Michaud had put it. When Michaud had obtained a definite acceptance, he parted from his companion, rubbing his hands at the thought that he had just achieved a great victory, and congratulating himself for having been the first to think of a marriage which would put all the zest back into their Thursday evening gatherings.

While Michaud strolled along the embankment chatting with Laurent, Madame Raquin was having an almost identical conversation with Thérèse. When her niece, as pale and frail-looking as ever, was about to retire for the night, the old lady kept her back for a while. She questioned her in affectionate tones, begging her to answer honestly and tell her why it was that she was so very depressed. Then, having received only vague answers, she started talking about the emptiness of a widow's life, gradually working her way round to mentioning the possibility of a new marriage, until in the end she asked Thérèse straight out whether she did not secretly want to marry again. Thérèse threw up her arms in horror, saying that nothing was further from her mind, and that she would always stay faithful to Camille. Madame Raquin burst into tears. Pleading against the instincts of her own heart, she tried to convince Thérèse that despair could not go on for ever, and finally, when the young woman exclaimed that she could never, ever replace Camille, she responded by suddenly pronouncing Laurent's name. Then she burst into a torrent of arguments about the suitability and the advantages of such a union, repeating aloud all the things that had been on her mind during the evening and painting, with unthinking selfishness, a picture

of the happiness of her final years, with her two dear children
by her side. Thérèse listened with head bowed, resigned,
docile, and more than ready to satisfy her wishes.

'I love Laurent like a brother,' she said in anguished tones
when her aunt had fallen silent. 'Since it is your wish, I shall
try to love him like a husband. I want to make you happy
. . . I had been hoping you would leave me to cry in peace,
but I'll dry my eyes for the sake of your happiness.'

She kissed the old lady, who was overcome with astonishment at having been the first to forget her son. As she got
ready for bed, Madame Raquin sobbed bitterly, reproaching
herself for being less strong than Thérèse and wanting for
purely selfish reasons a marriage which the young widow was
accepting out of pure abnegation.

The next morning Michaud and his old friend had a brief
conversation in the arcade, outside the shop door. They
informed each other of the success of their schemes and agreed
to push straight ahead with their plan and force the young
pair into an engagement the same evening.

When Laurent came into the shop that evening at five,
Michaud was already there. As soon as the young man had
sat down, the former superintendent whispered in his ear:

'She accepts!'

This blunt announcement was heard by Thérèse, who remained pale but kept her gaze imprudently fixed on Laurent
The two lovers looked hard at each other for a few seconds,
as if to ask each other's advice. They both realized at once
that they had to accept the situation without hesitating, and
finish the whole thing once and for all. Standing up, Laurent
went over and took the hand of Madame Raquin, who was
struggling to hold back her tears.

'Dearest mother,' he said, 'Monsieur Michaud and I discussed your future happiness, yesterday evening. Your children
wish to make you happy.'

Hearing herself called 'Dearest mother', the poor old lady
could not stop her tears from flowing; she seized Thérèse's
hand and placed it in Laurent's, quite unable to speak.

The two lovers felt a shiver go through them as their skin
touched. They kept their fingers tightly intertwined in a burning, nervous embrace. Laurent went on hesitantly:

'Thérèse, do you wish us to make your aunt's existence a happy and peaceful one?'

'Yes,' she replied in a weak voice, 'we must fulfil our duty.'

Then, very pale, he turned to Madame Raquin and added:

'When Camille fell into the water, he screamed to me: "Save my wife, I place her in your care." I believe that by marrying Thérèse I shall be carrying out his last wish.'

On hearing these words, Thérèse let go of Laurent's hand. It was as if she had received a blow to the heart. She was stunned by her lover's effrontery, and stared dazedly at him while Madame Raquin managed to stammer through her tears:

'Yes, yes, my friend, do marry her and make her happy; my son will thank you from the depths of his grave.'

Laurent felt himself wilting, and went to lean against the back of a chair. Michaud, who was also moved to tears, pushed him towards Thérèse with the words:

'Kiss each other, to mark your engagement.'

As his lips touched the widow's cheeks, the young man was filled with a strange uneasiness, and she recoiled as though her lover's two kisses had burned her. It was the first time that he had ever behaved affectionately towards her in front of other people; all the blood rushed to her face and she felt herself go burning red, she who knew nothing of modesty and had never once blushed for shame in all her illicit love-making.

After this moment of crisis, the two murderers could breathe easily again. Their marriage was decided upon, and at last the goal that they had been pursuing for so long was in sight. The details were settled that same evening. On the following Thursday the forthcoming marriage was announced to Grivet, Olivier, and his wife. As he broke the news, a delighted Michaud kept rubbing his hands together and saying:

'It was all my idea, I persuaded them to marry ... Just you see what a fine couple they'll make!'

Suzanne came up to Thérèse and embraced her in silence. This poor, deathly-pale creature had taken a liking to the cold, reserved young widow, and loved her as a child would, with a sort of respectful awe. Olivier congratulated the aunt and her niece, while Grivet came out with a few *risqué* jokes which were not too well received. In general, the company was thrilled and delighted, and everyone declared that all was for the best;

in fact, they were already imagining themselves at the wedding.

Thérèse and Laurent maintained a prudent and dignified attitude. They acted towards each other with friendly consideration and affection, nothing more, and gave the appearance of performing an act of supreme devotion to duty. Their expressions gave away nothing of the fears and desires with which they were racked. Madame Raquin looked on at them with wan smiles, full of meek gratitude and benevolence.

There were a few formalities to be completed. Laurent had to write to his father to ask his consent. The old peasant from Jeufosse, who had almost forgotten that he had ever had a son in Paris, sent a four-line reply saying that he could marry and be hanged if he wished, and making it clear that, although he was determined Laurent would never get a penny from him, he was leaving him free to do what he wanted with his person and make whatever idiotic mistakes he thought fit. Laurent was very worried by the tone of this permission.

Madame Raquin, after reading this unnatural father's letter, had a kindly impulse which led her into a foolish mistake. She made over to her niece her capital of more than forty thousand francs, thereby giving everything away to the young couple and leaving herself with nothing; she was entrusting herself to their generosity, for she wanted her whole happiness to depend on them alone. Laurent was to contribute nothing to their joint finances, and even let it be understood that he would not continue in his job for ever, but might go back to painting. However, the future of the little family seemed assured; the income from the forty thousand francs or so, added to the profits from the haberdashery business, should easily provide for three people. There would be just enough for them to be happy.

The wedding preparations were speeded up and the formalities cut to a minimum. It was as if everyone were in a hurry to push Laurent into Thérèse's bedroom. And so the longed-for day finally arrived.

XX

THAT morning Laurent and Thérèse both awoke, in their separate rooms, with the same deeply joyful thought, that their
last night of terror was over. No more sleeping on their own;
from now on, they could defend each other against the
drowned man.

Thérèse looked around her and smiled at the size of her
double bed. Then she got up and dressed slowly, waiting for
Suzanne to come and help her with her wedding dress.

Laurent sat up in bed and stayed there for a few minutes,
taking his leave of the attic which he found so abhorrent. He
was going to get out of this kennel at long last, and have a wife
of his own. It was December and he started shivering, but as
he leapt out on to the tiled floor, he told himself that he would
be warm enough that evening.

The previous week Madame Raquin, knowing how hard
up he was, had slipped into his hand a purse containing five
hundred francs, her whole savings. He had felt no scruples
about accepting it and had bought himself a complete new
outfit. On top of this, the old haberdasher's money had allowed
him to give Thérèse all the customary presents.

His black trousers and tail-coat, as well as his white waistcoat, shirt, and silk tie, were laid out on two chairs. Laurent
washed using plenty of soap, and sprayed himself with Eau
de Cologne, then started to dress with minute care. He wanted
to look handsome. As he was attaching his collar, which was
tall and stiff, he felt a most painful sensation in his neck; his
fingers fumbled with the collar stud and he began to grow
impatient, as the starched linen felt as if it were cutting into
his flesh. Looking to see what was wrong, he raised his chin
and saw Camille's bite standing out bright red; the collar had
slightly grazed the scar. Laurent pursed his lips and went quite
pale; the sight of that blotch discolouring his neck scared him
and filled him with anger. He crumpled up the collar and
picked out another one, which he put on with all possible

precautions. When he had gone downstairs, his new clothes made him walk stiffly and he did not dare turn his head; his neck felt imprisoned by the stiffened cloth, and, with every movement that he made, a fold pinched the deep wound left by the drowned man's teeth. He could still feel a painfully sharp pricking sensation as he climbed into a cab and went to collect Thérèse, to take her off to the town hall, and then the church.

On the way, he picked up an Orleans Railway employee and old Michaud, who were to act as his witnesses. When they arrived at the shop, everyone was ready; Grivet and Olivier, Thérèse's witnesses, were there, as was Suzanne, gazing at the bride like a little girl who has just dressed her doll. Although she could no longer walk, Madame Raquin insisted on being with her children all the time, so they hoisted her into the carriage and set off.

At the town hall and the church everything passed off satisfactorily. The calm, modest attitude of the couple was noticed and greeted with approval. They spoke the sacramental word 'yes' with a degree of emotion which moved even Grivet himself. They felt as if they were in a dream. But while they sat and knelt peacefully side by side, furious thoughts were raging within them despite themselves, tearing apart their peace of mind. They avoided looking each other in the face. When they got back into the carriage, they felt more like strangers than before.

It had been decided that the dinner would be a family affair, held in a cheap little restaurant up the hill in Belleville.* Only the Michauds and Grivet were invited. While they were waiting for it to turn six, the wedding party drove all round the boulevards;* then they went to the restaurant, where a table had been laid for seven in a little, yellow-painted private room reeking of wine and dust.

The meal was less than jolly, as the couple were in a serious, pensive mood. Since that morning they had been having peculiar sensations which they made no attempt to understand. They had been dazed right from the start by the speed of the formalities, and the ceremony which had just tied them to each other for ever. Then the long ride down the boulevards, which seemed to go on for months, had lulled them into a state of drowsiness; they had patiently let themselves be carried along through the monotonous streets, looking at the shops and the passers-by with blank eyes, overcome by a numbing lethargy which they tried to shake off with bursts of forced laughter. When they finally entered the restaurant, they felt weighed down by overwhelming fatigue and a growing apathy.

Sitting opposite each other at table, they smiled fixedly, then subsided into oppressed pensiveness; they ate, spoke when spoken to, and moved their limbs automatically, like machines. The same sequence of fleeting thoughts kept breaking through the listless inertia that filled their minds. They were married and it did not feel any different, which they found most strange. In their imagination they were still separated by a gaping chasm, and they wondered from time to time how they could ever cross it. They felt as if they were still in the period before the murder, when a material obstacle still stood between them. Then, suddenly, they remembered they would be sleeping together that very evening, in a few hours time, and looked at each other in amazement, not properly understanding why that should be allowed. They did not feel united; on the contrary, they dreamed that they had been violently separated and flung apart in opposite directions.

When the guests, laughing fatuously, demanded to hear them talk to each other in more intimate tones, to clear the air of any embarrassment, they stammered and blushed bright red, unable to force themselves to act like lovers in front of everyone else.

Waiting had blunted the force of their desire, and the past had ceased to exist. Their violent, erotic appetites had gone, and they had even forgotten the joy they had felt that same morning, the deep joy that had come over them at the thought that from now on they would not be afraid any more. Now they were simply weary and bewildered at everything that was happening to them, and the day's events were going round and round in their heads, monstrous and incomprehensible. So they sat there, smiling and speechless, not expecting or hoping for anything, while in the depths of their despondency a vague but painful anxiety began to grow.

And Laurent, every time he moved his head, felt a burning sensation in his neck, as his collar pinched and cut into the wound left by Camille's bite. While the mayor was reading out the marriage regulations, while the priest was going on about God, and during every other minute of that long day, he had felt the drowned man's teeth sinking into his skin. At times he imagined there was a rivulet of blood running down his chest and making a red stain on his white waistcoat.

Privately, Madame Raquin was grateful to the couple for their gravity, for any boisterous display of joy would have hurt the poor mother's feelings; to her, her son was there throughout, invisibly handing Thérèse over to the care of Laurent. Grivet's attitude was quite different; he was bored by the wedding and was trying in vain to liven things up, despite warning looks from Michaud and Olivier which glued him to his seat whenever he was thinking of standing up and coming out with something idiotic. However, on one occasion he did manage to get to his feet, to propose a toast:

'To the children of Monsieur and Madame,' he said in a ribald tone of voice.

They could not avoid drinking to that. On hearing Grivet's words, Thérèse and Laurent turned extremely pale. It had never occurred to them that they might have children, and now the thought sent an icy shudder running through them. They nervously clinked glasses and looked hard at each other, surprised and scared at being there together, face to face.

The meal did not last long. The guests wanted to accompany husband and wife back to the nuptial chamber. It was scarcely more than half past nine when the wedding party returned to the shop in the arcade. The costume jewellery woman was still sitting in her cubby-hole, behind the box lined with blue velvet. She looked up out of curiosity and smiled at the newly-weds. They caught her glance, and it terrified them. Perhaps the old woman knew all about their past assignations, and had seen Laurent slipping into the little side-passage.

Thérèse withdrew almost at once to the bedroom with Madame Raquin and Suzanne. The men remained in the dining-room while the bride was made ready for the night. Laurent felt limp and enervated, and not in the least impatient, and listened tolerantly to the vulgar jokes that Michaud and Grivet were able to crack to their hearts' content now that the ladies were out of the way. When Suzanne and Madame Raquin emerged from the bridal chamber and the old haberdasher told Laurent in emotional tones that his wife was waiting for him, he shuddered and stood still for a moment as if stunned. Then he shook the hands they were holding out to him and went into Thérèse's room, hanging on to the door for support like a man drunk.

XXI

LAURENT closed the door carefully behind him and stayed leaning against it for a while, looking around the room with an anxious, embarrassed expression on his face.

A fire was burning brightly in the grate, casting swathes of dancing yellow light on to the ceiling and walls and illuminating the room with a strong, flickering glow which made the lamp on the table seem feeble by comparison. Madame Raquin had wanted to arrange the room prettily, and it was all perfumed and decked out in white, like a nest for young, innocent love; she had taken particular pleasure in adding a few pieces of lace around the bed and filling the vases on the mantelpiece with great bouquets of roses. The room was full of gentle warmth and lingering scents, and bathed in a calm, soothing atmosphere redolent of relaxed sensuality. From time to time the crackling of the fire broke the silence of trembling anticipation. It was like some delightful wilderness, a warm and sweet-scented hideaway shut off from the bustle of the outside world, one of those secret places which form the perfect background to passion and sensual pleasure, providing the sense of mystery that is their necessary accompaniment.

Thérèse was sitting on a low chair to the right of the fireplace, her chin cupped in her hand, staring fixedly into the flames. She did not look round when Laurent came in. Her lace-trimmed petticoat and bodice stood out stark white in the brilliant light of the fire. The bodice had slipped down, revealing a pink patch of shoulder half hidden by a lock of her black hair.

Laurent moved a few steps forward, without speaking. He took off his tail-coat and jacket. When he was in his shirt-sleeves he looked again at Thérèse, who had not moved. Then he caught sight of her exposed shoulder and bent down, trembling, to press his lips to the piece of bare flesh. But she turned abruptly round, withdrawing her shoulder, and gave Laurent such a strange look of revulsion and fear that he backed away, disconcerted and ill at ease, as if himself smitten with fear and loathing.

He sat down opposite Thérèse, on the other side of the fireplace, and there they remained, silent and motionless, for a whole five minutes. Now and again jets of reddish flame would shoot forth from the burning wood, casting blood-red reflections over the faces of the murderers.

It was almost two years since the lovers had found themselves in the same bedroom together, without witnesses and able to give themselves up entirely to each other. They had not had a single amorous assignation since the day when Thérèse had come round to the Rue Saint-Victor, bringing with her the idea of murdering Camille. As a prudent calculation they had weaned their bodies off each other, scarcely even allowing themselves an occasional hand-clasp or furtive kiss. After the murder of Camille, when new desires had seized them, they had contained their lust and decided to await their wedding night, promising themselves extraordinary pleasures once they could enjoy them with impunity. Now that the great night had finally arrived, they just sat there face to face, suddenly overcome with panic and unease. They only had to stretch out their arms to fall together in a passionate embrace, but their arms felt limp, as though they were already tired out and satiated with love. The torpor of the day's events weighed more and more heavily on them and they looked at each other without any desire, afraid, embarrassed, and upset at their own frigid, silent behaviour. Thus their passionate dreams had led them into a peculiar situation in which, having succeeded in killing Camille and getting married to each other, all it had taken to cool their ardour to the point of horror and disgust was for Laurent's lips to have brushed against Thérèse's shoulder.

They started desperately searching within themselves for a little of the passion that had burned in their hearts long ago. Their bodies no longer seemed to contain either muscles or nerves, and their embarrassment and worry grew until they became horribly ashamed of just sitting, glum and silent, opposite each other. They wished they could find the strength to throw themselves into a crushing embrace, so as not to

appear complete fools in their own eyes. After all, they belonged to each other, didn't they? They had killed a man
and played out a gruesome comedy so as to be free to wallow
in constant sensual gratification, and now there they were,
sitting stiffly on opposite sides of the fireplace, exhausted, troubled in mind, and utterly lethargic of body. After a while,
they both began to feel that such an outcome was just too
ridiculously horrible and cruel. So Laurent tried to speak of
love and conjure up memories of the past, calling upon his
imagination to revive their former tender feelings.

'Thérèse,' he said, leaning over to the young woman, 'do
you remember our afternoons in this room ... I used to come
in through that door ... Today, I came in through this one
here ... We are free now, and we'll be able to love each other
in peace.'

He spoke hesitantly and without conviction. Thérèse,
hunched up in her low chair, was still staring absently into
the flames, not listening. Laurent continued:

'Do you remember that dream of mine? I used to dream
I was going to spend a whole night with you, and fall asleep
in your arms and be woken in the morning by your kisses.
Now I'm going to make the dream come true.'

Thérèse shuddered, as if suprised by a voice muttering in her
ear, and turned towards Laurent, on whose face the fire was
at that moment casting a reddish glow; at the sight of this
bloody visage, a shiver ran through her.

He went on, disconcerted now and even more anxious:

'We have done it, Thérèse, we have removed all the obstacles
between us and we belong to each other ... The future is
all ours, isn't it? A future full of peace and happiness, and
contented love ... Camille isn't there any more ...'

He stopped short, his throat dry, gasping for air, unable
to carry on. The name of Camille had come as a blow to
Thérèse, hitting her in the pit of her stomach. The two murderers stared dumbfounded at each other, pale and shaking.
The yellow light of the fire still danced across the walls and
ceiling, a warm scent of roses hung in the air, and the fire
crackled away in the silence.

Now their memories had been let loose, the ghost of Camille
had been invoked, and it had come to seat itself between the

newly-weds, in front of the blazing fire. Thérèse and Laurent smelt again the same cold, damp stench of the drowned man in the warm air that they were breathing; they both sensed the presence of a corpse there with them, and gazed at each other, not daring to move. Then the whole appalling story of their crime unfolded once more before their mind's eye. The victim's name was enough to bring the past flooding back and force them to relive the anguish of the murder all over again. Without opening their lips they stared at each other, and both experienced the same nightmare and read the start of the same cruel story in each other's eyes. This exchange of terrified looks, and the wordless narrative of the murder which they were about to recount to each other, filled them both with intolerably acute apprehension. With their nerves thus stretched to breaking-point, they were on the verge of screaming and coming to blows. In an attempt to drive away the memories, Laurent wrenched himself out of the terrified fascination that held him transfixed in Thérèse's gaze and moved a few steps away, taking off his boots and putting slippers on; then he went back to sit down by the fireplace and tried to make trivial conversation.

Thérèse understood his intentions and made herself respond to his questions. They chatted about this and that, trying to force themselves to make small talk. Laurent declared that it was hot in the bedroom, and Thérèse replied that nevertheless a draught was coming in under the door to the back stairs; and they both turned towards the little door with a sudden shudder. So Laurent quickly changed the subject, talking about the roses, the fire, and anything else he could see in the room; with a great effort, she found monosyllabic replies to keep the conversation going. They had moved further apart and assumed an air of unconcern; they were trying to forget who they were, and to behave towards each other like strangers thrown together purely by chance.

Yet oddly, despite all their efforts to exchange empty nothings, each could guess the thoughts that the other was hiding beneath the banality of his or her speech. They were quite unable to stop thinking about Camille, and their eyes carried on telling the story from the past as they conversed silently but insistently in glances beneath the aimless conversation they were holding out loud. The occasional words they spoke were meaningless, disconnected, and contradictory, for their whole being was straining towards a silent exchange of terrifying memories. When Laurent spoke of the roses, or the fire, or whatever else, Thérèse understood perfectly that he was reminding her of the struggle in the boat and the muted splash made by Camille, and, whenever she replied to a trivial question with a yes or a no, Laurent understood that she was saying she did or did not remember a particular detail of the crime. And in this way they discussed what was on their minds, with no need of words, and while talking about something else. Moreover, they were not really aware of what they were saying, for they were busy following the train of their secret thoughts, one idea after another; had they suddenly carried on with their confidences aloud, they would have understood perfectly well what each other was talking about. Gradually, this kind of mind-reading, caused by their memory's stubborn insistence on constantly forcing upon them the image of Camille, began to drive them frantic; they realized they could each see what the other was thinking and that, if they did not keep quiet, words would come unbidden into their mouths to name the drowned man and retell the story of the murder out loud. Whereupon they brought the conversation to an end and kept their lips sealed.

But in the dreadful silence that followed, the two murderers still went on conversing about their victim. Each felt as if the other's gaze were piercing his or her flesh with sharp, pointed phrases. Sometimes they thought they heard each other speaking out loud; their senses were becoming distorted, their vision turning into a strange, delicate kind of hearing; they could read each other's faces so clearly that the very thoughts acquired a peculiar, strident sound of their own which shook their organisms to the core. They could not have understood each other better if they had both screamed in heart-rending tones: 'We killed Camille, and his body is still here between us, turning our limbs to ice.' And the terrible confessions went on flowing between them, more visible and resounding than ever, in the calm, damp air of the room.

Laurent and Thérèse had begun communicating their unspoken story to each other by recounting the day of their first meeting, in the shop. Then other memories had come back one by one, in order; the hours of ecstasy, the moments of hesitation and anger, and the terrible instant of the murder. It was at this point that they had sealed up their lips and stopped their small talk, for fear of suddenly naming Camille without meaning to. Yet their thoughts did not stop there, but took them on through the panic and the fearful waiting that had followed the murder. And so into their minds came thoughts of the drowned man's corpse stretched out on a slab in the Morgue. With one look, Laurent told Thérèse all about the horror he had felt, and Thérèse, pushed beyond endurance and forced by a hand of iron to unseal her lips, suddenly took up the conversation out loud:

'So you saw him at the Morgue?' she asked Laurent, without naming Camille.

Laurent seemed to be expecting this question; he had already been reading it for a while on the young woman's blanched face.

'Yes,' he replied in a choked voice.

A shudder ran through the murderers; they moved closer to the fire and held their hands out to the flames, as if an icy draught had suddenly whistled through the hot room. They remained silent for a while as they huddled there together in the warmth. Then Thérèse continued in an undertone:

'Did he look as though he had suffered much pain?'

Laurent was unable to answer, but made a shocked gesture, as if to ward off some revolting vision. Then he jumped up and went over to the bed, before coming back over to Thérèse with his arms open in a violent gesture.

'Give me a kiss,' he said, stretching out his neck to her.

Thérèse had risen to her feet, looking terribly pale in her night attire, and was leaning back with one elbow on the marble of the fireplace. She looked at Laurent's neck. Amid the white of the flesh she could see a pink blotch, which a rush of blood was now enlarging and turning a fiery red.

'Kiss me, kiss me,' he said again, with his face and neck aflame.

She leaned even further back to avoid kissing him, then, pressing a finger-tip to Camille's bite-mark, she asked her husband:

'What's that? I didn't know you had hurt yourself.'

Thérèse's finger felt as if it were boring a hole in his throat; the contact made him pull away, wincing in pain.

'That,' he stammered, 'it's . . .'

He hesitated, but found he could not lie and had to admit the truth.

'It's Camille; you see, he bit me, in the boat. It's nothing, it's all right now . . . Kiss me, kiss me!'

Then the wretched fellow held out his smarting neck once more. He wanted Thérèse to kiss him on the scar in the hope that it would soothe the thousand stings which were torturing his flesh. Chin held up and neck thrust forward, he offered himself again, but Thérèse, by now almost lying along the fireplace, made a gesture of utter repugnance and cried out in a beseeching voice:

'No, no, not there . . . it's all bloody.'

She slumped down trembling into the low chair and held her head in her hands. Laurent stood there, not knowing what had happened. He lowered his chin and looked uncomprehendingly at Thérèse. Then, all of a sudden, he seized her head between his great hands in an animal-like embrace and forced her lips towards his neck, down on to the bite. He held her head there for a few seconds, crushed against his skin. Thérèse had given up resisting and was emitting muffled moans, unable to breathe against his neck. When she managed to escape from his clutches, she wiped her mouth violently and spat in the fire. She had not said a word.

Ashamed at his brutality, Laurent began to walk slowly up and down between the bed and the window. It was pain alone, that terrible smarting, that had made him demand a kiss from Thérèse, and when her cold lips had pressed against the burning scar the pain had been even greater. This kiss obtained by violence had shattered him; nothing in the world could have made him wish for a second, so painful had the shock been. And as he looked at the woman with whom he was now obliged to live, trembling and hunched up in front of the fire, with her back to him, he told himself over and again that he no longer loved her and she did not love him. For nearly an hour Thérèse sat slumped in her chair while Laurent paced silently up and down. They were each facing up to the terrifying fact that their passion was now dead, and that in killing Camille they had also killed off their own desire. The fire was slowly dying down, leaving a great mass of glowing embers. The heat in the room had gradually become stifling; the flowers were drooping, thickening the air with their heavy, drowsy scents.

Suddenly Laurent thought he was having a hallucination. As he was turning round to walk back from the window to the bed, he saw Camille in a shadowy corner, between the fireplace and the wardrobe. His victim's face was all green and contorted, just as he had seen it on the slab at the Morgue. He stood there rooted to the spot, weak at the knees, leaning against a piece of furniture. Hearing his low gasp of terror, Thérèse looked up.

'There, over there,' he whimpered.

With arm outstretched, he pointed to the shadowy corner where he could see the ghastly face of Camille. Thérèse, caught up in his fear, ran over and clung to him.

'It's his portrait,' she whispered, as if the painted figure of her former husband could hear her.

'His portrait?' Laurent repeated, his hair by now standing on end.

'Yes, you know, the painting you did of him. My aunt was going to move it into her room today; she must have forgotten to take it down.'

'Of course . . . his portrait . . .'

For some time the murderer did not recognize the canvas. In his fear and confusion, he had forgotten that he himself had drawn the crude features and daubed on the muddy colours which so terrified him now. Panic made him see the painting as it really was, repulsive, ill-composed, and murky, a grimacing death's head on a black background. He was astounded and overwhelmed by the unspeakable ugliness of his own creation; above all there were the two white eyes swimming in their spongy, yellowish sockets which exactly reminded him of the decomposing eyes of the drowned man at the Morgue. He stood there for a while panting for breath, thinking that Thérèse was lying in order to reassure him. Then he made out the frame, and began to calm down.

'Go and take it down,' he said to her in a whisper.

'Oh no! I'm too scared!' she replied with a shudder.

Laurent started shaking again. At times the frame seemed to disappear and he saw only the two white eyes staring hard at him.

'Please,' he begged his wife, 'will you take it down?'

'No, I can't.'

'We'll turn it round to face the wall, then it won't be able to scare us any more.'

The murderer, craven and cringing, pushed Thérèse towards the canvas, hiding behind her to avoid the drowned man's stare. However, she freed herself, so he decided to take the risk himself and went up to the picture with arm raised, fumbling for the hook. But the portrait gave him such a long, repulsive, crushing look that, having tried to out-stare it, Laurent was overwhelmed and forced to admit defeat, backing away and muttering:

'No, you're right, Thérèse, we can't . . . Your aunt can take it down tomorrow.'

Head bowed, he resumed his pacing up and down, feeling sure that the portrait was still staring at him, following him around with its eyes. He could not stop himself from casting a furtive glance at the painting now and again, and each time he saw the drowned man's blank, lifeless stare looming out of the shadows. The thought that Camille was there in the corner, spying on him, observing his wedding night, scrutinizing Thérèse and himself, drove him utterly crazy with fear and desperation.

A small thing which would have made anyone else smile caused him to lose his head altogether. As he was by the fireplace, he heard a sort of scratching sound. He turned pale, convinced that it was coming from the portrait and imagining that Camille was getting down from his frame. Then he realized that it was actually coming from the door to the back stairs. He looked at Thérèse, who was again gripped by panic.

'There's someone at the top of the stairs,' he hissed. 'Who could it be, coming in that way?'

She made no reply. Their minds both turned to the drowned man, and an icy sweat broke out on their foreheads. They fled to the far side of the room, expecting the door to fly open and Camille's corpse to fall in onto the floor. As the scratching continued, louder and more erratic, they imagined their victim tearing at the wood with his nails in an attempt to get in. For almost five minutes they did not dare to move. Then at last there came a miaow, and, as Laurent went over to look, he realized that it was Madame Raquin's tabby cat, which had been shut in the bedroom by mistake and was trying to get out by rattling the door with his claws. François was frightened by Laurent; in a single bound he leapt up on to a chair and, with fur bristling and legs out rigid, he stared straight at his new master with a hard, cruel look in his eye. Laurent did not like cats, and François was close to frightening him, for in this overwrought atmosphere of fear he thought the cat was about to leap at his face to avenge Camille. The creature must know everything; it was thinking thoughts behind its round, strangely dilated eyes. Faced with the fixity of this animal stare, Laurent had to look away. He was on the point of giving François a kick when Thérèse cried out:

'Don't hurt him!'

Her shout affected him strangely and brought an absurd idea into his head.

'Camille has entered that cat's body,' he thought. 'I shall have to kill it . . . It looks so human.'

He did not deliver the kick, for fear of hearing François speak to him with Camille's voice. Then he remembered the jokes Thérèse used to make in the days of their great passion, when the cat had been a witness to all their embraces, and he told himself that the creature knew too much and would have to be thrown out of the window. But he lacked the courage to go through with his plan. François was still ready for battle: with claws out and back arched in annoyance, he followed his enemy's every movement with superb detachment. Laurent was disconcerted by the steely glint in his eye; he hastened to open the door into the dining-room and the cat fled with a high-pitched miaow.

Thérèse had resumed her seat by the hearth, where the fire had now gone out; Laurent went back to pacing up and down between the bed and the window; and thus they waited for dawn. They had no thought of going to bed; the life had quite gone out of their hearts and their bodies, and they had just one desire, to get out of that suffocating room. Being shut up together and having to breathe the same air made them feel utterly sick; they would have liked someone else there to interrupt their intimacy and rescue them from the cruel embarrassment of being in each other's presence, unable to utter a word and quite incapable of resurrecting their passion. Their prolonged silences, heavy with bitter, despairing recriminations and unspoken accusations, which they could nevertheless hear quite distinctly in the calm air, were a torture to them.

Daylight came at last, dirty and grey, bringing with it a biting chill.

Once the room was filled with pale light, Laurent shivered but felt rather calmer. He looked squarely at Camille's portrait and saw it as it really was, trivial and childish; with a shrug he took it down, thinking how silly he had been. Thérèse stood up and went to unmake the bed, so as to deceive her aunt into thinking they had spent a blissful night together.

'Now look here,' said Laurent brusquely, 'I hope we'll get a bit more sleep tonight. This kind of childishness just can't go on.'

Thérèse gave him a deep, serious look.

'You know', he said, 'I didn't get married for sleepless nights ... We're behaving like children ... It's your fault; when you put on your graveyard expression like that, it flusters me. Do try and be a bit more cheerful tonight and not scare me to death.'

He gave a forced laugh, for no particular reason.

'I'll try,' she replied in an undertone.

Such was their wedding night.

XXII

THE nights that followed were even more cruel. The murderers had wanted to be with each other at night to defend themselves against the drowned man, yet, strangely, being together only increased their fear. They became exasperated, got on each other's nerves, went through agonies of appalling terror whenever they exchanged the least word or look. As soon as any sort of conversation began between them, when they were on their own, they would both see red and become quite irrational.

Thérèse's impassive yet highly-strung constitution had had a peculiar effect on Laurent's stolid, sanguine one. Long before, at the time of their great passion, the difference in their temperaments had bound them powerfully together as a couple, establishing a kind of equilibrium between them based on the complementarity of their organisms. He put in something of his sanguine nature, she contributed her nerves, and they lived hand in glove in this way, needing the kisses they exchanged to regulate the mechanism of their being. But now the balance had been disrupted. Thérèse's over-wrought nerves had become dominant, and Laurent suddenly found himself plunged into a state of nervous hypersensitivity; under the passionate influence of his wife, his temperament had gradually become that of a young girl suffering from an acute neurotic condition. It would be interesting to study the changes, determined by circumstances, which sometimes come about in certain organisms; these changes begin in the body but quickly communicate themselves to the brain, and thence to the whole individual.

Before he met Thérèse, Laurent had the typical heavy calm, the prudence and the sanguine approach to life, of a peasant, eating, drinking, and sleeping like an animal. Come what may, throughout his everyday existence he breathed steadily and placidly, and was always satisfied with himself; once he began to run to fat, he lost any sharpness he may have had. Only every once in a while, deep down in his fleshy body, did he feel any stirrings. But Thérèse had turned these stirrings into horrible convulsions of lust, and caused a nervous system of astonishing sensitivity to develop within this great flabby frame. Laurent, who, before all this, had enjoyed life through his blood rather than his nerves, now developed a far less raw sensuality. At the first kisses from his mistress, a whole new and poignant life of the nerves was revealed to him which increased his erotic satisfaction many times over and gave him such acute pleasure that at first it almost drove him mad. He rushed headlong into these intoxicating delights to which his own sanguine nature had previously never had access. So a strange process took place within him; he developed a nervous disposition which became dominant over the sanguine one and so modified his whole nature; he lost his ponderous calm and became much more alive. The point came when his nerves and his blood were in balance; this was his moment of deepest pleasure, when existence seemed perfect. Then the nerves began to dominate, and he fell victim to all the agonies and fears which torture those whose minds and bodies are disturbed.

Thus it was that shadows in a corner could make Laurent shake with fear like a cowardly child. This shivering, haggard creature, the new individual which had just emerged from the skin of the stolid, brutish peasant, was going through all the fears and anxieties experienced by those of a nervous disposition. Everything that had happened, from Thérèse's wild caresses, to the tension of the murder and his apprehensive expectation of physical pleasure afterwards, had conspired to drive him almost out of his mind, inflaming his senses by sudden and repeated attacks on his nerves. Insomnia had inevitably followed, together with hallucinations, and at that point Laurent fell into the intolerable existence of permanent horror with which he was now struggling.

His remorse was purely physical. Only his body, with its over-stretched nerves and trembling flesh, was afraid of the drowned man. His conscience had nothing to do with the terror he felt, and he did not in the least regret having killed Camille; in periods of calm when the ghost was not there, he would have committed the murder all over again if he had thought it was in his interests to do so. During the day he mocked his own fears and swore to himself that he would be strong, constantly chiding Thérèse for unsettling him. For, as he put it to her, she was the one who was afraid, she was the sole cause of the terrible scenes that occurred each night in the bedroom. But as soon as night fell and he was shut in the room with his wife, beads of chill sweat appeared on his skin and he was riven with childish fears. Thus he went through periodic crises, attacks of nerves which deranged his senses and made his victim's green and revolting face appear to him every evening. It was like the onslaught of some fearful illness, a sort of murderer's hysteria, for illness and nervous affliction were truly the only terms in which to describe the terrors Laurent was going through. His face became twisted, his limbs went rigid, and all his sinews stood out in knots. His body was suffering terribly but his soul remained absent; the wretched fellow did not feel in the least repentant. Thérèse's passion had infected him with a terrible sickness, and that was all.

Thérèse, too, was experiencing profound disturbances, but in her case it was simply because her fundamental nature had become abnormally amplified. Since the age of ten she had been troubled by nervous disorders, due in part to the way she had been brought up in the fetid, nauseating air of little Camille's sick-room. Thus there had built up within her an accumulation of stormy impulses and powerful fluids, which would give rise in later life to truly tempestuous outbursts. Laurent had given her, as she had given him, a brutal shock. From their first amorous embrace, her inflexible but sensual temperament had developed with furious intensity and she had lived solely for her passion. As she had given herself over more and more completely to the desires burning within her, she had sunk into a sort of unhealthy stupor in which everything that happened seemed to overwhelm her and drive her nearer to madness. She responded to the frights she had received with more womanly weakness than her new husband; she had a vague sense of remorse, and some regrets which she would not acknowledge, and she sometimes felt tempted to throw herself down on her knees and implore Camille's ghost to forgive her, swearing to appease him by repenting. It may be that Laurent noticed these cowardly urges in Thérèse, for whenever they found themselves in the grip of a common terror, he would take it out on her and treat her harshly.

For the first few nights they could not bring themselves to go to bed at all. They sat in front of the fire waiting for dawn, as they had done on their wedding night, for the thought of lying side by side in bed filled them with horror and repugnance. By an unspoken agreement they avoided any sort of embrace, and never even looked at the bed that Thérèse unmade every morning. When exhaustion overcame them they would fall asleep for an hour or two in their armchairs, only to be jolted awake by the sinister climax of some dreadful nightmare. When they woke, with stiff and aching limbs and blotchy faces, shivering with cold and feeling thoroughly unwell, they would look at each other in stupefaction, each amazed at seeing the other there. They always behaved with peculiar modesty towards each other, as if ashamed of revealing their revulsion and their terror.

They would fight against sleep for as long as they could, sitting at either side of the fireplace and talking about a thousand trivial things, taking care not to let the conversation flag. There was a wide gap between them, in front of the hearth, and whenever they turned their heads they imagined that Camille had pulled up a chair and was sitting there, toasting his toes with a lugubrious and mocking air. The apparition which they had seen on their wedding night was now coming back every night. This horribly disfigured corpse which was always there, silently observing and ridiculing their conversations, filled them with constant anxiety. They did not dare move, but blinded themselves by staring straight into the flames; and then, when they could no longer prevent themselves from looking nervously round, their eyes, dazzled by the burning coals, actually created the apparition and imparted to it a sinister red glow.

In the end Laurent refused to sit down at all, though he would not tell Thérèse the reason. She realized that he must be seeing Camille, just as she was, so she declared in her turn that she found the heat too much and would feel better a few feet away from the fire. She pushed her armchair over to the foot of the bed and huddled there instead, while her husband resumed his pacing up and down the room. From time to time he would open the window, letting the cold January nights fill the room with their freezing air, in order to cool his fever.

For a week the newly married couple spent the whole of every night like this. They would doze off and take a little rest during the day, Thérèse behind the counter in the shop, Laurent at his office; but at night they were entirely prey to pain and fear. Yet the strangest thing of all was their attitude to each other. They spoke not one loving word, but pretended to have forgotten the past, seeming merely to live in mutual toleration, like sick people who feel a secret sympathy for each other's sufferings. Each hoped to conceal his or her fear and loathing from the other, and neither seemed to notice anything strange about the way they were spending their nights, which should have taught them a lot about each other's state of mind. When they stayed up until morning, hardly speaking, turning pale at the slightest sound, they looked as if they thought all couples behaved the same way in the first days of their married life. Theirs was the inept hypocrisy of two insane people.

Soon they were so utterly worn out that, one evening, they made up their minds to lie down on the bed, but without undressing. So, still in their clothes, they threw themselves down on the bedspread, fearful lest their skin should touch, for they felt as if the slightest contact would give them a painful shock. Then, after they had dozed fitfully like that for two nights, they ventured to take off their clothes and slip in between the sheets. But they still kept apart and took precautions to avoid accidently touching each other. Thérèse would get in first and take up her position along the far edge of the bed, against the wall. Laurent would wait until she had stretched out properly, then lie down himself along the near side, right by the edge. Between them there was a wide gap; that was where Camille's corpse lay.

When the two murderers were lying under the same sheet, with their eyes closed, they thought they could feel their victim's clammy body lying between them in the middle of the bed, and it made their flesh icy cold. It was like a repulsive obstacle between them. They were seized by a feverish delusion which made the obstacle seem real: they could touch the body, see it stretched out there like a greenish, half-putrefied lump

134 *Thérèse Raquin*

of meat, and smell the revolting stench given off by this mass of decomposing humanity. All their senses were in the grip of hallucinations which heightened everything they felt to the point where it became unbearable. The presence of this foul bedfellow made them lie there quite still, not speaking, petrified with terror. Occasionally Laurent thought of taking Thérèse violently into his arms, but he dared not move, thinking that he could not stretch out an arm without getting a handful of Camille's spongy flesh. Then it occurred to him that the drowned man was deliberately lying down between them in order to prevent their embracing, and he realized that Camille was jealous.

Occasionally, however, they did try to exchange a furtive embrace, to see what would happen. Laurent would teasingly order his wife to give him a kiss, but their lips were so cold that death seemed to have come and taken up position between their two mouths. They both felt sick. Thérèse shuddered in horror and Laurent, hearing her teeth chattering in fear, became angry with her.

'What are you shaking for?' he shouted at her. 'Surely you're not scared of Camille, are you? Where he is now, the poor devil can hardly object!'

They both avoided telling each other the real reason for their fear. Whenever one of them saw the drowned man's pallid mask in a hallucination, they would shut their eyes and lock his terror up inside them, not daring to speak to the other of what they had seen for fear of bringing on an even more appalling crisis. When Laurent, at the end of his tether, accused Thérèse in a despairing frenzy of being afraid of Camille, the name spoken aloud always made their terror worse than ever. By now the murderer was becoming quite hysterical.

'Yes, yes,' he stammered at her, 'you're scared of Camille, aren't you? It's as clear as day, for God's sake . . . Stupid bitch, you haven't an ounce of courage . . . Don't worry, you can sleep tight all right; or do you think your first husband is going to come and drag you out of bed by the feet, just because I'm in here with you?'

At the very idea that the drowned man might come and tug at their feet, Laurent's hair stood on end. He went on even more violently, torturing himself:

'I shall have to take you down to the cemetery one night ... We'll open up Camille's coffin so that you can see what kind of a putrefied mess there is inside! Then perhaps you won't be so scared of him! In any case, it's not as if he knows we shoved him in the water!'

Muffled groans were heard from Thérèse, who had buried her head in the bedclothes.

'Look, we chucked him in because he was getting to be a nuisance,' continued her husband, 'and we'd chuck him in again if we had to, wouldn't we? So stop being childish and get a grip on yourself. It's silly to upset our happiness like this ... Don't you see, my dear, when we're dead and buried, the fact that we shoved a poor idiot in the Seine won't make a blind bit of difference to what happens to us, but we will have enjoyed each other to the full, and that's the main thing ... So come on and give me a kiss.'

She did kiss him, frigid and panic-stricken, and he was shaking just as much as she was.

For more than a fortnight Laurent wondered how on earth he could kill Camille again. He had pushed him into the river, but somehow he wasn't dead enough, and he kept coming back at night and getting into Thérèse's bed. Just when the murderers thought they had finished the job and could enjoy their passionate pleasures in peace, their victim came back to life again and turned their bed to ice. Thérèse was not a widow, and Laurent found himself married to a woman who already had a drowned man for a husband.

XXIII

LITTLE by little, Laurent fell into a state of raving fury. He resolved to chase Camille away from his bed. First he had gone to bed with all his clothes on, then he had avoided touching Thérèse. In the end, driven by rage and despair, he made up his mind to clasp his wife to him and crush her to death if necessary, rather than leave her to his victim's ghost. It was a brutal and domineering gesture of defiance.

In fact, the hope that Thérèse's kisses would cure his insomnia was the only thing that had induced him to enter her bedroom. Once he was there as her master, his body, racked by even more atrocious agonies, lost all interest in attempting a cure. For three weeks he remained utterly cast down, quite forgetting that he had done everything he had done in order to possess Thérèse, and unable to touch her without increasing his suffering, now that she was indeed his.

The sheer scale of his anguish finally jolted him out of his depression. In the first moment of stupor, in the strange desperation of their wedding night, it was not surprising that he should have forgotten the reasons which had pushed him towards marriage. But the repeated assaults of his appalling dreams had filled him with a smouldering annoyance which finally overcame his cowardly tendencies and gave him back his memory. He remembered that he had married Thérèse in order to drive away his nightmares by holding her tight in his arms. So one night, all of a sudden, that is just what he did, dragging her roughly to him even at the risk of having to lean across the drowned man's corpse.

She too was at the end of her tether; she would have flung herself into the fire, had she thought that the flames would purify her flesh and deliver her from her pain. She returned Laurent's embrace, determined either to be consumed by the fire of his caresses or to find in them relief.

They hugged each other in a horrible embrace. Pain and terror took the place of desire. When their limbs touched, they

felt as if they had fallen on to a pile of glowing embers. They
let out a scream and clung more tightly to each other, so as
not to leave any room for the drowned man between their
bodies. But they could still feel pieces of him squashed revolt-
ingly between them, freezing their skin in some places while
the rest of them was burning hot.

Their kisses were appallingly cruel. Thérèse felt with her
lips for the bite-mark on Laurent's stiffened, swollen neck,
and feverishly clamped her mouth to it, for that was the gaping
wound in their relationship, and, once that was cured, the
murderers could sleep easy. She realized this, and was trying
to cauterize the scar with the fire of her kisses. But she burned
her own lips, and Laurent pushed her violently away, letting
out a low moan as he did so, for he felt as if someone had
held a red-hot iron to his neck. Thérèse, half crazed, came
back and tried again to kiss the wound; she felt a bitter thrill
in putting her lips to the place where Camille's teeth had sunk
into Laurent's neck. The thought flashed across her mind of
biting her husband in the same place, tearing out a great chunk
of flesh and making a new, deeper wound which would take
away all sign of the first one; she would no longer be afraid
if the only imprint she saw was that of her own teeth. But
Laurent protected his neck against her kisses; the smarting
feeling was too overwhelming, so every time she brought her
lips near he pushed her away. They continued fighting each
other in this way, groaning desperately and struggling in their
horrible embrace.

They fully realized that all they were doing was making their
suffering worse. However hard they hugged each other in
terrible embraces, burning and bruising each other until they
both cried out in pain, they were unable to calm their horror-
struck nerves. Every hug simply increased their loathing, and,
while they were exchanging such terrible kisses, they were
haunted by terrifying hallucinations, imagining that the
drowned man was tugging at their feet and shaking the bed
violently beneath them.

At one point they released each other, out of overwhelming
revulsion and complete nervous rejection. Then they decided
they were not going to admit defeat and fell back into each
other's arms, only to be forced to let go again, feeling as if

red-hot needles had been stabbing their limbs. They tried several times to overcome their repugnance in this way, and to find oblivion in the exhaustion of their nerves. But every time their nervous excitement and tension caused them such frustration that the strain might have killed them if they had remained in each other's arms. However, this battle against their own bodies had worked them up into such a fury that they were determined to persevere and win. Suddenly, they were shattered by a spasm more acute than the others, and the unparalleled violence of the shock made them think they were going to have a seizure.

Thrown to opposite sides of the bed, burned up and bruised by their passion, they both began to cry.

And, through their sobbing, they thought they could hear the triumphant laugh of the drowned man, as he slipped between the sheets once more with howls of derision. They had not succeeded in driving him out of their bed; they were beaten. Camille lay down quietly between them while Laurent shed impotent tears and Thérèse shuddered lest the corpse should try to take advantage of its victory and seize her in turn in its decomposing arms, as her legitimate master. They had tried the ultimate remedy, and, now that it had failed, they realized that they would never again dare exchange the least kiss. The furious paroxysm of the senses which they had tried to induce as a way of killing off their fears had merely plunged them even deeper into horror. Feeling the chill contact of this corpse which was now going to keep them apart for ever, they shed tears of blood and wondered anxiously what was to become of them.

XXIV

JUST as old Michaud had hoped when he had worked to set up the marriage of Thérèse and Laurent, once the wedding was over Thursday evenings regained all their former jollity. Camille's death had put them in great danger, for the guests had ventured into the grieving household only with great reluctance; each week they feared that they would be bid a definitive farewell. The thought that the door of the shop would doubtless soon be closed to them appalled Michaud and Grivet, for they clung to their habits with the instinctive stubbornness of animals. They kept telling themselves that one fine day the old mother and the young widow would go off to mourn their dear departed in Vernon, or somewhere else, leaving them out in the cold on Thursday evenings, with nothing to do; they had visions of themselves wandering pathetically about the arcade, dreaming of never-ending domino games. Meanwhile, as they waited for these bad days to arrive, they timidly enjoyed the last remnants of their happiness, dropping round to the shop with concerned and conciliatory expressions on their faces and telling themselves that this might be the last time. These fears remained with them for more than a year, and, faced with Madame Raquin's tears and Thérèse's silence, they never dared let themselves go and have a good laugh. They no longer felt at home, as they had in Camille's day; they seemed, as it were, to be stealing every evening spent sitting round the dining-room table. It was in these desperate circumstances that old Michaud's selfishness had induced him to try his master-stroke of marrying Thérèse off to Laurent.

On the Thursday following the wedding Grivet and Michaud made a triumphal entrance. They had won. The dining-room was theirs once more, and they no longer had to fear being asked not to come again. They arrived well pleased with life, made themselves thoroughly at home, and trotted out all their old jokes one after the other. It was easy to see from their smug and confident airs that they thought a revolution had come about. Camille's memory was no longer there; the dead husband, that life-chilling ghost, had been chased away by the living husband, and now the past with all its joys had come alive again. With Laurent replacing Camille, there was no longer any reason for gloom, the guests could laugh away without hurting anyone's feelings; in fact, it was their positive duty to laugh and cheer up this splendid family who were kind enough to invite them into their home. So Grivet and Michaud, who had been coming round for almost eighteen months on the pretext of consoling Madame Raquin, could now put their little hypocrisy to one side and turn up quite openly, and once more nod off in their chairs opposite each other to the clicking of dominoes.

Every week another Thursday evening would come round, and every week these grotesque death's heads which Thérèse had always found so exasperating would gather once more around the table. She talked of throwing them out, for their mindless laughter and stupid comments were getting on her nerves. But Laurent convinced her that it would be a mistake to send them packing, for it was vital to keep the present as much like the past as possible, and vital above all to stay on the right side of the police, those imbeciles who were protecting them from all suspicion. Thérèse gave way, the guests were well received, and they saw a long line of blissful, cosy evenings stretching ahead of them.

It was around this time that husband and wife began to lead a kind of double life.

In the morning, when daylight came to chase away the terrors of the night, Laurent would hastily throw on his clothes. He was only really at ease once he was in the dining-room, where his self-centred calm returned as he sat at the table before a huge bowl of milky coffee prepared by Thérèse. Madame Raquin, now such an invalid that she could scarcely walk downstairs to the shop, watched him with motherly smiles while he ate. As he swallowed his toast and filled his stomach, he gradually became more self-assured. After the coffee, he would drink a small glass of cognac, which would make him feel quite all right again. Then he would say: 'See you this evening,' to Madame Raquin and Thérèse, without ever kissing them goodbye, and saunter off to work. Spring was on its way; the trees along the embankment were putting on leaves, clothing themselves in fine, pale-green lace. Down below, the river murmured caressingly past, while up above the early-morning sunlight had a gentle warmth to it. Laurent felt himself reawakening in the cool air as he filled his lungs with the scent of new life carried by these April and May breezes; he tried to keep in the sun, stopping to look at the silvery reflections sparkling on the Seine or listen to the noises along the embankment, letting the keen morning smells diffuse into him and enjoy the bright, happy morning with each one of his senses. He certainly had hardly a thought of Camille, although he did sometimes find himself staring idly at the Morgue, across the river; then his mind turned to the drowned man as someone brave might think back to a silly scare he had once had. With full stomach and freshly washed face, he recovered all his stolid peace of mind. Having arrived at his office, he always spent the day yawning and waiting for it to be time to go home; he was just like any other employee, bored stiff and without a thought in his head. The one idea he had was to hand in his notice and rent a studio, for he was vaguely dreaming of a new life of idleness, and that was enough to keep him busy until the evening. Memories of the shop in the arcade never intruded upon his thoughts, though in the evening, having longed since the morning for it to be time to go home, he would always leave unwillingly and walk back along the embankment in a worried, preoccupied frame of mind. However slowly he walked, he would eventually have to go back into the shop. And there, terror lay in wait for him.

Thérèse's feelings were similar. As long as Laurent was not with her, she felt at ease. She had got rid of the cleaning lady, saying that she did not clear up properly and there was dirt everywhere in the shop and the flat; she felt an overwhelming urge to tidy the place up. But the truth was that she was feeling the need to rush around doing things, to tire out her stiffened limbs. She bustled about all morning, sweeping, dusting, cleaning the bedrooms, washing crockery, and doing all the menial jobs that would have disgusted her in the past. These household tasks kept her on her feet, active but silent, until midday, leaving her no time to think about anything but cobwebs hanging from the ceiling or grease on the plates. Then she turned to cooking and started preparing lunch. At table, Madame Raquin complained that she was always jumping up to fetch the next course; she was upset and concerned about her niece's frantic activity, but when she chided her for it, Thérèse always answered that they had to save money. After the meal, she would get changed and finally make up her mind to go and join her aunt behind the counter. There, drowsiness would come over her and, exhausted by sleepless nights, she would doze off, giving in to the delicious lethargy that took hold of her whenever she sat down. These were only light dozes, full of vague charms, which calmed her nerves. The memory of Camille had receded and she was now tasting the profound peace which comes to sick people whose pain suddenly leaves them. Her whole body felt lithe again and her mind free, as she settled into a sort of warm, healing oblivion. Without these few moments of calm, her organism would have collapsed under the pressure of her nervous system, and it was from these dozes that she drew the strength to endure further suffering, and the horror which the following night would bring. Not that she really went to sleep, for she hardly even lowered her eyelids; she would simply be lost in peaceful dreams, and, whenever a customer came in, she would open her eyes and serve the few sous-worth of goods she required, before floating off back into her dream world. Three or four perfectly happy hours would go by in this way, with her answering her aunt in monosyllables and really enjoying drifting off into a semi-conscious state where thought was suspended and she was able to sink back into herself. Every once in a while she would glance out into the arcade, feeling particularly comfortable on grey days when it was dark in the shop and she could conceal her lassitude in the shadows. The dank and dreadful passage, with its stream of poor devils going past soaked by the rain, their umbrellas dripping on the flagstones, seemed to her like the entrance-way to some place of evil, a sort of filthy, sinister corridor where nobody would come looking for her and disturbing her peace. Occasionally, when she noticed the dingy gloom around her and smelled the acrid stench of damp, she imagined that she had been buried alive and was surrounded by earth, deep in a communal grave all crawling with corpses. She found this a consoling and peaceful thought, and told herself that she was safe now, she was going to die and would feel no more pain. At other times, when Suzanne dropped in to see her and stayed sitting by the counter all afternoon doing her embroidery, she was forced to keep her eyes open. Thérèse had now taken a liking to Olivier's wife, with her flabby face and sluggish movements, for she found the sight of the poor, timorous creature strangely comforting; she had made friends with her and liked to have her by her side, smiling her wan smiles, only half alive, bringing a stale cemetery smell into the shop. Whenever Suzanne's glassily transparent blue eyes gazed into hers, she felt a chill sense of well-being in her bones. Thérèse would wait around in this way until four o'clock. Then she would go back to the kitchen in order to tire herself out preparing Laurent's dinner with frantic haste. Whenever her husband appeared in the doorway, her throat went tight and her whole being was again overtaken by panic.

Every day, husband and wife experienced almost the same sensations. In the daytime, while they were apart, they could enjoy hours of delicious rest; in the evenings, as soon as they were together again, a nagging sense of unease overcame them.

However, the evenings were quiet enough. Thérèse and Laurent, who both shuddered at the prospect of going back into the bedroom, always stayed up as long as they could. Madame Raquin, half lying in a big armchair close by, chatted placidly to them. She spoke of Vernon, always thinking about her son but avoiding his name out of a kind of delicacy of feeling; she would smile at her dear children as she planned out their future for them. The lamp cast its pale glow on her white face, and her words sounded extraordinarily quiet in the dead, silent atmosphere. All the while the two murderers were sitting, silent and still, at her side, apparently listening devoutly to what she was saying; in reality, however, they made no effort to follow the poor old woman's ramblings, but were just glad of this quiet flow of words which prevented them from hearing their own clamorous thoughts. They did not dare to look at each other, but kept their eyes on Madame Raquin to ensure that their faces always wore the appropriate expression. They never mentioned going to bed and would have stayed there until morning, listening to the old haberdasher's soothing babble, bathed in the calming influence which surrounded her, had she not shown a desire for her own bed. Only then did they leave the dining-room and retire despairingly to their room, rather as if they had been about to fling themselves into an abyss.

Soon, they began to find Thursday evenings very much preferable to these more intimate occasions. When they were alone with Madame Raquin, they could not lose themselves in company; the tenuous thread of their aunt's voice and her affectionate gaiety could not drown out their inner cries of anguish. As they felt bedtime approaching, they shuddered whenever their glance happened to settle on the door to the bedroom, and the wait for the moment when they would be alone became more and more cruel as the evening wore on. On Thursdays, however, they could become drugged by idiotic conversation and forget each other's presence completely, so that they suffered less. In the end even Thérèse began to look forward passionately to the days when guests were due, and if Michaud and Grivet had not arrived she would have gone to fetch them herself. With people from outside in the room between herself and Laurent, she felt less agitated, and she would have liked to have guests and noise all the time, something to distract and insulate her. In company, she put on a kind of nervous gaiety. Laurent too brought out again all the coarse jokes of his peasant origins, his belly-laughs and art student's pranks. Never had the evening gatherings been such jolly and noisy affairs.

So it was that, once a week, Thérèse and Laurent were able to face each other without shuddering.

It was not long before a new fear presented itself. Madame Raquin was gradually becoming paralysed, and they could foresee the day when she would be fixed immovably in her chair, physically helpless and unaware of her surroundings. The poor old woman was beginning to mutter in disconnected phrases, her voice was failing, and her limbs were becoming useless, one after the other. She was turning into a vegetable. With horror, Thérèse and Laurent watched this creature who could still keep them apart from each other, and whose voice shook them out of their bad dreams, slipping away from them.

Once the old haberdasher had lost her mind for good and just sat there stiff and silent in her chair, they would be on their own, with no way of escaping the face-to-face confrontation they feared every evening. When that happened, their dreadful ordeal would begin at six o'clock, rather than midnight; it would drive them mad.

So they tried by every means to preserve Madame Raquin's health, which meant so much to them. They called doctors in to see her and looked after her every need, finding that the job of sick-nurse brought a forgetfulness and a peace of mind which encouraged them to renew their efforts. They were anxious not to lose the third person who made their evenings together bearable; they did not want the dining-room, and the whole house, to become as awful and unpleasant as their bedroom. Madame Raquin was extremely touched at their zeal in caring for her, and kept tearfully congratulating herself on having united them and handed over to them her forty thousand or so of capital. Never, after her son's death, had she expected to receive so much affection in her last days, and the tenderness of her dear children warmed her old age; she did not feel the relentless advance of the paralysis which, despite all their efforts, was making her less mobile by the day.

Meanwhile, Thérèse and Laurent continued to lead their double lives. It was as if there were two quite distinct people in each of them: one, nervy and terrified, who started shaking as soon as darkness fell, the other sluggish and unconcerned, who breathed easily as soon as the sun was up. They were living two different existences, screaming in terror when they were left on their own, smiling serenely when there were other people there. In public, their faces never ever hinted at the agonies which tortured them in private; they appeared peaceful and happy, and instinctively concealed their sufferings.

Nobody who saw them behaving so peacefully during the day could have guessed what hallucinations tormented them every night. They seemed like a couple blessed by heaven, living a perfectly happy existence together. Grivet's gallant name for them was 'the turtle-doves'. When long nights without sleep left them with bags under their eyes, he joked about it and asked when the christening was to be, which always provoked general mirth. Laurent and Thérèse hardly paled, and managed to raise a smile; they were becoming used to the old employee's innuendoes. So long as they were still in the dining-room, they were able to master their terrors. But it was impossible to guess the awful transformation which came over them as soon as they shut themselves up in the bedroom. On Thursday evenings in particular, the change was so violent and brutal that it seemed to be happening in a supernatural world. The strangeness and wild excesses of their nightly dramas defied belief, and were kept hidden deep down in their tortured minds. If ever they had spoken about them to anyone else, they would have been taken for mad.

'What a happy pair of lovers they are!' old Michaud was fond of remarking. 'They don't say much, but they don't think about it any the less. I bet they devour each other with kisses when we aren't there!'

That was certainly the view of the whole company. Soon Thérèse and Laurent were being held up as an ideal couple. Their affection, quiet happiness, and apparently endless honeymoon were celebrated right through the Passage du Pont-Neuf. They alone knew that the corpse of Camille lay between them in bed, and only they could feel beneath the calm surface of their faces the nervous contractions which, at night, horribly distorted their features and changed their placid expressions into hideous, aching masks.

XXV

AFTER four months Laurent started to think about reaping some of the benefits he had expected from marriage. He would have abandoned his wife and fled from the ghost of Camille three days after the wedding, had self-interest not kept him tied to the shop in the Passage du Pont-Neuf. He accepted the nights of terror, and stayed in that suffocating atmosphere of fear, so as not to forgo the rewards of his crime. If he left Thérèse, he would slide back into poverty and be forced to keep on working; as long as he remained with her, on the other hand, he could indulge his taste for lazing around and living the good life, with no need to work, on the income that Madame Raquin had settled on his wife. He might well have run off with the forty thousand francs if only he had been able to cash them in, but on Michaud's advice the old haberdasher had taken the precaution of safeguarding her niece's interests in the contract. Thus Laurent found himself tightly bound to Thérèse. In compensation for the appalling nights he was enduring, he meant at least to be supported in pleasant idleness, with plenty to eat, warm clothes to wear, and enough money in his pocket to indulge his whims. Only at that price was he prepared to sleep next to the drowned man's corpse.

One evening he announced to his wife and Madame Raquin that he had handed in his resignation and would be leaving the office at the end of the fortnight. As Thérèse looked worried, he hastened to add that he was going to rent a small studio, where he would go back to his painting. He went on at length about the inconvenience of his job and the broad horizons that art would open up for him; now that he had a bit of money behind him he could make a bid for success, and he wanted to see whether he was capable of doing something really great. The tirade which he came out with on this subject merely concealed a burning desire to go back to the studio life he had been leading before. Thérèse remained tight-lipped, for she had no intention of letting Laurent fritter away the small fortune on which her freedom depended. When her husband pressed her with questions in an attempt to gain her assent, she replied drily, pointing out that, if he left his office, he would no longer be bringing in any money, so he would have to depend entirely on her. While she was speaking, Laurent looked at her sharply in a disconcerting way that made the rejection she was about to pronounce stick in her throat; she thought she could read in her accomplice's eyes the menacing threat: 'If you don't agree, I'll spill the beans.' She began to stammer. Then Madame Raquin exclaimed that her dear son's wish was only fair and that they must provide him with the means of becoming a man of talent. The good lady was spoiling Laurent as she had spoiled Camille; the attentions he lavished on her had thoroughly softened her up, and she was now in his pocket and always ready to agree with whatever he said.

And so it was decided that the artist would rent a studio and receive a hundred francs a month to cover his various expenses. The family budget was arranged in the following way: the profits from the haberdashery would pay the rent on the flat and the shop, and would almost cover the household's regular outgoings; Laurent would take the rent for the studio and his hundred francs a month out of the investment income of just over two thousand francs, and the rest would go on things they all needed. Thus the capital would remain untouched, which somewhat reassured Thérèse. She made her husband swear never to go over his allowance. In any case, she reflected, Laurent could never get his hands on the forty thousand without her signature; she resolved never to sign any papers.

The very next day Laurent rented a little studio near the bottom of the Rue Mazarine which he had had his eye on for a month. He did not intend to leave his job without first finding a retreat where he could spend his days in peace, away from Thérèse. At the end of the fortnight he bade farewell to his colleagues. Grivet was stunned at his departure. A young man with such a fine future ahead of him, he observed, a young man who in only four years had reached a salary that had taken him, Grivet, twenty years to attain! He was even more astounded when Laurent told him that he was going to devote himself entirely to painting again.

Finally the artist moved into his studio. It was a sort of attic some five or six metres square with a steeply sloping ceiling into which was let a large window, which shed a harsh, white light on the floor and the grubby walls. The noises of the street did not rise to that height. The silent, pale-looking room, with its opening high up, out on to the sky, was like a hole in the ground, a burial vault dug out of grey clay. Laurent furnished it after a fashion, bringing up two chairs in need of recaning, a table which he propped against the wall to stop it collapsing on to the floor, an old kitchen dresser, his paint box, and his old easel; the only touch of luxury was provided by a huge divan he had picked up from a second-hand furniture dealer for thirty francs.

He went two weeks without even dreaming of taking up his brushes. He would arrive between eight and nine o'clock, lie down on the divan and smoke, and wait for midday, pleased that it was still morning and there were still long hours of daylight ahead of him. At noon he would go home for lunch, then hurry back so as to be on his own and not to have to look at Thérèse's pale face any longer. Then he would wait for his food to go down, dozing and lounging about until evening. His studio was a haven of peace where he felt no fear. One day his wife asked if she could visit his precious retreat. He refused, but she came knocking on the door anyway; he did not open it, and told her that evening that he had spent the day at the Louvre. He was afraid that Thérèse might bring the ghost of Camille in with her.

In the end he grew bored with doing nothing, so he bought a canvas and some paints and set to work. Not having enough money to pay models, he resolved to paint whatever his imagination suggested, without bothering whether it was true to life. He began with a male head.

Nor did he stay cooped up indoors as much as he had done in the past; he would work for two or three hours each morning, then spend the afternoon strolling around Paris or one of the suburbs. He was on his way back from one of these long walks when, just outside the Institute, he bumped into an old school friend who had just had a triumph, thanks to the support of his friends, at the last Salon.

'What, you?' exclaimed the painter. 'Laurent, you poor

fellow, I'd never have recognized you! You've got thinner.'

'I'm married now,' said Laurent with embarrassment.

'You, married? I'm not surprised to see you looking so odd, then. So what are you up to these days?'

'I'm renting a little studio, and doing a bit of painting in the mornings.'

Laurent said a little about his marriage, then launched into an excited account of his future plans. The friend looked at him with an astonished expression which both flustered and worried him. The truth was that the painter was finding it difficult to reconcile this husband of Thérèse's with the rough, common fellow he had known in the old days. Laurent now seemed to be cutting a much more distinguished figure; his face had slimmed down and had become fashionably pale, while his whole bearing was more dignified and graceful.

'But you're turning into quite a dandy,' the artist could not help exclaiming; 'you look just like an ambassador, and all got up in the latest style, too. So whose school are you working for?'

Laurent found the scrutiny to which he was being subjected unpleasant, but did not dare break off the conversation abruptly.

'Would you like to come up to my studio for a minute?' he finally asked the friend, who was making no move to go.

'I'd be delighted to,' he replied.

Unable fully to understand the changes he was seeing, the painter was keen to visit his old friend's studio. He was not going to climb up five storeys just to see Laurent's new works, which would almost certainly make him feel queasy; all he wanted to do was satisfy his curiosity.

Once upstairs, he glanced at the canvases hanging on the walls and was even more astonished. He saw five studies, two female and three male heads, painted with real energy; they were all solidly and confidently constructed, each standing out in magnificent patches of colour against a light grey background. The artist rushed forward, astounded and not even trying to conceal his surprise:

'Did you do these?' he asked.

'Yes', Laurent replied. 'They're sketches for a big picture I'm working on.'

'Come on, stop pulling my leg; are you really the one who put those together?'

'Of course; why shouldn't I be?'

The painter did not dare to reply: 'Because they are the work of a real artist, and you have never been more than a hopeless botcher.' He stood for a long time in silence before the studies. They were clumsy, of course, but they had a strange quality to them, and such power that they bore witness to a highly developed artistic sensibility. It was as if they had been painted from experience. Never before had Laurent's friend seen sketches so full of the highest promise. When he had studied them properly, he turned towards their creator:

'Well, honestly, I would never have thought you were up to painting stuff like that; where on earth did you learn to be so talented ? It's not normally something they can teach you.'

And he looked closely at Laurent, whose voice seemed gentler and whose every movement had a kind of elegance about it. He could never guess what terrible shock had changed this man, giving him the nervous sensitivity and the acute and delicate sensations of a woman. Some strange transformation had undoubtedly come about in the organism of Camille's murderer. It is difficult for analysis to penetrate to such depths. Perhaps Laurent had become an artist in the same way that he had become a coward, as a result of the drastic upheaval that had thrown his body and his mind off balance. In the past, he was weighed down and stifled by his sanguine temperament, and his vision was blocked by the dense vapours of good health which surrounded him; now that he was thinner, and more sensitive, he had the restless vitality and keen, direct sensations of those of nervous temperament. In the life of terror he was leading, his mind was released from reason and could soar to the dizzy ecstasies of genius; the quasi-moral sickness, the neurosis which afflicted his whole being, had developed in him a peculiarly lucid artistic sensibility; since he had killed a man, his body felt lighter, his frantically working brain seemed immense, and, in this abrupt enlargement of his intellect, exquisite creations, poetic reveries, passed before his mind's eye. And so it was that his movements had suddenly become elegant, and his paintings works of beauty, for they were now much more personal and full of life.

His friend did not try to probe any deeper into the birth of the artist. He left, with his astonishment intact. Before going, he looked at the canvases once more and said to Laurent:

'I've only one criticism to make, which is that all your studies have a certain family likeness; they look too similar. Even the women have something violent about them which makes them look like men in disguise ... So you see, if you want to turn these sketches into a picture, you'll have to alter some of the faces; they can't all be brothers and sisters, it would make people laugh.'

He went out of the studio, then on the landing outside he said with a smile:

'Seriously, though, it's been really good to see you again, old chap. From now on, I'll believe in miracles ... You're certainly making quite a go of it!'

He set off downstairs, and Laurent went back into the studio in a deeply troubled frame of mind. When his friend had remarked on the family likeness between his pictures he had turned abruptly away to hide the fact that his face had gone white, for he himself had already been struck by the unavoidable resemblance between them. He walked slowly over and stood in front of the canvases; as he contemplated them and looked across from one to another, a chill sweat ran down his back.

'He's right,' he muttered, 'they do all look alike ... They all look like Camille.'

He backed away and sat down on the divan, unable to tear his eyes away from the painted heads. The first had the face of an old man with a long white beard, beneath which the artist could make out Camille's weak chin. The second represented a fair-haired girl, and she looked back at him with his victim's blue eyes. Each of the other three had one or other of the drowned man's features. It was as if Camille had been dressed up as an old man or a young girl, taking on whatever guise it pleased the artist to give him but always keeping the same underlying appearance. There was another dreadful point of resemblance between these heads: they all seemed to be terrified and in pain, they all seemed overwhelmed by the same feeling of horror. Each had a slight wrinkle to the left of the mouth which gave them a grimacing air. This wrinkle, which Laurent remembered seeing on the drowned man's face, was the sign of their repulsive family relationship.

Laurent realized that he had spent too much time at the Morgue gazing at Camille, and that the image of the corpse had become deeply etched in his mind. Now, without him being in any way aware of it, his hand kept tracing out the features of that dreadful face whose memory followed him wherever he went.

Gradually, as he lay back on the divan, the painter began to see the figures coming to life. Then there were five Camilles in front of him, five Camilles created by the power of his own hands, who by a strange and horrifying process had taken on the appearance of different ages and both sexes. He jumped up, slashed the canvases to bits, and flung them out of the door, telling himself that he would die of fear in his studio if he went on filling it like that with portraits of his victim.

He had just been struck by a new dread: he was afraid that he would never again be able to draw a head without it taking on the drowned man's appearance. He resolved to find out immediately whether or not he was in control of his own hand. He set a blank canvas on the easel, then, in a few quick strokes with a piece of charcoal, he roughed out a face. It looked like Camille. Quickly he erased that sketch and tried another. For a whole hour he fought against the compulsion that was directing his fingers. With each new attempt he came back to the drowned man's face. However strongly he exerted his will to avoid the lines he knew so well, they were the ones he kept drawing, as, despite himself, he obeyed the promptings of his rebellious nerves and muscles. He had started by sketching as fast as possible, then he worked at controlling the charcoal much more slowly. The results were the same: Camille, with his agonizing, contorted look, kept appearing on the canvas. Laurent sketched a great variety of heads one after the other, from angels, to virgins with haloes, to helmeted Roman warriors, pink-skinned, fair-haired children, and old scar-faced ruffians; always, always it was Camille who reappeared, as angel, virgin, warrior, child, or ruffian. So Laurent launched into caricature, exaggerating features, inventing monstrous profiles and grotesque heads, but he only succeeded in making the striking portraits of his victim even more horrible to look at. He finished up by drawing animal heads, dogs and cats, and these, too, looked vaguely like Camille.

By now Laurent was boiling with sullen rage. He punched a hole through the canvas with his fist, thinking despairingly of his great picture. There was no question now of completing it, for he realized that from now on all he would ever be able to paint was Camille's portrait, and, as his friend had told him, a collection of faces that all looked the same would make people laugh. He visualized his great work as it would have been, and, on the shoulders of all his characters, men and women alike, he saw the pasty, terrified face of the drowned man; this strange vision struck him as appallingly ridiculous and filled him with exasperation.

So he would not dare to paint ever again, for fear of bringing his victim back to life at the least stroke of his brush; if he wanted to live in peace in his own studio, he must never paint there. The thought that his fingers had an unavoidable and involuntary ability to keep on reproducing Camille's portrait made him stare at his hand in terror. It felt as if it no longer belonged to him. NO free will

XXVI

THE attack that had been hovering over Madame Raquin finally came. Suddenly, the paralysis which for several months had been creeping along her limbs and threatening at any moment to take her body into its embrace, seized her by the throat and bound her hand and foot. One evening, as she was chatting peacefully to Thérèse and Laurent, she stopped in mid-sentence, her mouth gaping open, feeling as if she were being strangled. When she tried to scream and call for help, she could only come out with rasping noises. Her tongue had turned to stone, her hands and feet had gone stiff. She had been struck dumb and immobilized.

Thérèse and Laurent got to their feet, horrified at this thunderbolt which had struck the old lady down in a matter of seconds. Seeing her unable to move and gazing imploringly up at them, they plied her with questions to try and find out what had caused the problem. She could not reply but kept looking at them in horrible anguish. So they realized that what they had in front of them was now no more than a body half alive, which could see and hear them, but not speak. This attack plunged them into despair, not because they were concerned at the paralysed woman's sufferings, but out of self-pity, because they would have to live from now on with only each other for company.

From that day forth, the couple's life became unbearable. They spent evenings of torment sitting in front of the aged invalid, who could no longer calm their fears for them with her rambling conversation. She sat slumped in a chair like some inanimate bundle, and they were left on their own, at either end of the table, embarrassed and fearful. This semi-corpse could no longer keep them apart; at times they forgot that it was there, or took it for part of the furniture. Then their nocturnal terrors would come over them again and the dining-room became, like the bedroom, a terrible place where the ghost of Camille kept rising up before them. As a result, their suffering now went on for an extra four or five hours a day. As soon as it was dusk, they would start to tremble and lower the lampshade to avoid having to look at each other, trying to believe that Madame Raquin would soon say something and so remind them of her presence. The only reason they kept her there rather than getting rid of her was because her eyes were still alive, and they occasionally felt slightly comforted to watch them shining and moving around.

They always sat the old invalid right in the glare of the lamp, to keep her face well lit and so that they would always have her in front of them. This wan and formless face would have been an unbearable sight to other people, but they felt such a desperate need of company that their gaze rested on it with real joy. It looked like a decayed death mask with two living eyes in the middle; they alone could move, rolling rapidly from side to side in their sockets; the cheeks and the mouth seemed petrified in their terrifying immobility. Whenever Madame Raquin gave in to sleep and let her eyelids close, her still, chalky-white face really became that of a corpse; Thérèse and Laurent, feeling that there was nobody with them any more, would then make a noise until the paralytic opened her eyes again and looked at them. In this way they forced her to stay awake.

They regarded her as a distraction from their nightmares. Since she had become an invalid, she needed to be looked after like a child, and the things they had to do to care for her shook them out of their own preoccupations. In the morning, Laurent would lift her out of bed and put her in her chair, then take her back to bed again in the evening; she was still quite a weight, and it took all his strength to pick her up gently in his arms and move her. It was also he who shifted her chair around. All the other duties fell to Thérèse: she would dress the old lady, feed her, and try to understand what she wanted. For some days Madame Raquin retained the use of her hands, so she could write down what she wanted on a slate; then they too went dead and she could no longer raise them or hold a pencil, which left her with only the language of the eyes with which to make her niece guess what she wanted. Thus Thérèse devoted herself to the arduous task of being a sick-nurse, which kept her mind and body occupied and so did her a great deal of good.

To avoid being alone together, the couple would move the poor old lady's chair into the dining-room first thing in the morning. They brought her in to join them as if she were somehow necessary to their existence, and they made her sit at all their meals and listen to all their conversations. Whenever she indicated that she wanted to go back to her own room, they pretended not to understand. All that she was good for was to stop them being alone; she had no right to live her own life. At eight o'clock Laurent would go off to his studio, and Thérèse downstairs to the shop, leaving the paralysed old woman on her own in the dining-room until noon; then, after lunch, she would be alone again until six. During the day, her niece would often go upstairs and fuss around to make sure she had everything she wanted. The friends of the family could hardly find words to extol the virtues of Thérèse and Laurent.

The Thursday evening gatherings continued, with the invalid present as before. They pulled her chair up to the table, and from eight o'clock to eleven she stayed wide awake, looking round from one guest to another with a penetrating gleam in her eye. The first few times, old Michaud and Grivet were somewhat embarrassed by the sight of their old friend's lifeless body; they did not know what expression to put on, their grief was not all that great, and they wondered how much of a display of sadness the situation required. Should they speak to this inanimate face, or take no notice of it at all? Gradually they came round to the idea of treating Madame Raquin as if nothing had happened, and in the end they would pretend to be quite unaware of her condition. They chatted to her, supplying the answers to their own questions, laughing on her account as well as their own, and never letting themselves be put out by the rigid expression on her face. It was an odd sight, for these men seemed to be talking rationally to a statue, behaving much as little girls do with their dolls. The paralytic woman sat there stiff and silent in front of them while they babbled away, waving their arms around excitedly and holding lively conversations with her. Michaud and Grivet kept congratulating themselves on their impeccable behaviour. They thought that, by acting in this way, they were showing their politeness; it also spared them the inconvenience of having to express sympathy in the customary way. They expected Madame Raquin to be flattered at being treated like a healthy person, and this, they thought, dispensed them from the slightest scruples about making merry in her presence.

Grivet developed a personal obsession. He claimed to be perfectly attuned to what Madame Raquin was thinking, and maintained that, as soon as she looked at him, he knew at once what she wanted. This was just another of his delicate attentions; the only problem was that he always got it wrong. He would often interrupt the game of dominoes, look hard at the paralysed woman whose eyes were quietly following the play, and declare that she was asking for such and such. But when they checked, Madame Raquin either wanted nothing at all, or something completely different. This never discouraged Grivet, who would triumphantly exclaim 'Now what did I tell you?' before starting again a few minutes later. It was quite a different matter when the invalid did actually want something; then, Thérèse, Laurent, and the guests would call out one thing after another, to see what it might be. In the course of this, Grivet always drew attention to himself by the inanity of his suggestions. He always said whatever came into his head, at random, and was forever offering her the opposite of what she wanted. Which did not prevent him from repeating:

'I can read her eyes like a book, I can. Look there, she's telling me I'm right. Aren't you, dear lady. . . . Yes, yes.'

In any case, it was far from easy to work out what the poor old woman wanted. Thérèse alone possessed the knack. She could communicate fairly easily with that walled-in intelligence, still alive but buried deep within a dead body. What was going on inside this poor creature who was just sufficiently alive to observe life going on around her but not to participate in it? She could see and hear, she could doubtless also think clearly, but she had neither the gestures nor the voice to externalize the thoughts that were welling up within her. Maybe her thoughts were choking her? She could not have lifted a hand or opened her mouth, even if one movement, one word, from her had been enough to decide the fate of the world. Her mind was akin to one of those people who are accidentally buried alive and who wake up in the darkness of the earth, two or three metres below ground; they struggle and shout, and others walk around on top of them without hearing their dreadful lamentations. Often, as he looked at Madame Raquin, with her lips shut tight and her hands stretched out on her knees, putting the whole of her life into her quick, darting eyes, Laurent would say to himself:

'Who knows what she's thinking about, on her own . . . There must be some cruel drama going on deep down in that useless body of hers.'

Laurent was mistaken. Madame Raquin was happy, quite happy in the care and affection of her dear children. She had always dreamed of ending her days like that, slowly, surrounded by devoted and loving attention. Naturally, she would have preferred still to be able to speak, so as to thank her friends for helping her die in peace. But she accepted her condition without resentment; the peaceful and retiring life that she had always led, and the gentleness of her temperament, prevented her from suffering too much from her enforced silence and immobility. She had regressed into childhood, living her days without worry, staring straight ahead and lost in thoughts of the past. In the end she even began to enjoy sitting still in her chair, like a good little girl.

Day by day her eyes became gentler, brighter, and more penetrating. She had learned to use them like a hand or a mouth, to make requests and thank people with, and in this strange but delightful way she was able to compensate for the organs she could no longer use. Her eyes shone forth with a celestial beauty amid the drooping, grimacing flesh of her face. Since her twisted, unmoving lips could no longer smile, she smiled adorable and affectionate smiles with her eyes instead, moist gleams and bright rays shining forth from them like those of the morning sun. It was really most strange to see those eyes laughing just like lips in such a dead face, the lower part of which remained sallow and mournful while the upper part was lit with a divine radiance. It was for her dear children in particular that she poured all her soul's gratitude and affection into a simple glance in this way. When Laurent picked her up in his arms, morning and evening, to move her around, she would thank him lovingly in looks of effusive tenderness.

She lived like this for several weeks, waiting for death and

believing herself safe from further misfortune, for she thought
that she had now had her fair share of suffering. But she was
wrong. One evening, she was shattered by an appalling blow.

It was useless for Thérèse and Laurent to sit her between
them, full in the light, for she was no longer sufficiently alive
to separate them and give them protection from their fears.
Whenever they forgot that she was there and could still see
and hear them, they were gripped by panic, saw the ghost
of Camille, and tried to drive it away. At such moments of
tension their speech became confused, and one day they let
slip an admission which unwittingly revealed the truth to
Madame Raquin. Laurent had a kind of fit during which he
talked like a man hallucinating. Suddenly the paralysed old
woman knew the truth.

A horrifying contortion passed across her face and she shuddered so much that Thérèse thought she was about to jump
up and scream; then she fell back, ramrod stiff in her chair.
This type of shock was all the more horrendous because it
seemed that it had suddenly galvanized a corpse. Her physical
sensitivity, having returned for a second, vanished again and
left the invalid looking even more sickly and downcast than
before. But her eyes, normally so gentle, had become hard
and black, like steel.

Never had despair fallen so brutally upon a human being.
The appalling truth, like a flash of lightning, scorched the paralytic's eyes and burned its way into her with the supreme violence of a thunderbolt. If she had been able to stand up and
bring out the scream of horror which was rising in her throat,
to curse her son's murderers, she would have suffered less
horribly. But, having heard and understood everything, she
was forced to remain silent and immobile, keeping the full
force of her anguish bottled up inside her. She felt as if Thérèse
and Laurent had tied her up and bound her to her chair to
prevent her from leaping to her feet, and that they were deriving
some unspeakable pleasure from telling her over and over
again: 'We killed Camille,' after fixing a gag over her mouth
to stifle her sobbing. Sensations of horror and panic coursed
up and down in her body, unable to find a way out. She made
superhuman efforts to lift the crushing weight from her chest,
and to clear a passage in her throat through which to let her

despair flood out. But it was in vain that she summoned up her last strength, for she could feel the tongue pressed cold against the roof of her mouth, and was quite incapable of making her deadened body obey; she was held rigid by a corpse-like impotence. Her feelings were like those of someone who has fallen into a death-trance and is being buried, with shovelfuls of earth thumping down on his head while he just lies there, bound and gagged by his own body.

The ravages brought about in her heart were even more terrible. She felt the collapse of everything, and was utterly crushed. Her whole existence was devastated, for all her affection, her kind feelings, her devoted care, had been brutally knocked down and trampled underfoot. Her life had been an affectionate and gentle one, and then, at the very last, when she was on the point of carrying her belief in the calm joy of existence with her into the grave, a voice had suddenly screamed out that it was all lies, nothing but iniquity. The tearing of this veil showed her, underlying the love and friendship which she had thought she could see, a terrifying spectacle of blood and shame. She would have cursed God if she had been able to utter the blasphemy. God had been deceiving her for more than sixty years, treating her like a nice, sweet little girl and placing false pictures of peace and joy before her eyes to amuse her. And she had remained a child, naïvely believing a thousand idiotic things and not seeing that real life was bogged down in the blood and mire of the passions. God was wicked; he should have told her the truth earlier, or else let her depart this world still blind and innocent. Now, the only thing left for her was to die denying love, denying friendship, denying devotion to others. Nothing existed except murder and lust.

So Camille had died at the hands of Thérèse and Laurent, who had thought up their crime while wallowing in the shame of adultery! This thought was such an abyss for Madame Raquin that she could not comprehend it with her reason, nor yet grasp its meaning in any clear and detailed way. Her only sensation was that of a horrible fall; she felt as if she were plunging into a cold, black hole. And she kept telling herself: 'I'm going to be smashed to bits when I hit the bottom.'

After the first shock, she found the sheer monstrosity of

the crime unbelievable. Then, once the certainty of adultery
and murder had taken root in her mind, she began to remember
little incidents from the past which she had not understood
at the time, and she feared she was going mad. Yes, Thérèse
and Laurent were indeed the murderers of Camille, Thérèse
whom she had brought up, Laurent whom she had loved with
a mother's devotion and affection. All that went round and
round in her head like a huge wheel, with a deafening din. She
guessed at such revolting details, went down to such depths of
deception, and relived in her mind such a horribly two-faced
display of duplicitous behaviour, that she would rather have
died than have to think about it any more. One single idea
went on grinding mechanically and implacably round in her
head with all the heavy relentlessness of a millstone, as she
repeated to herself: 'My children are the ones who killed my
child.' She could find no other way to express her despair.

In the abrupt reversal of all her feelings, she tried in a panic
to recognize her former self, but without success; she was overwhelmed by a brutal influx of vengeful thoughts which drove
all goodness from her life. After this transformation, an inner
darkness descended on her; she felt a new being, cruel and
pitiless, coming to life in her dying body, a being who wanted
to tear her son's murderers to pieces.

Once she had succumbed to the shattering embrace of paralysis, and realized that she would never be able to leap at the
throats of Thérèse and Laurent and carry out her dream of
strangling them, she resigned herself to silence and immobility,
and great tears rolled slowly from her eyes. Nothing could be
more heart-rending than this still, wordless grief of hers. The
tears running, one by one, down the lifeless face in which
not a wrinkle moved, this inert, waxen face unable to show
grief by its expression, and in which only the eyes cried, was
a most moving sight.

Thérèse was overcome by horror and pity.

'We must put her to bed,' she said to Laurent.

Laurent hastily pushed the paralytic through into her bedroom, then bent down to pick her up in his arms. At this
moment Madame Raquin hoped that some powerful mechanism would set her back on her feet, and made a supreme
effort to stand. God could not possibly allow Laurent to clutch

her to his chest, and a thunderbolt would strike him dead if he had the monstrous impudence to try. But no such mechanism came into play, and the heavens withheld their thunder; she remained passively slumped in her chair, like a parcel of laundry. Then she was seized, picked up, and moved, and had to go through the ordeal of feeling herself limp and helpless in the arms of Camille's murderer. Her head lolled on to Laurent's shoulder and she stared at him through eyes widened by fear.

'That's right, go on, take a good look at me,' he muttered; 'your looks won't eat me . . .'

And he flung her roughly down on the bed, where she passed out. Her last thought had been one of terror and revulsion. From now on she would have to submit, day and night, to Laurent's foul embrace.

XXVII

ONLY a terrible fit of panic could ever have induced the couple to break their silence and admit what they had done in front of Madame Raquin. Neither of them was cruel at heart, and they would both have avoided making any such revelation out of humanity, even if their own safety had not already made it imperative for them to keep quiet.

The following Thursday they became particularly worried. In the morning Thérèse asked Laurent whether he thought it was wise to let the paralysed old woman stay in the dining-room during the evening gathering. Now that she knew everything, she might alert the others.

'Oh come on!' said Laurent; 'she can't even move her little finger; she's hardly going to start blabbing to them.'

'She might find a way,' replied Thérèse. 'Since the other evening, I've been reading in her eyes that she's determined to do something.'

'No, no, you see, the doctor told me that it really is all over for her. If she does ever open her mouth again, it'll be her last gasp ... It's all right, she's not got long to go. It would be silly to put still more on our consciences, and prevent her from being there this evening ...'

Thérèse shuddered.

'That's not what I meant,' she exclaimed. 'You're quite right, there's been enough blood as it is ... I just thought we could lock her in her room and pretend she was feeling unwell and having a lie down.'

'Brilliant,' Laurent retorted; 'and then that idiot Michaud would walk straight in anyway, just to see his old friend ... That would be an excellent way of giving the game away.'

He hesitated, trying to appear unruffled, but anxiety made him stammer:

'We'd do better to let events take their course. That lot are as thick as planks; they'll certainly not pick up on the old girl's desperate silence. They'll never suspect a thing;

they're too far from the truth. Once we've carried out this test, we'll know that we won't have to worry any more about being imprudent ... You'll see, it'll be all right.'

That evening, when the guests arrived, Madame Raquin was in her usual place between the stove and the table. Laurent and Thérèse put on a show of good humour to hide their fear, and anxiously awaited the incident which could not fail to materialize. They had pulled the shade on the lamp right down so that only the oilcloth covering the table was in the light.

The guests began by engaging in the usual banal but noisy chit-chat preceding the first game of dominoes. Grivet and Michaud were careful to ask the paralytic the customary questions about her health, questions to which, as usual, they themselves provided most positive answers. After which the company took no more notice of the poor old woman, but plunged joyfully into the game.

Ever since she had found out the horrible secret, Madame Raquin had been fervently looking forward to this evening. She had pulled together the remnants of her strength in order to denounce the culprits. Right up to the last minute she had been afraid they would not allow her to be there; she thought that Laurent would get her out of the way, perhaps by killing her, or at least by locking her in her room. When she saw that they were going to let her stay after all, and later when she was there among the guests, she felt a hot flush of joy at the thought that she was going to try and avenge her son. Realizing that her tongue was now utterly lifeless, she tried a different type of language. By an astonishing effort of will she managed to galvanize her right hand, raising it slightly from her knee where it always lay inert, and making it crawl very gradually up the table leg in front of her until it lay on the table-cloth. Then she wriggled her fingers feebly to attract the attention of the others.

When the players noticed this white, soft, corpse-like hand in their midst, they were extremely surprised. Grivet paused with his arm in mid-air, just when he was about to lay down a triumphant double six. Since her stroke, the invalid had never once moved her hands.

'Hey, look, Thérèse,' exclaimed Michaud; 'look how

Madame Raquin is moving her fingers ... She must want
something.'

Thérèse could not speak; she, like Laurent, had followed
the paralytic woman's extreme efforts and was now staring
at her hand, chalk-white in the harsh lamplight, an avenging
hand that was about to speak. The two murderers waited,
holding their breath.

'Good lord, yes, she does want something,' said Grivet; 'we
understand each other famously, she and I ... She wants to
play dominoes ... Eh? That's right, isn't it, dear lady?'

Madame Raquin made a violent gesture of denial. She
stretched out one finger, bent back the others, and, with infinite
pains, began to trace out letters on the table. But she had
only made a few strokes when Grivet called out in triumph
once again:

'I know: she's saying how right I am to play the double
six!'

The invalid shot a ferociously scornful glance at the old
employee and went back to the word she was trying to write.
But Grivet constantly interrupted her, saying that she did not
need to go on, he now understood, then putting forward some
idiotic explanation. In the end, Michaud told him to keep
quiet.

'For heaven's sake, let Madame Raquin speak,' he said.
'Now, what is it you want to tell us, my dear?'

And he looked hard at the table-cloth, much as if he were
listening attentively. But the paralytic's fingers were growing
tired, for she had had to start the same word more than ten
times over, and now they could barely manage it, slipping
from side to side. Michaud and Olivier leaned closer, still
unable to make it out, and forced her to write the first letters
yet again.

'Ah!' Olivier suddenly exclaimed, 'this time, I've got it! She's
written your name, Thérèse ... Let's see: Thérèse and ...
Go on, dear lady, please finish.'

Thérèse almost cried out in fear. She watched her aunt's
fingers sliding over the table-cloth, and it seemed as if they
were tracing out her name and denouncing her crime in letters
of fire. Laurent had leapt violently to his feet, wondering
whether he should not throw himself on the old woman and

break her arm. He was convinced that all was lost, and, as he watched this hand coming back to life to divulge Camille's murder, he felt the chill weight of retribution bearing down on him.

Madame Raquin was still writing, but more and more hesitantly.

'That's right, I can read it clearly now,' Olivier continued a moment later, looking across to the husband and wife. 'Your aunt has written both your names: Thérèse and Laurent . . .'

The old lady made repeated signs of agreement, while giving the two murderers a look which quite crushed them. Then she tried to complete her sentence. But her fingers had gone stiff again, and the extraordinary will-power that had galvanized them was slipping away; she could feel the paralysis creeping back down her arm and taking hold once more of her wrist. She frenziedly traced another word, and Michaud read out:

'Thérèse and Laurent have . . . '

And Olivier asked:

'Yes, but what have they got, these dear children of yours?'

The murderers, now crazed with terror, were on the point of shouting out the end of the sentence. They were staring at the avenging hand with fixed and anguished gaze when, suddenly, it went into a spasm and flattened out on the table, before falling back down into the invalid's lap, like a lump of lifeless flesh. The paralysis had returned and put a stop to their retribution. Michaud and Olivier sat down again in disappointment, while Thérèse and Laurent felt such a stab of joy that they almost collapsed with the sudden rush of blood thumping through their hearts.

Grivet was annoyed that nobody had believed him, and now he thought the time had come to re-establish his reputation for infallibility by completing Madame Raquin's unfinished sentence. As everyone was wondering what it could mean, he intervened:

'It's perfectly clear, I can guess the whole sentence from the look in Madame's eye. I don't need things written out for me on a table, one glance from her is enough. What she meant to say is: "Thérèse and Laurent have taken good care of me."'

Grivet had reason to feel pleased with his powers of imagination, because this time the whole company agreed with him. The guests began to sing the couple's praises for having been so kind to the poor lady.

'It is quite clear', said Michaud gravely, 'that Madame Raquin wished to register her appreciation of the loving care her children are lavishing on her. It reflects most creditably on the whole family.'

And he added, picking up his dominoes again:

'So, let us continue; now, where were we ... Grivet was about to play the double six, I believe.'

Grivet put down the double six and the game proceeded, futile and monotonous.

The old paralytic stared at her hand, plunged in terrible despair; it had let her down. Now it felt as heavy as lead; she would never be able to raise it again. Heaven did not want Camille to be avenged, for it had deprived his mother of her only means of telling the world about his murder. And the poor unfortunate told herself that all she was good for now was to go and join her child under the earth. She lowered her eyelids, feeling herself quite useless, and wishing she were already locked away in the darkness of the grave.

XXVIII

FOR two months Thérèse and Laurent struggled on against the anguish generated by their union. They were the cause of each other's sufferings. Hatred slowly welled up in them both, to the point where they began to look at each other with fury in their eyes, and unspoken menace.

It was inevitable that it would come to hatred in the end. They had loved each other like animals, with the hot passions of the blood; then, in the nervous upheaval following their crime, love had turned to fear and they had felt a physical horror at the thought of their embraces; now, amid the pain of their married life, they were rebelling and constantly flying into tantrums.

Theirs was a terrible hatred, leading to frequent violent outbursts. They could feel that they were irritating each other, and they both felt that they would be able to lead a quiet life without the other's constant presence. When they were together, they each felt stifled by an enormous burden, a burden which they would have liked to push aside and do away with; they would purse their lips and their eyes would light up with thoughts of violence, as the desire to tear each other to pieces overcame them.

Deep inside, the same thought was gnawing away at each of them; they were frustrated with their crime itself, and despairing that it had ruined their lives for good. That was the origin of all their anger. They realized that the ill could not be cured and that they would have to suffer for Camille's murder until they died, and it was this idea of suffering in perpetuity that exasperated them. In the absence of anyone else to blame, they took it out on each other, with detestation.

They were not willing to admit openly that their marriage was the inevitable punishment for the murder; they refused to hear the inner voice which was shouting the truth at them, laying out before their eyes the story of their life. And yet, in their fits of anger, they could each see clearly enough what lay at the root of their annoyance, and were conscious of the furious egotism of their natures which, having led them into murder in order to satisfy their appetites, had now left them with such a desolate and intolerable existence. They remembered the past and they knew full well that the only thing that gave them any cause for remorse was their disappointed hope of sensual gratification, peace, and happiness; had they been able to enjoy each other's embraces undisturbed, they would certainly not have shed a tear for Camille—they would have grown fat on their crime instead. But their bodies had rebelled, refusing to accept marriage, and now they were wondering fearfully where all the horror and loathing were going to lead them. They could see only an appalling and painful future ahead, leading to a sinister and violent end. And so, like two enemies who had been tied together and were struggling in vain to escape from their enforced embrace, they tensed their muscles and nerves to breaking-point, but without being able to free themselves. Then, realizing that they would never be able to get free, exasperated at the cords biting into their flesh and sickened by their contact with each other, feeling their discomfort grow with each passing hour and forgetting that they themselves had tied the knot that bound them, they flung dreadful accusations at each other in an attempt to alleviate their sufferings; unable to bear their bonds a moment longer, they tried to heal their mutually inflicted wounds by deafening each other with their curses and screams of reproach.

Every evening some quarrel would break out. It was as if the two murderers were looking for an opportunity to let off steam and unwind their tensed-up nerves. They watched each other's slightest move, testing their reactions, probing every exposed wound to the quick, and taking a keen delight in making each other scream with pain. Their life was filled with constant irritations, for they were now so tired of each other that they could not bear the least word, or look, or gesture, without feeling aggrieved and flying off the handle. Their whole being was ready and waiting for violence, and the slightest cause of impatience or the most ordinary annoyance would swell to extraordinary proportions in their deranged organisms, and suddenly become heavy with brutality. The most trivial thing could whip up a storm which went on until the following day. A dish that was too hot, an open window, a denial or a simple remark was enough to provoke them to real fits of insanity. And at some point in the dispute, one would always fling at the other the name of Camille; then, one thing always led to another until they started blaming each other for the drowning at Saint-Ouen, at which point they really saw red and lost control completely. This led to the most dreadful scenes as, suffocating with rage, they exchanged blows, hurled foul abuse, and committed shameful acts of brutality against each other. It was usually after dinner that Thérèse and Laurent reached this degree of exasperation, locking themselves in the dining-room so that nobody would hear their desperate rowing. There, at the back of that damp, vault-like room lit only by the yellowish glow of the lamp, they could tear each other apart to their hearts' content. In the calm, still air their voices became horribly strident. They only stopped when they were worn out with exhaustion, for it was only then that they were able to enjoy a few hours' rest. Quarrelling became a kind of need for them, a means of achieving sleep by brutalizing their nerves.

Madame Raquin listened to all of this. She would be there the whole time in her chair, her hands hanging down on her knees, her head erect and her face unmoving. She heard everything, but never a shudder ran through her lifeless body; her gaze remained riveted unflinchingly on the two murderers; she must have endured the most appalling torments. In this way she discovered, detail by detail, everything that had happened before and after Camille's murder, and saw deeper and deeper into the disgusting crimes of those whom she had once called her dear children.

The quarrels between the two of them revealed to her all the circumstances, and laid out one by one before her terrified mind all the episodes of the horrible saga. And as she waded further into this bloody mire, she would pray for mercy and think that she had reached the bottom of their infamy, only to be forced to go deeper still. Every evening she found out some fresh detail, and still the awful story went on and on, until she felt as if she had lost her way in some endless, horrifying nightmare. Their first admission of guilt had been devastating and brutal, but she was hurt even more by these

repeated blows, these small details which the couple let slip
in their mad frenzy and which cast a truly sinister light on
their crime. Daily the mother had to listen to the story of her
son's murder, and every day the story became more horrible,
more detailed, and was screamed into her ears with even greater
violence and brutality.

Sometimes, Thérèse was smitten with remorse as she looked
at the pallid mask down which great tears were silently rolling.
Then she would point at her aunt and implore Laurent with
her eyes to keep quiet.

'What's the problem?' he yelled boorishly. 'You know she
can't give us away. D'you think I like it any better than she
does? Anyway, we've already got her money, so what does
it matter what I say?'

And the dispute would carry on, bitter and violent, killing
Camille all over again. Neither Thérèse nor Laurent dared
to give in to the impulse which they occasionally felt, to take
pity on the paralytic and shut her in her own room when they
were fighting, in order to spare her another account of the
crime. For they were afraid they would strike each other down
if they did not have this semi-corpse to keep them apart. And
so pity gave way to cowardice, and they forced unspeakable
suffering on Madame Raquin simply because they needed her
presence to protect them from their own hallucinations.

Their quarrels were always the same, and always brought
them back to the same accusations. As soon as the name of
Camille was spoken and one accused the other of having killed
him, a terrifying clash would occur.

At dinner one evening Laurent, looking for a pretext to get
angry, said that the water in the carafe was warm—warm water
made him feel sick and he wanted some that was cool.

'I couldn't get any ice,' Thérèse answered curtly.

'Right then, I shan't have anything at all to drink,' said
Laurent.

'It's perfectly good water.'

'It's warm and it tastes of slime. It might as well be river
water.'

'River water!' Thérèse repeated.

And she burst into tears, one idea having led to another.

'What are you crying for?' asked Laurent, who knew very

well why and was already turning pale.

'I'm crying', she sobbed, 'because ... You know perfectly well why ... Oh God, oh God! You killed him!'

'That's a lie!' shouted the murderer vehemently. 'Admit it's a lie! I may have pushed him in the Seine, but you put me up to it.'

'Me? Me!'

'Yes you! Don't play the innocent, don't make me beat the truth out of you; I need you to confess to your crime and take your share of the blame, to calm me down and let me have some relief.'

'But it wasn't me who drowned Camille.'

'Yes it most certainly was ... Oh! you can play surprised if you like, and pretend you've forgotten; perhaps I should refresh your memory?'

He got up from the table, went to lean over her, and purple with rage, screamed in her face:

'You were by the edge of the river, remember, and I whispered: "I'm going to push him in." And you agreed, you just got into the boat.'

'It's not true ... I wasn't thinking straight, I don't remember what I did but I never wanted to kill him; you did that, and you alone.'

These denials were a torture to Laurent. As he had said, the idea of having an accomplice was some comfort to him; had he dared, he would have tried to prove to himself that the full horror of the murder should fall on Thérèse. At times he felt like hitting her to make her confess that she was more guilty than he.

He started pacing up and down the room, screaming and raving, watched by the fixed stare of Madame Raquin.

'Ah, the bitch, the bitch!' he spluttered. 'She's trying to drive me mad! You, didn't you come to my room one evening like a whore and drive me wild with your caresses so I would agree to do in your husband? You couldn't stand him—whenever I came here to see you, you told me he stank like a sick child ... Three years ago, what did *I* know about this sort of thing? Was *I* a criminal? I was an honest man leading a quiet life, not doing anyone any harm; I wouldn't have hurt a fly.'

'You're the one who killed Camille,' Thérèse insisted with a desperate obstinacy which made Laurent utterly lose his head.

'No, it was you, I tell you, you!' he repeated with an awful scream. 'Now you be careful, don't get me worked up or it will be the worse for you! What, you miserable slut, you don't remember a thing? You gave yourself to me like a tart, there, in your husband's bedroom, and taught me how to get pleasures that drove me crazy. Admit it, you had it all worked out, you hated Camille and you'd been wanting to kill him for ages! Of course, that's why you took me as your lover, so that we would clash and I'd destroy him.'

'That's not true! It's monstrous, what you're saying! You've no right to hold my weaknesses against me. I can truly say, like you, that before we met I was an honest woman who had never done anyone any harm. If I drove you crazy, you drove me crazier still. Let's not argue, Laurent, do you hear me? I would have too much to say against you.'

'Such as what?'

'Oh, nothing . . . You made no effort to save me from myself, you took advantage of me when I was vulnerable, you enjoyed wrecking my life . . . I can forgive you all that . . . But for pity's sake don't accuse me of killing Camille. Keep your crime to yourself, and don't keep trying to make my life even more awful than it is.'

Laurent raised his arm to slap Thérèse across the face.

'Go on, hit me,' she added; 'I'd prefer that, it would hurt less.'

With that, she offered her face. He held back, then took a chair and sat down beside her.

'Now listen,' he said, trying to keep his voice steady; 'refusing to accept your share of the blame is just cowardice. You know full well we did it together, you know you are as guilty as I am. What makes you want to shift all the responsibility on to me and claim you are innocent? If you were, you would never have agreed to marry me; don't forget, it's two years now since the murder. Would you like to try a little test? I'm going to go and spill the beans to the Public Prosecutor; then you'll see if we aren't both found guilty together!'

They shuddered, and Thérèse went on:

'The world may condemn me, but Camille knows it was all your doing. He doesn't torment me at night as he does you.'

'Camille never bothers me,' said Laurent, pale and trembling; 'you're the one who sees him in your nightmares; I've heard you shouting out in your sleep.'

'Don't say that,' exclaimed Thérèse angrily; 'I've never said anything in my sleep, and I don't want the ghost to come back now. Ah! I understand, you're trying to divert it away from you . . . I am innocent, I am innocent!'

They looked at each other, terrified and exhausted, afraid that they might unwittingly have called up the drowned man's corpse. Their quarrels always ended like that, with them protesting their innocence and trying to deceive themselves in order to drive away their bad dreams. They were forever trying to shrug responsibility for the crime off onto each other and defend themselves as if they were in court, each levelling the most serious charges at the other. The strangest thing was that they never managed to believe in the truth of their own protestations, for they both recalled exactly what had happened and could read tacit admissions in each other's eyes, even when their lips denied everything. Their lies were childish and their claims ridiculous, mere battles of words fought by two pathetic creatures who lied for the sake of lying, unable even to hide the fact that they were lying. Each in turn took the role of accuser and, although their imaginary court case never came to a verdict, they played it out every night with cruel determination. They knew they would prove nothing, they could never erase the past, and yet they kept on trying, charging back into battle, spurred on each time by pain and fear, yet defeated in advance by the terrible reality of the situation. The only profit they gained from their disputes was the storm of shouts and screams, whose din numbed their senses for a while.

And through all their rows, all their accusations, the paralysed old woman's gaze never left them. Her eyes lit up with a glint of joy whenever Laurent raised his broad hand against Thérèse.

XXIX

NOW a new phase began. Thérèse, driven to distraction by fear and not knowing where to turn for the slightest consoling thought, began to shed tears for her drowned husband out loud in front of Laurent.

A sudden collapse occurred in her. Her over-stretched nerves snapped and her hard, violent nature softened. She had become over-emotional once before, in the first days of their marriage, and now her emotionalism came back in a kind of necessary and inevitable reaction. Having put all of her nervous energy into the struggle against Camille's ghost, having lived for several months in a state of smouldering irritation and revolt against her sufferings, and having tried to cure them by the strength of her will alone, she suddenly felt so weary that she was forced to bend and give in. Now she went back to being just a woman, a little girl even, and, with no strength left to resist and make a further desperate stand against her terrors, she let herself be swept along by pity, tears, and remorse, in the hope that they would bring her some relief. She tried to turn these weaknesses of mind and body to her advantage; perhaps the drowned man, who had been impervious to her tantrums, would give in to her tears; so this remorse of hers was quite calculated, as probably the best way to placate and satisfy Camille. Like certain devout ladies who think they can deceive God into forgiving them their sins by praying with their lips and adopting the humble pose of the penitent, Thérèse humiliated herself, beat her breast, and found words of repentance, when all she felt deep in her heart was fear and cowardice. Moreover, she took a kind of physical pleasure in letting herself go like this, feeling crushed and powerless and giving herself up unresistingly to grief.

She imposed the burden of her weepy despair on Madame Raquin. The old paralytic became an object for her everyday use, a kind of prayer-stool, a piece of furniture in front of which she could confess her sins without fear and beg for forgiveness. Whenever she felt the need to cry, to distract herself with sobbing, she would kneel down before the invalid and, choking and exclaiming in passion, act out by herself a remorse scene which allowed her to find relief in weakness.

'I am a vile creature,' she would say in a faltering voice; 'I don't deserve forgiveness. I deceived you, and sent your son to his death. You can never forgive me. But if you could only see what remorse there is now in my heart, if you only knew how I am suffering, perhaps you would have some pity ... No, no pity for me, I wish I could die at your feet, overwhelmed by shame and grief.'

She would go on in this vein for hours at a time, passing from despair to hope, condemning herself and then granting her own pardon; she always put on the voice of a sick little girl, sometimes demanding, sometimes plaintive; she would throw herself down on the floor and then immediately get up again, obeying each new impulse of humility or pride, repentance or defiance, that came into her head. Sometimes she would even forget that she was kneeling in front of Madame Raquin, and go on with her monologue as if in a dream. Once she was thoroughly intoxicated with her own words, she would stagger to her feet in a daze and go down to the shop, calmer and no longer afraid of bursting into nervous sobbing in front of her customers. But whenever a fresh need to repent came over her, she would hurry back upstairs and kneel once more at the invalid's feet. These scenes happened ten times a day.

It never occurred to Thérèse that her tears and displays of remorse must be causing unspeakable distress to her aunt. The truth was that anyone who had wanted to find a way of torturing Madame Raquin could not have invented anything more awful than the comedy of remorse acted out by her niece. She saw through to the selfishness underlying these effusions of grief. The long monologues which she was forced to endure at any moment of the day, and which kept taking her back to Camille's murder, put her through untold misery. She could never forgive, and was nourishing implacable thoughts of revenge made even more acute by her powerless state, yet all day long she had to listen to pleas for forgiveness and humble, cowardly entreaties. She would have liked to reply, some of the things her niece said brought crushing denials rushing to

her throat, but she had to stay silent and let Thérèse plead
her case, unable to interrupt her. Her inability either to shout
out or to stop up her ears filled her with indescribable torment.
And still, one by one, her niece's slow, plaintive phrases filtered
into her mind like some interminable chant. It even crossed
her mind that the couple were inflicting this torture on her
deliberately, out of diabolical cruelty. Her sole means of
defence was to shut her eyes as soon as her niece knelt down;
even if she still heard what she was saying, she did not have
to look at her.

Eventually, Thérèse took her effrontery to the point of kissing her aunt. One day, during a fit of repentance, she pretended
to have caught a glimmer of mercy in the old paralytic's eyes;
she crawled along on her knees and pulled herself up, shouting
frantically: 'You forgive me, you forgive me!'; then she kissed
the poor old woman, who could not throw her head back to
escape, on her forehead and cheeks. As her lips touched the
cold flesh, Thérèse felt extreme revulsion, but thought that
this, like her tears and remorse, would be an excellent way
of calming her nerves. So she carried on kissing the old lady
every day, as both a penance and a relief to herself.

'Oh! how kind you are!' she would sometimes exclaim. 'I
can see how touched you are by my tears. Your eyes are full
of pity . . . I am saved!'

And she smothered her aunt in caresses, resting her head
in her lap, kissing her hands, smiling happily at her and taking
care of her with every sign of deep affection. After a while
she began to believe that this play-acting was real, and to
imagine that Madame Raquin really had forgiven her; then
she could talk to her about nothing but how happy her forgiveness had made her.

This was all too much for the paralytic; it almost finished
her off. Her niece's kisses gave her the same bitter feeling of
disgust and rage that she felt every morning and evening when
Laurent picked her up in his arms to get her up or put her
to bed. She was obliged to submit to the filthy caresses of
the vile creature who had betrayed and killed her son; she
could not even raise a hand to wipe away that woman's kisses
from her cheeks, and for long hours afterwards she could feel
them smarting. In this way she became a plaything for

Camille's murderers, a doll to be dressed and undressed, turned this way and that, and used in accordance with their wishes and whims. She remained lifeless in their hands as if her insides had been full of sawdust, and yet inside her feelings were all still alive, and the slightest contact with Thérèse or Laurent knotted her stomach with anguish and defiance. What exasperated her most was the wicked mockery of her niece's pretending to see forgiveness in her eyes, when she actually wished she could blast her out of existence with a single look. She often made desperate attempts to cry out in protest, and put all her hatred into her eyes. But Thérèse, whom it suited to be able to tell herself twenty times a day that she was for-given, simply behaved in an even more affectionate way and refused to notice anything. The old lady was forced to accept effusions of gratitude which her heart utterly repudiated. Henceforth, she lived in a constant state of bitter, impotent irritation, with a niece who had made herself thoroughly sub-missive and kept looking for endearing and affectionate ways to repay her for what she called her heavenly goodness.

Whenever Laurent caught his wife kneeling in front of Madame Raquin, he would drag her roughly to her feet, saying:

'Stop all this play-acting. You don't see me crying and going down on my knees, do you? You're just doing it to annoy me.'

He found Thérèse's remorse strangely unsettling. Since his accomplice had started moping around him, her eyes red with crying and with a plea always on her lips, he had felt much worse. The sight of this walking confession redoubled his fear and further increased his unease; it was like having an eternal reproach lurking about the house. Moreover, he was scared that his wife's repenting urges might one day lead her to tell all. He would have preferred to see her still hard and menacing, and fighting to defend herself against his accusations. But her tactics had changed; she now readily admitted her part in the crime, levelled accusations against herself, made herself com-pliant and timorous, and then went on to plead for redemption with burning humility in her voice. This attitude annoyed Laurent, and every evening their quarrels became fiercer and more sinister.

'Listen,' Thérèse would say to her husband, 'we are both

terribly guilty, we must repent if we ever want any kind of peace again ... You can see how much calmer I've been since I started weeping. Do the same as me; let us say together that we are being justly punished for committing a terrible crime.'

'Hah!' snorted Laurent, 'you can say what you like. I know how devilishly cunning and two-faced you can be. Cry if it amuses you, but for heaven's sake don't keep going on about it.'

'Oh! you are wicked, you're rejecting your own feelings of remorse. But you're really a coward; you went for Camille when he wasn't looking.'

'You mean to say I'm the only guilty one ?'

'No. That's not what I'm saying. I am guilty too, more guilty than you are; I should have saved my husband from you. Oh! I know the full horror of my guilt, but I am trying to obtain forgiveness, and I shall succeed, Laurent, whereas you'll go on living a life of misery. You haven't even got the heart to spare my poor aunt your disgusting displays of temper, and you have never expressed a word of regret to her.'

With that she kissed Madame Raquin, who shut her eyes. She fussed around her, straightening the pillow behind her head and lavishing a hundred little attentions on her. Laurent was infuriated.

'Hey! Leave her alone', he shouted; 'can't you see she hates the sight of you and your fussing! If she could raise a hand, she'd slap you round the face.'

His wife's measured, plaintive speech and resigned attitude would slowly work him up into a blind fury. He could see easily enough what her tactic was: she wanted to stop making common cause with him and set herself apart, in order to bury herself in her regrets and so escape the embrace of the drowned man. At times he thought that she was perhaps on the right track, that tears of repentance might be a cure for his terrors, and the thought of having to suffer and be afraid on his own certainly made him shudder. He, too, would have liked to feel remorse, or at least pretend to, just to see; but he could not find the right words, or the necessary tears, so he would resort to violence once more and shake Thérèse in an attempt to annoy her and drive her into the same state of mad fury as himself. She maintained a studied calm, responding with tearful submissiveness to his shouts of rage and making herself all the more humble and contrite as he grew more violent. As always in their rows, Thérèse put the finishing touch to his fury by singing the praises of Camille and intoning a list of his virtues.

'He was such a good man', she said, 'and we must have been horribly cruel to turn against such a kind-hearted fellow, who never had a bad thought.'

'He was good, yes, I know,' sneered Laurent; 'you mean he was stupid, don't you? Or have you forgotten? You used to tell me how the things he said got on your nerves, and how he could never open his mouth without coming out with something idiotic.'

'Don't mock ... All that's missing now is for you to insult the man you murdered ... You know nothing about a woman's heart, Laurent; Camille loved me, and I loved him.'

'You loved him did you, really? Ah! that's a good one! I suppose it was because you loved him so much that you took me for a lover! I can still remember the day when you were crawling all over me and telling me that Camille made you feel sick when your fingers sank into him as if he were made of clay. Oh, I know full well why you fell in love with me: you needed stronger arms than that poor fool could offer you!'

'I loved him as a sister. He was the son of my benefactress, he had all the delicate feelings of someone with a weak constitution, he was always noble and generous, kindly and affectionate ... And we killed him, Oh God! Oh God!'

And she would burst into tears and swoon, while Madame Raquin looked daggers, indignant at hearing Camille's praises sung by such a person. Laurent, powerless against this flood of tears, stalked feverishly up and down trying to find some ultimate means of stifling her remorse. All the good that he kept hearing her speak of his victim ended up by making him deeply worried, for he sometimes let himself be taken in by his wife's heart-rending lamentations and started actually to believe in Camille's virtues, which only served to increase his fears. But what finally made him lose his head and commit acts of real violence was the comparison that the drowned man's widow never failed to make between her first and her second husband, always to the advantage of the former.

'Oh yes!' she would shout, 'he was better than you; I would much rather he were still alive and you were there in the ground instead.'

At first Laurent would just shrug his shoulders.

'Say what you like,' she went on, becoming more agitated; 'I may not have loved him while he was alive, but when I think back, I love him now ... I love him and I hate you, can't you see that? You, you're a murderer ...'

'Will you shut up!' screamed Laurent.

'... and he's just a victim, an honest man killed by a villain. Oh! You don't frighten me ... You know very well what a petty, brutal wretch you are, with no heart and no soul. How can you expect me to love you now that you're covered in Camille's blood? Camille was all affection for me, and I would kill you, do you hear me? kill you, if that would bring him back and give me his love again.'

'Shut up, you bitch!'

'Why should I? I'm telling the truth. I would buy forgiveness if it cost me your blood. Oh! How I cry and grieve! It's my fault that this swine killed my husband ... I must go, one night, and kiss the ground where he lies; it will be my final joy.'

Laurent, drunk with rage and infuriated by the dreadful pictures that Thérèse kept holding before his eyes, threw himself upon her, knocked her to the ground, and held her down with his knee while raising his fist.

'That's right,' she screamed, 'hit me, kill me ... Camille never lifted a finger to me, but you, you are a monster.'

And Laurent, goaded on by her words, would shake her in his rage, beating and bruising her body with his clenched fist. On two occasions he almost strangled her. She went limp beneath his blows, deriving a bitter pleasure from being hit; she yielded to him and offered herself, provoking him into beating her more harshly still. For her, this was one more remedy for all the suffering in her life, and she slept better at night for having been beaten in the evening. Madame Raquin was filled with exquisite pleasure when Laurent dragged his wife across the floor like this, raining kicks on her back.

The murderer's existence had been unbearable since the

day Thérèse had conceived the hellish idea of expressing her remorse and grief for Camille out loud. From that moment on, the wretched man had lived perpetually with his victim; at any moment of the day he had to listen to his wife praising her first husband and bemoaning her loss. Anything at all could be a pretext: Camille used to do this, Camille used to do that, Camille had such and such a quality, Camille had loved her in such and such a way. Always Camille, always sorrowful phrases and tears of regret for his death. Thérèse put all her vindictiveness into making this torment, which she was inflicting on Laurent to protect herself, as cruel as she could. She went into the most intimate details, told him a thousand trivialities from her childhood with sighs of regret, and so managed to link the drowned man's memory with each and every event in their daily lives. The corpse, which had already been secretly haunting the household, was now brought in explicitly. It sat on the chairs and installed itself at the table, lay on the bed and made use of the furniture, and anything that was lying around. Laurent could not pick up a fork, a brush, or anything else, without Thérèse making him feel that Camille had touched it before him. As he was constantly being brought up against the man he had killed, the murderer began to feel a strange sensation which drove him almost insane: through being constantly compared to Camille, and constantly using the things Camille had used, he imagined that he *was* Camille, and began to identify with his victim. Then his control always snapped and he flung himself at his wife to silence her, so as not to have to listen to her words which were driving him out of his mind. All their quarrels ended in violence.

XXX

THE time came when Madame Raquin, to escape the suffering that she was enduring, had the idea of letting herself starve to death. Her courage was exhausted, she could no longer stand the martyrdom of the murderers' constant presence, and she started dreaming of death as her ultimate release. Every day, whenever Thérèse kissed her or Laurent picked her up and carried her in his arms like a child, her anguish deepened, until she made up her mind to evade these kisses and embraces which were causing her such horror and revulsion. Since she was already insufficiently alive to avenge her son, she preferred to be thoroughly dead and leave nothing in the murderers' hands but a corpse without feeling, which they could treat as they pleased.

For two days she refused all food, summoning her last strength to clench her teeth together, and spitting out whatever they did manage to force into her mouth. Thérèse was at her wits' end, wondering where on earth she would take herself to cry and repent when her aunt was not there any more. She lectured her endlessly to prove that she had to go on living; she wept and even lost her temper, reverting to her rages of the past and forcing the old lady's jaws apart as if she were a recalcitrant animal. But Madame Raquin held firm. It was a disgusting struggle.

Laurent stayed utterly neutral and indifferent to all this. He was very surprised at the frenzy Thérèse put into preventing the invalid's suicide. Now that her presence was of no further use to them, he hoped she would die. He would not have killed her himself, but since she wanted to die anyway, he could see no reason to deny her the means of doing so.

'For heaven's sake leave her alone,' he shouted at his wife. 'It'll be good riddance ... Perhaps we'll be better off when she's gone.'

These words, which were repeated several times in front of her, produced a strange emotional reaction in Madame

Raquin. She began to fear that Laurent's hopes might be realized, and that, once she was dead, the couple might indeed
enjoy happy, peaceful times. Then she told herself that wanting to die was cowardly and that she had no right to depart
before she had seen the sinister saga through to its resolution.
Only then would she be able to slip away into the darkness,
and say to Camille: 'You are avenged.' The thought of suicide
was hard to bear when she remembered that she would be
taking her ignorance with her to the grave; there, in the cold
and silent earth, she would lie asleep, tormented for ever by
not knowing whether her torturers had been punished. In order
to enjoy the sleep of death, she needed to feel the keen joy
of vengeance as she passed into insensibility, she needed to
take with her a dream of hatred fulfilled which she could dream
for all eternity. So she took the food which her niece offered
her and consented to live a while longer.

In any case, she could see that the end could not be far
off. Every day the situation between husband and wife was
becoming more tense and unbearable. At any moment there
must come an explosion which would wreck everything. Hour
by hour Thérèse and Laurent were squaring up to each other
in a more menacing way. It was no longer just at night that
they found their enforced proximity a trial; their whole day
was spent in an atmosphere of anxiety and dreadful conflict.
Everything became a cause of fear and pain to them. They
lived in a hell in which they were constantly wounding each
other, making everything they said and did as bitter and cruel
as possible, trying to push each other over the brink of the
precipice which they felt yawning at their feet, and into which
they were in fact both already plunging.

The thought of a separation had occurred to them both.
They had each dreamed of running away and finding some
kind of peace far from the Passage du Pont-Neuf, where the
damp and the filth seemed made to go with the barrenness
of their lives. But they could not, they dared not flee. The
idea of not having each other to tear to pieces, of not suffering
and inflicting suffering together, seemed an impossibility to
them. They were stubborn in their pursuit of hatred and
cruelty. A sort of combined repulsion and attraction simultaneously pushed them apart and bound them together, and

they always felt like two people who, after a row, want to leave each other and yet keep coming back to shout fresh abuse. Then there were material difficulties in the way: they did not know what to do with the invalid, nor what to say to the Thursday guests. If they did run away, perhaps people would suspect something; then they could see themselves being hunted down and sent to the guillotine. So they stayed put out of cowardice, wretchedly dragging out their horrific existence together.

Whenever Laurent was not there, in the morning or afternoon, Thérèse would wander aimlessly between the dining-room and the shop, anxious and disturbed, not knowing how to fill the emptiness which seemed to stretch further ahead of her by the day. Whenever she was not weeping at Madame Raquin's feet, or being beaten and cursed by her husband, she was at a loss for what to do. As soon as she found herself alone in the shop, she would sink into a heavy depression and gaze out at the people walking through the dark and dirty arcade with a dazed expression on her face, feeling utterly dejected in this gloomy tomb with its graveyard stench. In the end she asked Suzanne to come and spend whole days with her, hoping that the poor, pallid creature's gentle presence would make her feel calmer.

Suzanne was delighted to accept her offer; she still liked her and felt a kind of friendly respect for her, and for a long time now she had wanted to come and work with her while Olivier was out at the office. She brought her embroidery along and sat down behind the counter in the place vacated by Madame Raquin.

From that day on, Thérèse began to be less attentive to her aunt. Now that she had something else to occupy her, she went upstairs less often to weep in her lap and kiss her lifeless face. She made an effort to seem interested in Suzanne's interminable chatter about her household problems and all the banal details of her monotonous life; it drew her out of herself, and she was sometimes surprised to find herself taking a real interest in such nonsense, something which later brought a bitter smile to her lips.

Gradually she lost all her regular customers. Since her aunt had been confined to her chair upstairs, she had let the shop go to rack and ruin, abandoning her goods to the dust and the damp. There was a lingering mouldy smell, spiders hung from the ceiling, and the floor was hardly ever swept. But what really drove the customers away was the strange reception they sometimes received from Thérèse. Whenever she was upstairs being beaten by Laurent, or going through a fit of panic on her own, and the shop bell gave its insistent ring, she had to rush down almost without having time to tie her hair up or wipe away her tears; then she would serve the waiting customer with bad grace, or even save herself the trouble by shouting from the top of the wooden stairs that she had run out of whatever it was they wanted. Such unaccommodating behaviour was not calculated to make people want to come back. The little seamstresses of the locality, accustomed to Madame Raquin's gentle and solicitous manner, ran away in the face of Thérèse's surly attitude and crazed looks. Once she had Suzanne at her side, the exodus became complete, for, in order not to be disturbed in the middle of their conversation, the two women always found a way of getting rid of the last customers who persisted in coming. From then on, the haber-dashery business contributed not one penny to the household expenses, so they had to break into the forty-odd thousand francs of capital.

Sometimes Thérèse would go out for whole afternoons at a time. Nobody knew where she was going. She had probably invited Suzanne round not just for the company, but also to mind the shop while she was away. When she returned in the evening, worn out and with black rings of fatigue round her eyes, she would find Olivier's little wife sitting hunched behind the counter, still smiling distantly, in exactly the same position as when she had left her five hours before.

About five months after she was married Thérèse had a ter-rible shock. She became convinced that she was pregnant. The idea of having a child by Laurent seemed monstrous to her, although she could not explain why. She was vaguely afraid of giving birth to a drowned baby; it was as if she could feel inside her the cold presence of a soft, half-dissolved corpse. So she determined at all costs to get rid of this icy foetus which she could not bear to carry any longer. She said nothing to her husband, then one day, after she had cruelly provoked him and he had raised his foot to kick her, she offered her stomach to the blow. She allowed herself to be kicked almost to death in that way, and the next day she had a miscarriage.

Laurent too was leading a miserable existence. The days all seemed unbearably long to him, and each one brought the same anguish, the same depressing boredom, which came over him at particular times with devastating regularity and monotony. So his life dragged on; every evening he was terrified by memories of the past day and by expectations of the one to come. He knew that from now on all his days would be the same, all bring him an equal dose of pain. And he could see the weeks, months, and years which stretched ahead of him, grim and implacable, waiting to fall on him in turn and gradually smother the life out of him. When the future is without hope, the present tastes appallingly bitter. Laurent had lost all his defiance; he was letting himself go and starting to slide into the void which already threatened to overwhelm him. Idleness was killing him. As soon as day broke he would leave home, with no idea where he was going, sickened at the thought of doing the same thing as the day before and yet forced to do it again despite himself. He always made for his studio, as a matter of habit, or obsession. This room with its grey walls, where the only view was a blank square of sky, filled him with gloom and despair. He would fling himself face down on the divan and just lie there with his arms dangling, thinking leaden thoughts. He no longer dared pick up a brush. He had made a number of fresh attempts, but each time the face of Camille started leering at him from the canvas. To avoid sliding into insanity he ended up flinging his paintbox away into a corner and deciding to do nothing at all. He found this enforced idleness unbelievably hard to bear.

In the afternoon he would wonder frantically what to do with himself. He often spent half an hour standing around on the pavement in the Rue Mazarine, hesitating and turning over in his mind the various distractions he could indulge in. Having rejected the idea of going back up to his studio, he would set off down the Rue Guénégaud and then stroll along the embankment. And until evening he would go wherever his feet took him, walking along in a daze and shuddering suddenly when his gaze fell upon the Seine. Whether he was up in his studio or down in the street, he was always equally depressed. The next day he would start all over again, spending the morning lolling on his divan and the afternoon walking up and down the embankment. This had been going on for months, and it might go on for years more.

Laurent occasionally reflected that he had killed Camille in order to lead a life of idleness afterwards, and he was always astonished to find, now that he was actually doing nothing, what misery he was going through. He would have liked to force himself to be happy; he proved to himself that he was wrong to be unhappy, that he had actually attained the ultimate in happiness, which is to sit back with arms folded and do nothing, and that he was a fool for not enjoying this felicity in peace. But his reasoning did not stand up to the reality of the situation. He was forced to admit in his heart of hearts that idleness made his torment even worse, because it left him all the hours of the day to contemplate his despair and appreciate to the full its incurable awfulness. Idleness, this animal-like existence which he had so coveted, had become his punishment. There were moments when he longed earnestly for an occupation to take him away from his own thoughts. But then he always let himself drift again, falling back under the influence of that inexorable fatality which had fettered his limbs, the more surely to crush him.

The truth was that his only relief came from beating Thérèse of an evening, which allowed him to throw off his painful sluggishness for a while.

His most acute suffering, both physical and moral, came from the bite in the neck that Camille had given him. There were moments when it seemed to him as if the scar covered the whole of his body. Whenever he forgot about the past for a moment, he would feel a stabbing pain which brought both his mind and his body back to the murder. He could never stand in front of a mirror without something happening which he had often noticed, but which still horrified him: driven by the emotion he was feeling, the blood would rush to his neck, turn the scar deep red, and make it eat into his skin. This wound, which was living on him like a parasite, coming alive, reddening, and gnawing him at the slightest sign of emotion, caused him much fear and was a real torment. In the end, he started to believe that the drowned man's teeth had

actually buried some animal there in his neck which was
devouring him. The part where the scar was did not seem
to belong to his body any longer; it was like a piece of foreign
flesh that had simply been stuck on, like a chunk of poisoned
meat which was rotting his own muscle away. Thus he carried
around with him everywhere he went a living, devouring
reminder of his crime. Whenever he was beating Thérèse, she
would try and scratch him there, and sometimes succeed in
digging her nails in, which made him scream with pain. Normally, she pretended to cry whenever she saw the scar, so
as to make it even more unbearable to Laurent. Of all her
brutalities towards him, using this bite as a way to hurt him
gave her the greatest sense of revenge.

Many times when shaving, he had been tempted to cut into
his neck to try and remove the marks left by the drowned
man's teeth. In front of the mirror, when he raised his chin
and caught sight of the red patch showing through the foamy
white lather, he would suddenly be filled with rage and bring
the razor up close, on the point of chopping straight into the
flesh. But the cold feel of the blade on his skin always brought
him to his senses, and then he would go weak at the knees
and have to sit down, until the balance of his cowardly nature
was restored and he could finish his shave.

He only ever shook off his sluggishness of an evening, when
he flew into blind, childish rages. When he was tired of quarrelling with Thérèse and beating her, he would start acting like
a child, kicking the walls and looking for something to smash.
All this brought him relief. He particularly hated François the
tabby cat, who rushed to take refuge in the invalid's lap as
soon as he saw Laurent coming. The only reason Laurent
had not killed him already was that he really did not dare
touch him. The cat looked at him with great round eyes,
unmoving and diabolical. It was these constantly staring eyes
that exasperated him and made him wonder what they wanted,
until in the end he became really scared and started imagining
the most absurd things. If he chanced to turn his head suddenly
and caught François scrutinizing him with his heavy, implacable look, something which could happen at any moment,
at table, in the middle of a quarrel, or even during a long
silent pause, he would turn pale, lose his head, and be on

the point of shouting at the cat: 'Hey you! Say something, tell me what it is you want.' Whenever he had an opportunity to step on one of his paws or his tail, he would do so with a joy that quite scared him, and the poor creature's squeals always left him feeling vaguely uneasy, as if it had been a human cry of pain. He was literally afraid of François. Particularly since the cat had taken to living on Madame Raquin's lap, as in some impregnable fortress from which he could train his green eyes on the enemy with impunity, Laurent had begun to notice a strange similarity between the angry creature and the paralysed old woman. He told himself that, like her, the cat knew all about the crime, and would denounce him if the day ever came when he could speak.

Finally, one evening François stared so fixedly at Laurent that, overwhelmed with fury, he decided that enough was enough. He opened the dining-room window wide, then came over and picked the cat up by the scruff of its neck. Madame Raquin realized what was going to happen; two great tears rolled down her cheeks. The cat began to spit and tensed itself, trying to roll over and bite Laurent's hand. But he held on, then whirled it round his head a couple of times and flung it with all the strength in his arm against the great black wall opposite. François smashed into the wall and fell, crushed to pieces, on to the glass roof of the passage. The whole night long the wretched creature dragged itself along the gutter, its back broken, screeching raucously in pain. That night, Madame Raquin mourned François almost as much as she had Camille, and Thérèse had a bad attack of nerves. The cat's moans were sinister, in the darkness just beneath the windows.

Soon, Laurent had something else to worry about. He became concerned at certain changes he had noticed in his wife's behaviour.

Thérèse had become sullen and taciturn. She no longer lavished effusions of repentance and grateful kisses on Madame Raquin; she had gone back to her coldly cruel, selfishly indifferent behaviour towards the paralysed old lady. It was as if she had tried out remorse and found that it did nothing to relieve her, and so had decided to have a go at some other remedy. No doubt her sadness derived from an inability to bring any

calm into her life. She regarded the old lady with a kind of
disdain, like a useless object which could no longer even serve
as a consolation. She only took as much care of her as was
necessary to stop her dying of hunger. From that moment
on, she dragged herself around the house, silent and depressed;
she also took to going out increasingly often, sometimes as
much as four or five times a week.

These changes surprised and alarmed Laurent. He thought
that remorse was now taking a different form in Thérèse, mani-
festing itself in the gloom and apathy which he had noticed
in her. This apathy seemed to him much more worrying than
the garrulous despair which she had inflicted on him in the
past. Now she hardly ever spoke, and no longer argued with
him, but seemed to keep it all bottled up inside her. He would
rather have listened to her pouring out her suffering until she
had finished, than see her withdrawn into herself like this.
He was scared that her inner anguish would one day so overwhelm her that, to gain release, she would go and tell the
whole story to a priest or a magistrate.

So Thérèse's frequent outings took on a terrifying significance for him. He imagined that she was looking for someone
outside in whom to confide, and was preparing to betray him.
Twice he attempted to follow her, but lost her in the narrow
streets. He took to spying on her again. An obsessive thought
had taken hold of him: driven to extremes by what she was
going through, Thérèse was going to give the game away, and
he had to gag her and stop the confession in her throat.

XXXI

ONE morning, instead of going up to his studio, Laurent installed himself in a bar at the corner of the Rue Guénégaud, opposite the arcade. From there he examined all the people emerging on to the pavement of the Rue Mazarine. He was watching for Thérèse. The day before, she had told him that she would be going out early and would not be back until evening.

He waited for a full half hour. He knew that his wife always left by the Rue Mazarine, although for one moment he thought she might have given him the slip by taking the Rue de Seine, and it occurred to him to go back into the arcade and hide in the side-passage next to the house itself. Just as he was becoming restless, Thérèse hurried out of the arcade. The clothes she was wearing were colourful, and for the first time he noticed that in her long dress with a train she looked like a prostitute, flouncing provocatively along the pavement, eyeing up the men and gathering up the front of her skirt so high that she was showing off all her legs, from her laced boots to her white stockings. She set off up the Rue Mazarine. Laurent followed.

It was a pleasant day and the young woman walked slowly along, her head held high and her hair trailing down her back. Men who had seen her from the front would turn round as she passed and look at her again from behind. She went down the Rue de l'École-de-Médecine.* Laurent was terrified; he knew that there was a police station somewhere in the neighbourhood, and he was quite convinced that his wife was going to denounce him. So he promised himself that he would rush up to her if she went in through the door, that he would plead with her, hit her, and force her to keep quiet. On one street corner she looked at a passing policeman, and he started shaking when he saw her approach him; he hid in a doorway, suddenly terrified of being arrested on the spot if he showed himself. This walk was becoming a real torment to him; while his wife enjoyed the sunshine, nonchalantly and immodestly trailing her skirts along the pavement, he came along behind, pale and trembling, telling himself over and over again that all was lost, that there was no escape, that he would be sent to the guillotine. Every step she took seemed to him like a step towards retribution. Fear gave him a sort of blind certainty, and each of the young woman's movements added to it. And so he followed her, going wherever she went, like a man walking to his death.

Suddenly, as she emerged on to the former Place Saint-Michel,* Thérèse made for a cafe which at that time stood at the corner with the Rue Monsie r-le-Prince.* There she sat down at one of the tables on the pavement, in the midst of a group of women and students. She shook hands with everyone in a friendly way and ordered an absinthe.

She seemed quite at ease as she chatted to a fair-haired young man who seemed to have been waiting for her there for some time. Two tarts came and leaned over the table, and started talking familiarly to her in their husky voices. All around her there were women smoking cigarettes and men kissing women on the street, in full view of the passers-by, who did not even turn their heads. Laurent could hear their swearing and their ribald laughter from the other side of the square, where he was standing motionless in a doorway.

When Thérèse had finished her absinthe, she stood up, took the fair-haired young man's arm, and set off down the Rue de la Harpe.* Laurent followed them to the Rue Saint-André-des-Arts,* where he saw them go into a lodging-house. He stood in the middle of the road, looking up at the façade of the building. His wife appeared momentarily at an open window on the second floor; he thought he could make out the fair-haired young man's hands slipping around her waist. Then the window slammed shut.

Laurent realized what was going on. Without waiting any longer, he went calmly on his way, happy and reassured.

'Well!' he said, as he went back down to the embankment, 'I'm glad it's only that. At least it gives her something to do, and stops her creating trouble ... She's a damned sight more sensible than me.'

What he found astonishing was that he had not been the

first to think of embarking on a career of vice; it might be a good cure for his terror. It had not occurred to him before, because all the life had gone out of his flesh, and he no longer felt the slightest inclination to debauchery. His wife's infidelity left him utterly cold, and he felt no combative upsurge of the blood or the nerves at the thought of her being in another man's arms. On the contrary, he found it rather amusing; he felt as if he had been following a friend's wife, and he laughed at the fine trick she was playing on her husband. Thérèse had become so estranged from him that she was no longer alive in his heart at all, and he would happily have sold her into crime a hundred times over to buy himself an hour's peace of mind.

He began strolling along, savouring the sudden and joyful reaction that the switch from horror to reassurance had brought. He was almost grateful to his wife for going to visit a lover when he had thought she was on her way to the police. The whole adventure had turned out in a quite unexpected way, which had been an agreeable surprise. The clearest lesson from the whole thing was that he had been wrong to be afraid, and that he ought to look for a taste of vice himself, to see whether it might not bring him some relief by stupefying his mind.

That evening, as he returned to the shop, Laurent resolved to demand several thousand francs from his wife, and stop at nothing to get them. He reflected that promiscuity was expensive for a man, and felt vaguely envious of whores who can make money by selling their bodies. He waited patiently for Thérèse, who was not yet back. When she arrived, he was all charm and said nothing about having spied on her that morning. She was a little tipsy, and her dishevelled clothes were full of that reek of tobacco and strong drink which always lingers in bars. Shattered, with her face covered in livid blotches, she was unsteady on her feet and clumsy with the shameful fatigue of her day's work.

Dinner was silent. Thérèse ate nothing. When it came to dessert, Laurent propped his elbows on the table and demanded five thousand francs, straight out.

'No,' she snapped. 'If I let you have your way, we'd soon be completely broke ... Don't you know how we stand? You'd be plunging us straight into poverty.'

'Maybe,' he said in an unconcerned voice, 'I don't care, I just want the money.'

'No, a thousand times no! You chucked in your job, the drapery business has gone right down, and we can hardly live on the interest on my dowry! Every day I have to break into the capital just to feed you and give you the hundred francs a month that you extort from me. You're not having any more, do you hear me?'

'Just think about it, don't refuse point blank; I tell you, I want five thousand francs, and I'll get it, and you're going to give it to me whatever you say.'

His calm insistence annoyed Thérèse and took away the last bit of clarity from her thinking.

'Ah! I see,' she shouted, 'you want to finish just as you began ... For four years now we've been providing for you. You only ever came round to fill yourself with food and drink, and since then you've carried on sponging off us. His Lordship does nothing all day, his Lordship has fixed it so that he can live at my expense, without lifting a finger ... No, you shan't have a thing, not one penny ... Do you want me to tell you what you are? All right, you're a ...'

And she swore horribly. Laurent laughed and shrugged his shoulders, simply replying:

'You've picked up some delightful expressions in the circles you move in nowadays.'

That was the only allusion he allowed himself to Thérèse's amorous exploits. She straightened her head and retorted snidely:

'At least I don't go with murderers.'

Laurent turned very pale. He remained silent for a moment, his eyes riveted on his wife. Then he said, in an unsteady voice:

'Listen, my girl, let's not get upset; there's no point, either for you or for me. I'm at the end of my tether. The sensible thing for both of us would be to come to an understanding, if we don't want something dreadful to happen to us. I asked for five thousand francs because that is what I need; I can even say that I intend to use it to guarantee us a peaceful existence.'

A peculiar smile came to his lips as he continued:

'Come now, think about it, what do you say?'

'No need to think about it,' she replied. 'I've already told you, you're not having a penny.'

Her husband rose abruptly to his feet. She was afraid he was going to hit her, so she hunched herself into a ball, determined not to give in to his blows. But Laurent did not even go near her; he merely contented himself with declaring coldly that he was fed up with life and was going to tell the whole story of the murder to the local police.

'You've driven me to distraction,' he said; 'you're making my existence a misery. I'd rather end it all now. We'll both be tried and condemned together, that's all there is to it.'

'Do you think you can scare me?' his wife shouted. 'I'm as tired of it all as you are. If you don't go to the police, I shall, so there! I'm quite ready to follow you to the scaffold; I'm not so much of a coward as you are. Come on then, let's go straight round to the police.'

She was already on her feet and heading for the stairs.

'Er, all right,' Laurent stammered nervously, 'let's go together.'

But once they were down in the shop they stood staring at each other, scared and hesitant. It was as if they were glued to the spot. The few seconds it had taken them to walk down the stairs had been enough to show them in a flash what the consequences of a confession would be. Both of them simultaneously saw gendarmes, prison, court-room, and guillotine pass quickly and distinctly before their eyes. And they felt, deep down, a weakening which made them want to throw themselves at each other's feet and plead with each other not to go, not to give the game away. Fear and embarrassment held them rooted there for two or three minutes in silence. It was Thérèse who finally resolved to say something, and gave in.

'After all,' she said, 'it's silly of me to quarrel with you about that money. Sooner or later you'll find a way of wasting it all for me anyway. I might as well let you have it straightaway.'

She made no further attempt to disguise her defeat, but sat down at the counter and signed him a credit note for five thousand francs which he could cash at the bank. Nothing more was said that evening about going to the police.

As soon as Laurent had the money in his pocket, he got drunk, went off whoring, and generally gave himself up to a noisy and dissolute life. He stayed out all night and slept all day, wandering about in the dark looking for thrills and trying to escape from reality. But he only succeeded in making himself more depressed. When he was surrounded by shouting and laughter, he only heard the great awful silence inside himself; when he was in the arms of a mistress, or downing glass after glass, the sating of his appetite merely left him with a leaden sadness. His days of debauchery and gluttony were behind him, for his whole being, which had become frigid and numb within, now found kissing and feasting a source of irritation. Already disgusted before he began, he was never able to work up his imagination and excite his senses or his appetite. By forcing himself into debauchery he simply made himself feel a little worse, and that was all. Then, when he came home and saw Madame Raquin and Thérèse sitting there, his tiredness laid him open to dreadful attacks of terror, and he would swear never to go out again, but to live with his suffering instead, and try to get used to it and overcome it.

Thérèse, for her part, was going out less and less. For a month she lived like Laurent, on the streets and in cafés. She would go home for a while in the evening to feed Madame Raquin and put her to bed, then go out again until the next day. On one occasion she and her husband went for four days without seeing each other. Then she was overcome with deep loathing and realized that vice did not suit her any better than her play-acted remorse. In vain had she hung around all the lodging-houses of the Latin Quarter, in vain had she led a life of indecency and disorder. Her nerves were completely shattered; debauchery and physical pleasure could no longer shake her out of herself violently enough to make her forget. She was like a drunkard whose scorched palate has become so insensitive that even the strongest alcohol has no effect. She lay there unmoved while making love, and no longer expected anything but boredom and fatigue from her lovers. So she left them all, realizing that they were no use to her. Despairing idleness came over her and she took to hanging around at home in an unwashed petticoat, her hair uncombed, her face and hands dirty; she was losing herself in slovenliness.

And so, when the two murderers found themselves face to face once more, worn out and having exhausted every possible means of escaping from each other, they realized that they did not have the strength to carry on struggling any longer. Debauchery had rejected them and had flung them back into their agonies. They returned once more to their damp and gloomy lodgings in the arcade, and from now on that was their prison, for they had repeatedly tried to escape but never managed to break the bloody bonds that held them to each other. Now they gave up any thought of attempting the impossible. They felt so strongly driven, squeezed, and shackled together by their situation that any attempt to rebel would be futile; they went back to living together, but their hatred for each other had turned into raving fury.

Their evening rows began again—in fact, the shouts and kicks now went on throughout the day. Hatred was now accompanied by suspicion, and suspicion finally drove them completely mad.

They became afraid of each other. Soon, the scene that had followed the demand for the five thousand francs was repeated morning and night. Each became obsessed with the idea that the other was going to denounce them, and they could not get away from this idea. When one of them said or did something, the other imagined that he or she was planning to go to the police. So they fought, or pleaded with each other. They would shout out in their anger that they were going to tell all, scaring each other to death, then tremble and take it all back, promising each other with bitter tears to keep silent. They were going through dreadful torment, but they did not have the courage to administer a proper cure by cauterizing the wound with a red-hot iron. If they kept threatening to confess, it was simply in order to terrify each other and drive all such thoughts from their minds, for they would never have had the strength to speak up and find peace in retribution.

More than twenty times they went as far as the police station door, one behind the other. Sometimes it was Laurent who was determined to own up to the murder, sometimes Thérèse

who was in a hurry to turn herself in. But always they would
meet up again in the street outside and, after exchanging insults
and pleading earnestly with each other, make up their minds
to wait a little longer.

Each fresh row left them more suspicious and timorous than
before.

They spied on each other from morning to night. Laurent
never left the flat in the arcade, for Thérèse would not let
him go out alone. Their suspicions and their dread of possible
revelations brought them together and united them in a horrible intimacy. Never, since their marriage, had they lived so
tightly bound to each other, and never had they suffered so
much. But despite the anguish which they imposed on each
other, they never took their eyes off one another, preferring
to endure the most extreme pain rather than be apart for an
hour. If Thérèse went down to the shop, Laurent would follow
her for fear of what she might tell a customer; if Laurent stood
in the doorway, watching people walking through the arcade,
Thérèse would station herself beside him to make sure he did
not speak to anyone. On Thursday evenings, when the guests
were there, the murderers would give each other pleading looks,
each listening in terror to what the other was saying, each
expecting to hear some admission of guilt and reading com-
promising meanings into every new sentence that the other
began.

Such a state of war could not go on much longer.

Thérèse and Laurent both came round independently to
the idea of escaping from the consequences of their first crime
by committing a second. One of them absolutely had to disappear if the other was to find any peace. This thought occurred
to them both at the same time; each felt the urgent necessity
of a separation, and each became intent on making it an eternal
one. The idea of murder which came into their heads seemed
natural, inevitable, a necessary consequence of the murder of
Camille. They did not even debate it in their own minds; they
accepted it as the only plan that would save them. Laurent
decided to kill Thérèse because she was an embarrassment
to him, because a word from her could destroy him, and
because she was making him go through unbearable torment;
Thérèse decided to kill Laurent for the same reasons.

The firm decision to commit another murder calmed them down somewhat. They each made their arrangements. They were acting in the heat of the moment, without taking proper precautions; they only gave vague thought to the probable consequences of a murder done without any guarantee of escape or means of avoiding punishment. They were each simply obeying their overwhelming urge to kill, in the manner of wild beasts. Nothing could have made them confess to their first crime which they had concealed so cunningly, yet they were going to risk the guillotine for a second which it never occurred to them to make any attempt to hide. This was a contradiction in their behaviour which they never even noticed. They simply assumed that, if they managed to get away, they would go and live abroad with the money. Two or three weeks earlier Thérèse had withdrawn the last few thousand francs of her dowry and was keeping it in a drawer which Laurent knew all about. Not for one moment did they consider what would become of Madame Raquin.

A few weeks before, Laurent had bumped into one of his old school friends, who was then working as a laboratory assistant for a famous chemist and expert in toxicology. This friend had shown him round the laboratory where he worked, pointing out the different bits of apparatus and telling him the names of the drugs. One evening, after he had made up his mind to murder Thérèse, she was drinking a glass of sugared water in front of him, and this reminded him of having seen in the laboratory a little stoneware bottle containing prussic acid. Recalling what the young assistant had told him about the terrible effects of this poison, which kills instantly but leaves few traces, it occurred to him that this was just what he needed. The next day he managed to slip out, went to see his friend, and, while his back was turned, stole the bottle.

That same day Thérèse took advantage of Laurent's absence to have sharpened a long kitchen knife which was used for breaking up loaf sugar and had lost its edge; she hid this in a corner of the sideboard.

XXXII

THE following Thursday the party at the Raquins' (as the guests persisted in calling their hosts) was a particularly jolly affair. It went on until half past eleven. As he was leaving, Grivet declared that he had never in his life spent such a pleasant few hours.

Suzanne, who was pregnant, spoke to Thérèse the whole time about her pains and joys. Thérèse pretended to listen with great interest; with her eyes staring straight ahead and her lips pursed, she occasionally nodded her head and her eyelids cast shadows right across her face as they closed. Laurent, for his part, listened intently to the stories old Michaud and Olivier were telling. These two went on and on, and Grivet was hardly able to get a word in edgeways between two sentences from father and son, though in any case he had a certain respect for them, as he regarded them as good conversationalists. Since the customary game had been replaced that evening by chat, he exclaimed naïvely that the ex-superintendent's conversation was almost as diverting as a game of dominoes.

In the almost four years since Michaud and Grivet had been spending Thursday evenings at the Raquins', they had never once grown tired of these monotonous functions which came round with annoying regularity. Never for one moment had they suspected what a drama was going on in this home which, whenever they arrived, was always so pleasant and peaceful. Olivier usually said, as his little policeman's joke, that in the dining-room there was a whiff of honesty in the air. Grivet, not wanting to be outdone, had called it the Temple of Peace. Two or three times in recent weeks Thérèse had explained away the blotches and bruises on her face by telling the guests that she had had a fall. But in any case, not one of them would have recognized the marks of Laurent's fist; they were all convinced that the two of them were a model couple, all gentleness and love.

The old paralytic had not made any further attempt to bring

to their notice the infamies concealed behind the dull and tranquil façade of these Thursday evenings. In the face of the destructive conflict between the murderers, and sensing the crisis that must burst upon them one day or another under the inevitable pressure of events, she had finally realized that the situation had no need of her. From then on she deliberately withdrew into the background and allowed the consequences of Camille's murder to unfold towards the deaths, in their turn, of the murderers. She simply prayed heaven to let her live long enough to witness the violent outcome that she could now foresee; her last wish was to feast her eyes on the spectacle of the supreme agonies which would finally mark the destruction of Thérèse and Laurent.

That evening Grivet came over to sit next to her and chatted for a long time, as usual both asking and answering all the questions. But he did not manage to get even a glance out of her. When the clock struck half past eleven, the guests all jumped to their feet.

'We are so happy in your house', Grivet exclaimed, 'that we never dream of leaving.'

'It's a fact', said Michaud in confirmation, 'that I'm never sleepy here, although I normally go to bed at nine.'

Olivier felt that it was his turn to say something funny.

'You see,' he said, displaying his yellow teeth, 'there's such a whiff of honesty in the air; that's why we're always so comfortable here.'

Grivet, annoyed at having been pre-empted, began declaiming with an emphatic gesture:

'This room is the Temple of Peace . . .'

Meanwhile, Suzanne was tying her bonnet strings and saying to Thérèse:

'I'll come round tomorrow morning at nine.'

'No,' Thérèse replied hastily, 'no, don't come until the afternoon . . . I'll probably be out all morning.'

As she spoke, her voice was strangely troubled. She accompanied the guests out into the arcade; Laurent went down too, carrying a lamp. Once they were alone, husband and wife both gave a sigh of relief; they must have been eaten up with concealed impatience right through the evening. Since the day before, they had been behaving in a darker, more anxious way

towards each other. Now they avoided looking at each other
and went back upstairs in silence. Their hands were shaking
in a slightly convulsive way, and Laurent was forced to put
the lamp down on the table so as not to drop it.

Before putting Madame Raquin to bed, they usually tidied
the dining-room, prepared some sugared water for the night,
and busied themselves doing things for the old woman, until
everything was ready.

That evening, once they were back upstairs, they sat down
for a moment and stared into the distance, their lips pale.

'Well then, aren't we going to go to bed?' asked Laurent
after a short silence, seeming to have jolted awake out of a
dream.

'Yes, yes, let's go to bed,' answered Thérèse with a shiver,
as though she were freezing cold.

She rose and picked up the water jug.

'Let me,' exclaimed her husband in as natural a voice as
he could manage; 'I'll make the sugared water; you see to
your aunt.'

He took the jug from Thérèse's hands and poured out a
glass of water. Then, half turning away, he emptied the little
stoneware bottle into it and added a lump of sugar. Meanwhile,
Thérèse had bent down in front of the sideboard, picked up
the kitchen knife, and was trying to slip it into one of the
large pockets that hung from her waist.

Just then that strange feeling which warns us of approaching
danger made husband and wife instinctively turn their heads.
They looked at each other. Thérèse saw the little bottle in
Laurent's hand and he noticed the glint of the knife between
the folds of her skirt. They stared at each other like this for
a few seconds, chilled and speechless, he standing near the
table, she half kneeling by the sideboard. They understood.
Each was frozen with horror at finding his own thought in
the mind of the accomplice; each read the secret intention
on the other's devastated face, and both were filled with pity
and horror.

Madame Raquin, sensing that the end was near, gazed at
them with a fixed, piercing stare.

Suddenly, Thérèse and Laurent burst into tears. An overwhelming crisis broke them and flung them into each other's

arms, as weak as children. They both felt something gentle and tender awakening in their bosom. They cried, unable to speak, thinking of the sordid life they had led and would go on leading, if they were cowardly enough to go on at all. Then, as they thought back over the past, they felt so weary and disgusted with themselves that they were filled with an immense need for rest, for oblivion. They exchanged a final glance, a glance of gratitude, before the knife and the glass of poison. Then Thérèse took the glass, drank half of it, and handed it to Laurent, who swallowed the rest straight down. Instantly they fell on top of each other, struck down as if by a thunderbolt, finding consolation at last in death. The young woman's mouth fell across her husband's neck, on the scar left by Camille's teeth.

The two bodies remained on the dining-room floor all night long, twisted and slumped in death, lit by the flickering yellow glow of the shaded lamp. And for more than twelve hours, until around noon the following day, Madame Raquin, stiff and silent, contemplated them there at her feet, feasting her eyes and annihilating them with the hatred in her gaze.

EXPLANATORY NOTES

4   *two or three men ... a book*: Zola is alluding here to the support
      he had already received from the much-respected critics Sainte-
      Beuve and Hippolyte Taine, to whom he refers again some
      lines later as 'the great critics, those of the methodical, Natural-
      ist school'. Apparently at his repeated request, Taine had writ-
      ten him a generally encouraging letter about *Thérèse Raquin*
      earlier in 1868, while Sainte-Beuve was to do so shortly after
      the publication of the second edition of the novel. Both letters,
      which provided Zola with useful ammunition against his critics,
      are reprinted in the Documents section of the Garnier–Flam-
      marion edition of *Thérèse Raquin* (see Select Bibliography).

5   *'Thérèse Raquin is the study ... natural manner'*: Without
      acknowledgement, Zola is here quoting almost verbatim from
      Taine's private letter to him on the subject of *Thérèse Raquin*
      (see above). Comparing Zola's work to that of Shakespeare,
      Dickens, and Balzac, Taine had praised his overall intentions
      but encouraged him to set the action of his future books in
      a broader social context. The result, we may assume, was the
      Rougon-Macquart cycle.

6   *'putrid literature'*: the title of the hostile attack on *Thérèse Raquin*
      published by 'Ferragus' (Louis Ulbach) in *Le Figaro* of 23 Janu-
      ary 1868 (see Introduction, p. ix).

7   *the Passage du Pont-Neuf*: the Passage du Pont-Neuf, of which
      a photograph can be found in Zola's *Œuvres complètes*, i. 524
      (see Select Bibliography), was built in 1823 on the site of the
      former Comédie-Française theatre; it was demolished in 1912
      to make way for the Rue Jacques-Callot. Most of the events
      in the novel take place in a small area of the sixth *arondissement*
      of Paris, on the left bank of the Seine.

11   *Vernon*: a small, undistinguished town on the left bank of the
      Seine, some 35 miles north-west of Paris.

20   *the Orleans Railway*: one of six large regional companies
      brought into being under Napoleon III to rationalize the mass
      of small, often uneconomic railway concerns which had grown
      up since the 1820s. The line which gave the original smaller
      company its name was opened in 1843, and had as its Paris

terminus the Gare d'Orléans (the present-day Gare d'Austerlitz).

20 *the Institute*: the seventeenth-century Palais de l'Institut, since
1805 the seat of the Institut de France (which is composed
of five learned Academies, including the Académie Française);
it is situated on the left bank, a little way downstream of the
Île de la Cité.

the Jardin des Plantes: the botanical and zoological gardens of
central Paris, situated in the fifth *arondissement*, on the left bank
nearly a mile upstream from the Institute. When they were
established, in 1635, they would have been near the edge of
the city.

the Port aux Vins: the quays on the left bank where the wine
barges used to dock, just upstream from Notre-Dame. Next
to them was the large warehousing area of the Halle aux Vins,
the wholesale wine markets of Paris.

the station: the Gare d'Orléans, headquarters of the Orléans
Railway; now called the Gare d'Austerlitz (the present building
dates from 1867).

Buffon: Georges Louis Leclerc, comte de Buffon (1707–88),
a naturalist and essayist who supported the idea that science
should be founded on experiment.

Thiers: Louis Adolphe Thiers (1798–1877), opposition politi-
cian and historian whose *History of the Consulate and Empire*
was published between 1845 and 1862. He was exiled in 1851
for opposing the *coup d'état* of Louis Napoleon and the establishment of the Second Empire.

Lamartine's History of the Girondins: Alphonse de Lamartine
(1790–1869), poet and statesman, published his *History of the
Girondins* in 1847, shortly before the abortive 1848 revolution,
to instruct the public in revolutionary morality. His political
career was brought to an end by the *coup d'état* of 1851.

31 *the Rue Saint-Victor*: a small street in the fifth *arondissement*,
situated to the south of what is now the Boulevard Saint-Germain, some half a kilometre back from the Seine, and just to
the west of the Halle aux Vins.

48 *the Batignolles district*: Les Batignolles was one of a number
of independent *communes* to the north of Paris (including Mont-
martre, La Chapelle, La Villette, and Belleville) lying beyond
the wall of the Fermiers-généraux (see below), which until 1859
marked the administrative boundary of Paris. In that year they
(and other *communes* to the south and west) were incorporated

into the city, and the number of *arondissements* was increased
from twelve to the present twenty. Les Batignolles, already a
working-class district in Zola's day, now makes up the less
affluent half of the seventeenth *arondissement*; immediately
beyond the present city boundary to the north lies the indus-
trial town of Clichy.

49   *the Pitié hospital*: one of the large Parisian hospitals, located
near the then Gare d'Orléans and the Jardin des Plantes; the
late eighteenth-century building which Zola knew, which
extended onto the site currently occupied by the Paris Mosque,
was demolished in 1912.

57   *Saint-Ouen or Asnières*: small rural towns just to the north and
north-west of central Paris, lying on broad meanders of the
Seine and popular with excursionists, but long since industria-
lized and swallowed up by the metropolis. Saint-Ouen was a
famous rowing centre.

58   *the fortifications*: since medieval times, Paris had been encircled
by a wall and defensive bastions. As the city expanded, these
fortifications were successively demolished and rebuilt further
out. Until 1859 the line of the eighteenth-century wall of the
Fermiers-généraux, which ran a little over half-way out between
the centre and the modern city boundary and was largely
designed for the enforcement of customs regulations, marked
the administrative limit of Paris. In 1840, however, Louis-Phi-
lippe ordered the building of an even greater wall, and by the
time of the Second Empire there was a fortified boundary running all round the city just outside the line of the present-day
boulevards extérieurs, beyond which lay a *zone militaire*, a broad
band of land on which no building was officially allowed. These
'fortifs', as they were popularly known, and the shanty-town
slums which had grown up in 'la Zone', were finally demolished
after 1920 to make way for new housing, sports facilities and
other developments.

59   *the Tuilerie gardens*: situated along the right bank of the Seine,
between the Louvre and the Place de la Concorde, and opposite
the Gare d'Orsay (which has now been turned into a great
museum of nineteenth-century art). The gardens of the Tuilerie
Palace, a royal residence for much of the century (but burnt
down during the Commune insurrection of 1871), were laid
out in Classical style by the famous landscape gardener Le
Nôtre in 1649.

67   *the Clichy barrier*: one of sixty rotundas (of which a number
still survive) housing customs and police posts which controlled

access to the city, through gateways in the wall of the Fermiers-généraux. The Clichy barrier stood on the site of the present-day Place de Clichy, with central Paris to the south and Les Batignolles to the North.

74 *the Morgue*: Throughout the nineteenth century the Morgue stood on the south side of Île de la Cité, first on the quai du Marché-Neuf, then, from 1864, on the quai de l'Archevêché behind Notre-Dame (where it was transferred on the orders of Haussmann). Both buildings (the latter on the site of present-day public gardens, near the eastern tip of the island) would have been very visible to walkers along the south bank of the river. The invaluable *Dictionnaire historique des rues de Paris* (see Select Bibliography) gives a description of the later site which confirms details of Zola's picture: 'the room where the bodies were displayed, divided off by a glass partition, was freely open to the public. Behind the screen, twelve black marble slabs, sloping towards the onlookers, awaited the corpses. From July 1830 the victims' clothes were also displayed as an aid to identification. . . . A refrigeration system was not installed until 1881'. (i. 101).

88 *the annual Salon*: founded in 1737 and named after the 'salon carré' of the Louvre in which they were first held, the Salons were annual art exhibitions organized by the Académie des Beaux-Arts in which the 'best' of the year's new work was given official recognition. By the mid-nineteenth century the judges were admitting only safe, academic pictures, such as those which, Zola later tells us, Laurent's art-school friend liked to paint. In 1863 many artists whose work had been rejected (including some of the great names of later nineteenth-century French painting) appealed directly to the Emperor, who ordered the setting-up of a Salon des Refusés; Manet's *Déjeuner sur l'herbe*, for instance, was first seen there. Zola, like Baudelaire before him, published controversial review-guides to a number of the Salons, castigating the lack of originality and 'temperament' in the offerings on display (see his *Salons* of 1866 and 1868 in *Œuvres complètes*, xii).

114 *Belleville*: originally an independent *commune* on the north-east boundary of Paris (see note to p. 48 above), in Zola's day it was already a populous working-class district. Since 1859 it has made up the southern part of the nineteenth *arondissement*.

the boulevards: Zola is probably referring here to the so-called 'Grands Boulevards', broad avenues which were laid out in the 1680s running in an arc along the northern edge of the

second and third *arondissements*. Thérèse and Laurent would
have had a majestic (if rather indirect) drive across the Place
de la Concorde in the west, past the Église de la Madeleine,
round the present site of the Opéra (begun in 1862 but not
completed until thirteen years later), to the Place de la Républi-
que in the east, before turning off up the Rue de Belleville
to their restaurant. The ring of boulevards was only completed
to the south in 1866, with the construction of the western
section of the Boulevard Saint-Germain (see below); the eastern section had been driven through from the river (Quai de
la Tournelle) to intersect with the Boulevard Saint-Michel in
1855.

the Rue de l'École-de-Médecine: a small street in the sixth
arondissement which, before the completion of the present-day
Boulevards Saint-Germain and Saint-Michel, ran between
the Rue Mazarine and the Rue de la Harpe (see below). When
Zola was writing *Thérèse Raquin*, many of the streets in the
student quarter through which Thérèse walks had recently
either disappeared completely or, like this one, been trun-
cated and made unrecognizable by Haussmann's grand road-
building and redevelopment schemes.

194   *the former Place Saint-Michel . . . the Rue Monsieur-le-Prince*: in
stead of carrying on to the end of the Rue de l'École-de-
Médecine, Thérèse must have turned right into the Rue
Monsieur-le-Prince. After walking about half a kilometre up
the hill to the south, she would have come out on to what today is called the Place Edmond-Rostand, by the eastern corner
of the Luxembourg gardens. This name was transferred to the
famous Parisian landmark we know today, down by the river at
the northern end of the Boulevard Saint-Michel, 'in the early
1860's, no later than 1864' (Geoff Woollen, 'How Streetwise
was Zola?', *Bulletin of the Émile Zola Society*, 16 (September
1997), 24–28, p. 26). Woollen points out that the Boulevard
Saint-Michel, a linear extension of the Boulevard de Sébastopol
on the other side of the Seine (and until 1867 called the
Boulevard de Sébastopol-rive-gauche) was begun at the river
end, by the Pont Saint-Michel, in 1855, but was only completed at its southern end, where it joins 'the former Place Saint-
Michel' at the Luxembourg, in 1859 or 1860. He also reminds
us that 63, rue Monsieur-le-Prince (near the Luxembourg end)
was Zola's first address in Paris, when he arrived in 1858 with
his mother and maternal grandfather (op. cit., p. 27).

Rue de la Harpe . . . the Rue Saint-André-des-Arts: Thérèse now
walks back down the hill, towards the river. Before the Boulevard Saint-Michel was completed, obliterating it along two-
thirds of its length to leave only the narrow, picturesquely-wind-
ing northern section, the Rue de la Harpe used to run from the
former Place Saint-Michel down to the Rue de la Huchette, in
the fifth *arondissement*. From there, the Rue Saint-André-des-
Arts led westwards, across the present Place Saint Michel, back
to the Rue Mazarine. Thérèse's whole walk is around two kilo-
metres in length, but only about half of it could be done along
the same streets today. Zola's use of detailed topographical references from before Haussmann's transformation of the area
thus helps date the action of his novel. The evident absence
from the picture of the Boulevards Saint-Germain and Saint-
Michel means that it must be set before 1860 at the latest,
while the fact that the Rue Monsieur-le-Prince was only called
that along its full present-day length from 1851 onwards may
set a lower limit on the year in which the book ends. Woollen
(op. cit., p. 26) adduces Grivet's twenty-year service on the
Orleans railway as further evidence for 1860 as the most recent
date, since the company's terminus, the present Gare
d'Austerlitz, was not built until 1840, but this may not be con-
clusive as the railway was founded some two years earlier.
Moreover, although the Boulevard Saint-Michel was only completed in 1860, if Thérèse's walk occurred in or after 1855 she
would have had to cross either the completed northern section
of the new road, or its construction site, which Zola would
surely have mentioned (the same is true of the Boulevard Saint-
Germain, also present in the area from 1855).

MORE ABOUT   **OXFORD WORLD'S CLASSICS**

American Literature

British and Irish Literature

Children's Literature

Classics and Ancient Literature

Colonial Literature

Eastern Literature

European Literature

Gothic Literature

History

Medieval Literature

Oxford English Drama

Poetry

Philosophy

Politics

Religion

The Oxford Shakespeare

A complete list of Oxford World's Classics, including Authors in Context, Oxford English Drama, and the Oxford Shakespeare, is available in the UK from the Marketing Services Department, Oxford University Press, Great Clarendon Street, Oxford OX2 6DP, or visit the website at www.oup.com/uk/worldsclassics.

In the USA, visit www.oup.com/us/owc for a complete title list.

Oxford World's Classics are available from all good bookshops. In case of difficulty, customers in the UK should contact Oxford University Press Bookshop, 116 High Street, Oxford OX1 4BR.